The Communitarian Constitution

The Communitarian Constitution

Beau Breslin

The Johns Hopkins University Press
Baltimore and London

© 2004 The Johns Hopkins University Press
All rights reserved. Published 2004
Printed in the United States of America on acid-free paper

Johns Hopkins Paperbacks edition, 2006
9 8 7 6 5 4 3 2 1

The Johns Hopkins University Press
2715 North Charles Street
Baltimore, Maryland 21218-4363
www.press.jhu.edu

*The Library of Congress has cataloged the hardcover edition of this book
as follows:*
Breslin, Beau, 1966–
    The communitarian constitution / Beau Breslin.
        p.   cm.
Includes bibliographical references and index.
    ISBN 0-8018-7782-2 (hardcover : acid-free paper)
    1. Constitutional law—Philosophy. 2. Separation of powers.
3. Public interest. 4. Common good. 5. Constitutional law—United
States—Philosophy. I. Title.
K3165.B74   2003
342′001—dc21   2003006213

ISBN 0-8018-8538-8 (pbk. : alk. paper)

A catalog record for this book is available from the British Library.

For Martha and Molly

Contents

Preface

In the spring of 1861, soldiers in the Union army surrounded the Cockeysville, Maryland, farm of John Merryman and arrested him for allegedly participating in the destruction of several railroad bridges west of Baltimore. The Union soldiers were acting on orders from the president of the United States, who earlier that year had suspended the constitutionally protected writ of habeas corpus in an attempt to "preserve the union." President Lincoln's extraconstitutional act stemmed from the realization that the loss of Maryland would lead to the unraveling of the regime. If the Confederates seized control of Maryland, he was quick to point out, the nation's capital in Washington would be surrounded by hostile forces. Accordingly, the president ordered his troops to "arrest, and detain, without resort to the ordinary processes and forms of law, such individuals as [the Union forces] might deem dangerous to the public safety."[1]

The problem, of course, was that the president was not entrusted with the power to suspend habeas corpus: that authority rested with Congress by virtue of its placement in Article I, Section 9, of the Constitution. Indeed, both Congress and, more importantly, the federal judiciary reacted to the president's order by noting that such a violation of our Constitution was unprecedented. "The Government of the United States," exhorted Chief Justice Roger Taney, "is one of delegated and limited powers. It derives its existence and authority altogether from the Constitution, and neither of its branches—executive, legislative, or judicial—can exercise any of the powers of government beyond those specified and granted."[2] The chief justice insisted that the actions of the president were not explicitly granted nor assumed by the constitutional text and thus were inconsistent with the very concept of a written charter.

Lincoln, however, was undeterred. Merryman, although by this time largely forgotten in the public scuffle between the president and the chief justice, was eventually released from prison, but not before Lincoln himself called for the further expansion of his original unconstitutional act. Scores of additional Maryland citizens—including the mayor of Baltimore, the chief of police, the police commissioner, and thirty-one members of the Maryland legislature—were detained at Fort McHenry for their political views. No charges were ever handed down to these supposed criminals; they were held in custody merely because they presumably threatened the war effort. According to Union officials, they were conspirators bent on permanently fracturing the nation. Thus, the president never wavered in his conviction that they ought to remain behind bars until they renounced their insubordinate ways.

Lincoln's defiance in the wake of various judges' decisions to issue writs of habeas corpus on behalf of public officials, journalists, and other confederate sympathizers is now legendary. He presumably believed until the moment of his death that the power to suspend the constitutional rules of due process was his alone. Moreover, he recognized that even if the power rested elsewhere, the desperate moment demanded his most decisive action. The continued existence of the Constitution itself was at stake, argued Lincoln, and thus the times called for unsettled—and unsettling—action. Asked the president: "Are all the laws, *but one*, to go unexecuted, and the government itself to go to pieces, lest that one be violated? Even in such a case, would not the official oath be broken, if the government should be overthrown, when it was believed that disregarding the single law, would tend to preserve it?"[3]

Ex Parte Merryman, the case that emerged from the events of 1861, is important on a number of different levels. Principally, it is now studied by legal experts as an example of constitutional posturing: the president's defiance of a direct order from the judiciary, combined with his disagreement over the institutional authority to suspend habeas corpus, makes this a prime case for those interested in America's system of separated powers. However, few recognize that *Ex Parte Merryman* is also a case that tests the very foundation of constitutional government. Beyond the power play waged by Lincoln, the principle that provisions of the Constitution may be suspended by a government official not authorized to do so brings to the fore an ongoing debate about the impact and force of the rules of constitutionalism. One of the primary purposes for framing a constitution in the first place is to delimit the power of leaders to behave with unbridled capriciousness. A constitution is supposed to suppress the proclivity of government agents to rule by their own inclinations. In this sense, Lincoln's behavior was not only unconstitutional, it was *anticonstitu-*

tional; he was, in essence, ignoring the proposition that it is the Constitution that directs the actions of the president, and not the other way around. Indeed, Lincoln subordinated the Constitution in favor of his own will. There is little doubt that the president was motivated by noble and patriotic sentiments, but the fact remains that Lincoln, for that moment at least, became the enemy of the constitutionalist.

This raises the question: Why was Lincoln willing to take such drastic steps? Why was he disposed, in this instance, to suspend the constitutional rights of due process? Historically, of course, we can point to the Union forces' early defeats as contributing to Lincoln's unease. The Civil War had just begun, and it was not going particularly well for the North. The Confederacy's initial momentum had the president concerned that things might quickly spiral out of control, and thus, the story goes, he had little choice but to ignore the Constitution.

Yet there is a larger, more theoretical answer to these questions that relates more directly to the themes of this book: Lincoln was inclined to overlook the Constitution because he believed it was the right thing to do, because he thought that at that moment the future of the entire regime was in jeopardy. That is to say, the president was moved to disregard those provisions of the constitutional text that guaranteed an individual's right to a fair trial precisely because he believed they might bring about the end of the Union. And he was probably right.

Nonetheless, accurately reflecting the will of the community, even in an emergency, does not rescue one from the scrutiny of the constitutionalist. Lincoln's position can—and should—be reframed to reflect his belief that the interests of the community he represented were in direct conflict with the Constitution. Allowing Merryman and his cohort to engage in insurrection was obviously antithetical to the North's desire for stability and national unity. Logically, therefore, the community's wishes, as Lincoln understood them, called for swift action—even if that meant transgressing explicit provisions of the U.S. Constitution. At that precise moment, Lincoln faced a constitutional crisis. He could ignore the will of the community and risk the ultimate demise of the Union, or he could react to the commands of his constituency and risk subordinating the constitutional text. He chose the latter.

By nature, a communitarian would make the same decision, and that is what this book aims to uncover. My primary thesis, illustrated most accurately by the above example, is that the beliefs shared by most American communitarians are largely incompatible with the basic tenets of modern constitutionalism, and that the rules governing constitutionalism clearly dictate that the community's wishes, however powerfully expressed, must remain subordinate to the text itself. Indeed, the communitarian faces a constitutionalist challenge every time the will of the citizenry contrasts with that of the constitutional document. Where the communitarian looks appropriately to the community for guidance, the constitutionalist looks elsewhere. In fact, it is, as I have indicated, decidedly anticonstitutionalist to be governed primarily by the whim of the present community. Communitarians and constitutionalists often disagree about what source ought to play the most significant role in decision making, and thus they will resolve individual cases in fundamentally divergent ways. Much as Chief Justice Taney—the constitutionalist—chided President Lincoln—the communitarian—for abandoning the rule of law in *Ex Parte Merryman*, the modern constitutionalist is similarly troubled by the contemporary communitarian pronouncement that above all else it is the community's welfare that ought to prevail. This work takes the standoff between the communitarian principles espoused by Lincoln and the constitutionalist ones articulated by Taney and places it within the broader context of theory and practice. Much to the dismay of communitarians in general, I assert that the two sides cannot be reconciled.

At the outset, a few things should be made clear. First, this is primarily a work of constitutional theory. Those seeking insight into the realm of constitutional interpretation or judicial process more generally may be disappointed by what they read. Constitutional theory is a large and vast discipline, and it includes many different but importantly interrelated subjects. The present study seeks to flesh out the more foundational questions of constitutional order and organization, and not the equally important but derivative questions of constitutional interpretation. It attempts to understand the nature of constitutional government broadly and then apply the specific rules of constitutionalism to the contemporary community-centered argument. As such, the book also addresses the subject of constitution making. Analyzing constitutional foundings is a burgeoning field within political science, due in large part to a renewed interest in the American founding and more recent foundings around the world. This work, while not directly focused on the subject of constitution making, has much to say about the process of constitutional foundings and the prospect of future regime success.

Secondly, this is not a book about American constitutionalism per se.[4] As part of the overall analysis, I will draw heavily on the U.S. Constitution and the many illustrations—both past and present—that give meaning to that particular text. But my aim is not to condemn communitarianism from such a singular and narrow perspective but simply to place communitarian ideals within the broader context of constitutional thought. The analysis, therefore, works at two levels of abstraction: the higher level features principles of generic constitutionalism, while the lower, more specific level centers on the principles and structure of the American Constitution itself. Distinguishing between the two is not always easy since the contemporary model of generic constitutionalism has adopted many of the characteristics of the American example. But recognition of the distinctions is essential to any critical evaluation of communitarian thought. Communitarianism falters primarily because it cannot sustain the more general maxims associated with generic constitutionalism; the movement suffers only coincidentally because it cannot successfully replicate the American version.

Thirdly, like so many others, I have been profoundly influenced by the work of John Rawls. It is now a commonly accepted belief that the publication of Rawls' *A Theory of Justice* marks the beginning of a revival in political theory. Our most important intellectual traditions—from libertarianism to conservatism—were resurrected as a direct result of the book. But perhaps the theoretical position that has benefited most from Rawls' work is communitarianism. Indeed, one of the pillars of the communitarian canon, Michael Sandel's *Liberalism and the Limits of Justice*, is an essay whose sole purpose is to discredit the neo-Kantian image of liberalism made so famous by Rawls. Likewise, Alasdair MacIntyre's more conservative version of communitarianism and Michael Walzer's primarily liberal construction of community are both, in a sense, responses to Rawls' theory of justice as fairness.

We can now add this book to the growing list of works published in Rawls' considerable shadow. Insofar as Rawls was preoccupied with the ideal—with the normative theory of the state—then any contemporary study of constitutionalism is a Rawlsian enterprise; for constitutions are a polity's attempt at political perfection, they are a regime's principal effort to design a model political order, and they are rarely, if ever, fully resolved. Put another way, the enduring debate over constitutional government is a debate centered squarely on the ideal. From Aristotle to the Anti-Federalists of the late eighteenth century, from the American Civil War to the fall of the Berlin Wall, political societies and their defenders have been stirred by a common desire for perfection. Today we can add communitarians to that list. Indeed, contemporary communitarians have now unwittingly entered the discourse over political modeling. They articulate a normative vision for modern society that seeks to return a sense of community—a sense of connectedness, if you will—to the current pluralist and largely ambiguous state composed of atomized individuals. At its very core, then, what communitarians offer is a not only a glimpse into their own particular image of the ideal but also a way to reflect on ours. We can learn from communitarians about our own constitutional characteristics, and thus the cycle of constitutional deliberation continues unabated. For that reason alone, we ought to be delighted by their recent reemergence on the political landscape.

As a result of its emphasis on constitutional theory, this book, I hope, contributes to a body of literature that extends beyond the sometimes narrow confines of the liberal-communitarian debate. The subject of constitutional theory has enjoyed a bit of a renaissance lately, with the work of Bruce Ackerman, Walter Murphy, Jeffrey Tulis, Sotirios Barber, Sanford Levinson, Harvey Mansfield, William F. Harris, Wayne Moore, Anne Norton, Stephen Macedo, Mark E. Brandon, Stephen Griffin, Keith Whittington and many others representing some of the finest examples of contemporary political thought. But the topic is really as old as political theory itself. Aristotle was deeply interested in constitutional theory, as were Plato, Montesquieu, Locke, and Rousseau. Madison, Hamilton, Jefferson, Adams, Marshall, Paine, and later Tocqueville, Calhoun, Lincoln, Douglas, Field, and Harlan, were also enticed by the allure of constitutional inquiry. During the early part of twentieth century, Edward Corwin, Carl Friedrich, and Charles McIlwain were among the main figures still exploring the nature of constitutional government. And then there are the contemporaries listed above, each of whom has more than admirably sustained the high level of intellectual inquiry we have grown accustomed to within the realm of constitutional thought. For my part, it is both exciting and not a little intimidating to throw my own hat into the ring. Indeed, I can only hope that somehow this book contributes to one of the many threads that has emerged from this very long, and very illustrious, list of thinkers.

There is much to admire about the communitarian enterprise. For me, the most appealing characteristic of communitarian thought is the proposition, made by many, that the communities we inhabit are primarily responsible for the formation of our identities. Certainly I am living proof of the truth of that claim.

To put it mildly, I have been influenced by a number of different communities. The academy, for one, has provided a nurturing environment for my intellectual and professional growth. Indeed, I am convinced that absent the community of scholars in the Political Science Department at the University of Pennsylvania, this book would not have been written. Three members of that community deserve special recognition: Graham Walker, now of Oklahoma Wesleyan University, gently nudged me to think about constitutionalism as a political conception worthy of deep reverence. Joseph Carrig helped me to locate the intellectual boundaries of constitutional thought within the broader tradition of political philosophy. And William F. Harris II, my mentor and friend, encouraged me to visualize the entire landscape of constitutional theory. To a great extent, this book is a product of his wisdom and teaching. My debt to him cannot be overstated.

I have found the academic community at Skidmore College to be every bit as vibrant and stimulating as the one I left at Penn. Colleagues in and around the Government Department have repeatedly reminded me of the virtue of self-sacrifice; they are teacher-scholars in the model sense of the term. A few stand above the rest: Aldo C. Vacs, Mary Ellen Fischer, Steven A. Hoffmann, Roy H. Ginsberg, Kate Graney, Natalie Taylor, Flagg Taylor, John J. P. Howley, Grace Burton, Tadahisa Kuroda, Christopher Whann, Patricia Ferraioli, Chris DeLucia, and Ronald P. Seyb have all contributed to my intellectual well-being in ways they cannot imagine. My colleagues Robert C. Turner, Timothy W. Burns, and David R. Karp merit separate mention, for they have generously provided encouragement and counsel at crucial points along the way. Finally, it is a pleasure to publicly acknowledge Michael Korzi, Stephen Wasby, Joseph P. DiGangi, and Mark Silverstein for their support. Each, in his own way, has furthered my education and shepherded my creative impulses.

I thank Henry Tom of the Johns Hopkins University Press for his guidance and patience. Even as I was contemplating abandoning the project, Henry encouraged me to explore the connections between communitarianism and constitutional theory in more subtle and nuanced ways. The book is far more interesting because of those explorations. Others at the press—including Michael Lonegro and my copyeditor, Elizabeth Yoder—have provided invaluable aid. Repayment to those who took the time to read the manuscript—Wayne D. Moore, Douglas E. Edlin, Ned Breslin, and the anonymous reviewers commissioned by the Johns Hopkins University Press—will come, I hope, in hearing their voices in the pages that follow. A special thanks must be extended to Scott Galupo, the most extraordinary writer I know. He not only took the time to read and edit the book in its current form but also did the same at least three other times. I don't think it is too much of an exaggeration to say that he knows more about my argument than even I do.

My greatest debt is owed to my most important community: Indeed, my family has been my primary source of inspiration. My father, Jud, and my mother, Wendy, instilled in me a passion for learning, and my siblings—Jamie, Matt, David, Ned, and Lindsey—have each shown me the true meaning of compassion and loyalty. Above all else, my wife, Martha, and my daughter, Molly, deserve my gratitude. What can I say about their place in my life? They make it all worthwhile. Not only is it impossible to imagine this book being published without their unbending support, but it is equally difficult to imagine my own life without their love. For that reason, I dedicate this book to them.

The Communitarian Constitution

CHAPTER ONE

Introduction

Communitarianism, Constitutional Visions, and the Anti-Federalist Legacy

Traditionally, Americans have engaged in continuous and spirited debate. From slavery to abortion, we have vigorously defended our positions on the major moral and practical issues of the day. Some, like Herbert Storing, even claim that the principles of debate, deliberation, and compromise lie at the cornerstone of the American political experience.[1] Consider the contemporary importance of the First Amendment's freedom of speech clause. While some use its forceful protection to further one side of a debate, others simultaneously appeal to it to promote the opposing position. In referring to the significance of free expression in a republic, Justice Oliver Wendell Holmes once wrote: "If there is any principle of the Constitution that more imperatively calls for attachment than any other it is the principle of free thought—not free thought for those who agree with us but freedom for the thought we hate."[2] He was also heard to claim that the principles of debate and free speech form "the theory of our constitution."[3] Similarly, Justice William Brennan encouraged debate and discussion by writing in 1964, "A profound national commitment to the principle that debate on public issues should be uninhibited, robust and wide-open."[4]

Things were no different at the nation's founding. Surrounding the creation of the American constitutional system in the late eighteenth century were two simultaneously broad and fiercely argued debates. The first, and the one most familiar to students of the American Constitution, involved like-minded men who for four months in 1787 discussed the specifics of a new constitutional regime for America. The fifty-five participants in this debate agreed that the current constitutional order—as dictated by the then-impotent Articles of Confederation—was for many reasons incapable of ordering the citizens of the growing and more complex United States: "The Confederation, resting only on good faith, had no power to collect taxes, defend the country, pay the public debt, let alone encourage trade and commerce."[5] Moreover, the Articles permitted individual states to play off each other in foreign affairs, thus sowing confusion in the matching areas of diplomatic relations and international commerce. Economic difficulties at home also contributed to the realization that the federal government was powerless under the Articles of Confederation. Controlling many state legislatures in postrevolutionary America were radicals who chose to implement measures aimed at debt relief and price-fixing, but who also frightened the prerevolutionary elite. The problem for most landowners and businessmen of the period was that the one potential weapon against such legislation—the Articles of Confederation—was really no weapon at all.

Virginia's Edmund Randolph captured the overall attitude of the delegates in Philadelphia when he wrote: "The present federal government is insufficient to the general happiness, [and] the conviction of this fact gave birth to this convention." It was inferred that Shays' Rebellion and the response by the Massachusetts legislature granting most of the rebels' demands signaled the inherent problems associated with a loosely conjoined confederation. Even more damning was the reality that the Articles were not the supreme law of the land. As a national constitutional charter, they were in large measure subordinate to the wishes of the individual states. Consequently, the participants in Philadelphia believed that the Articles could no longer control the burgeoning relationships that existed between the states and the other institutions of American society. They felt that if the young nation was to be both powerful and prosperous, a new public order was warranted. Accordingly, the delegates to the Constitutional Convention convened in Philadelphia in the summer of 1787 and commenced a debate that centered on which comprehensive political design should be adopted for the newly independent confederation of states.

The debate, like the weather that summer, was pronouncedly heated as the delegates to the Convention differed on a number of important constitutional issues. Most prominently, a multitude of disparate proposals were raised regarding how to structure the necessary changes to achieve the crucial goal of a unified and powerfully constituted nation. Yet perhaps what ultimately fostered consensus in Philadelphia that summer was that the participants shared a common vision: a mutual and unwavering belief that the construction of a new constitutional order—one that unified the independent states into a single powerful entity—was the best political strategy for the American people. What brought these statesmen together was a collective desire for fundamental institutional change. They ultimately concurred on many broad theoretical ideas, from unification to federalism, and despite the faddish indictment of self-interested elitism, they even shared a common background as wealthy landowners.[6] Resolution of America's initial constitutional debate, therefore, depended upon urgency, and because the delegates to the Constitutional Convention were deeply committed to a broad notion of political change, consensus and compromise were possible.

The second debate surrounding the nation's constitutional founding, the one perhaps less familiar, was not so blessed. Unlike the exchange in Philadelphia's Independence Hall, the participants in this much deeper, more theoretical dispute did not enjoy the advantage of a common general purpose. Some even contend that this second debate has yet to be fully resolved.[7] What was the ultimate appeal of the liberal-democratic polity as envisioned by the delegates to the Constitutional Convention? Is the proposed text reflective of the values expressed at Independence? The forum for the second debate—involving ratification of the Constitution itself—was not limited merely to the confines of Philadelphia's Independence Hall, but rather concerned every community and, in a general way, every citizen of the original thirteen states. It rested on the broad claim that the country's newly drafted constitutional order was not the design most suited for the American polity. Instead, another political strategy—a return to the principles articulated in the Articles of Confederation, or an embrace of a classical republican constitutional framework—might be more appropriate. Perhaps, some argued, a constitutional scheme that does not place so much value on the principle of concentrated, centralized power might better conform to the political affections and historical tradition of the young nation. Maybe supporters of the Constitution were advocating fundamental change when it was not actually necessary. At the end of the eighteenth century, the proponents of this alternative position were known as Anti-Federalists. Today the descendants of that critical tradition are recognized broadly as communitarians.

The story of America's founding is in many ways a precursor to a similar story unfolding today. Contemporary American citizens are not presently engaged in the formal task of constitution making, nor are they likely to convene a constitutional convention any time soon. Radicalized pamphleteers do not regularly line America's streets seeking an audience to espouse their concerns about the merits of our constitutional charter, nor are our major newspapers filled with opinion pieces discussing the benefits of a federal system or an independent judiciary. Nonetheless, we are still witness to an intellectual exchange of the highest order, a debate that harks back to an era surrounding our nation's birth when the very *foundation* of politics was carefully scrutinized. We may not always realize it, but whenever we openly discuss questions of freedom and order, rights and responsibilities, community and individualism, we enter into a conversation that implicates the nation's first principles. A debate about free speech is not just a debate about what rights the individual retains but is also about what level of invasion a community can (and should) tolerate. Similarly, a discussion about welfare or social security or taxation is not just about individual entitlements but is also about the community's ability to control its own destiny. These conversations are constitutional in nature.

It is no exaggeration, then, to suggest that modern communitarians are a direct descendant of Anti-Federalism in both form and substance. They stand for many of the same ideals that were first articulated by the Anti-Federalists—republicanism, communalism, civic virtue, and the public good. Furthermore, they believe, much like their Anti-Federalist forebears two centuries ago, in the centrality of shared values and constitutive bonds. Even more critically, however, modern communitarians share with Anti-Federalists a lack of devotion to any political regime built primarily on the principles of autonomous individualism and private self-interest—a regime, most would acknowledge, that resembles the contemporary United States. They find fault with modern America's penchant for selfishness and egoism. They lament the overall loss of connectedness that has plagued American society since its founding. Like Anti-Federalists, the communitarians' problem with American society rests most concretely on a broad critique of our constitutional underpinnings.

The Communitarianism of Anti-Federalists

Pitted directly against the Federalist defenders of the constitutional vision during the American founding, Anti-Federalists called for the repudiation of the newly created constitutional text and a return to the status quo. By no means a homogeneous collective, Anti-Federalists represented vastly different social, economic, and geographical backgrounds. Furthermore, they differed greatly in the severity of their aversion to the 1787 document. As Herbert Storing has suggested, "It is not possible to read far among the Anti-Federal writings without being struck by an extraordinary heterogeneity."[8] Many, for instance, supported the basic structure of the constitutional body but were concerned that a list of protected rights was omitted. Others opposed ratification of the text altogether, citing the problems of scale and consolidation as insurmountable. Some were Anti-Federalists for a time and then defected to the Federalist camp; others were originally Federalists and then became Anti-Federalists. A few were even opposed to the ratification of the Constitution for very specific reasons but thought the centralization of government was a good idea. Still others were just plain stubborn.

Wayne Moore has observed a similar schizophrenia among Anti-Federalists. The "first lines of attack" for Anti-Federalists, he says, "focused on the size of the government and the scope of delegated powers. But once ratification became likely, Anti-Federalists shifted their efforts to securing an enumeration of rights."[9] Yet despite the generally accepted notion that Anti-Federalists were not all alike, historians like Storing and theorists like Moore also caution us not to think of the movement as entirely fragmented, for the Anti-Federalists did share a number of fundamental and profoundly constitutive principles in common. They were, for the most part, intensely conservative. They stood opposed to significant political change since they believed the concepts proclaimed by the Articles of Confederation were those that embodied the spirit of the American Revolution. The proposed Constitution, they maintained, did not adequately reflect the values of local autonomy and civic engagement. A substantial portion of Anti-Federalists also agreed that the design of the new constitution was confused and obscure. It was difficult to comprehend not only the general meaning of its complex provisions but also the mechanical particularities of the document. "A constitution," said one opponent of ratification, "ought to be, like a beacon, held up to the public eye, so as to be

understood by every man. This government is of such an intricate and complicated nature, that no man on this earth can know its real operation."[10] Opponents of the Constitution insisted that the text needed to be (among other
things) more explicit about those freedoms and liberties that were retained by
the American people. The Anti-Federalists were not persuaded by the Federalist argument that a constitution is itself a bill of rights, but instead uniformly
insisted that a list of constitutionally protected rights (or at least a promise that
one would be included) was necessary before ratification could be achieved.
Such solidarity contributed to an ultimate Federalist concession and the inclusion of a bill of rights in the constitutional text four years later.

Most notable of the Anti-Federalist similarities was their steadfast commitment to two related doctrines: the theory of small-scale republicanism, and the
corresponding principle of civic virtue, both of which now regularly appear
within the contemporary communitarian literature. The Anti-Federalist affection for small-scale republicanism—along the lines of Rousseau's Geneva or
Pericles' Athens—involved the issue of geographical dimension and was in
many respects predicated on their general embrace of civic virtue, the belief
that man's passion for his country and his fellow citizens could (and should)
be as forceful as his natural inclination toward self-interest. That is to say,
the issue of size and the concomitant Anti-Federalist concern that an extensive polity would be harmful to the citizenry sprang from a belief in the
importance of public virtue and the necessity of identifying and cultivating
shared values.[11] Large republics, thought most Anti-Federalists, enervated the
capacity of individuals to relate to each other in tangible ways; they diluted
the institutions most capable of providing inhabitants with a common tradition; and they foreclosed the possibility that citizens could share in a single
collective experience. Thus, extensive republics could rarely guarantee that
the interests of the community would transcend the selfishness of its individual residents.

To be sure, supporters of ratification also defended the need for civic virtue,
but only insofar as those qualities could be made compatible with large-scale
governance. Anti-Federalists, in contrast, maintained that governing was possible only "over a relatively small territory with a homogeneous population."[12]
Convinced that accompanying the shift in power from the independent states
to the federal government would be a corresponding corrosion of civic or
communal virtue, the Anti-Federalists pushed to preserve state autonomy. At
best, they insisted that the creation of an extensive national polity would

disfigure the shared moral values that had developed in each community over the prior century; at worst, it would culminate in political oppression or tyranny.

The Anti-Federalist concern about the size of the newly formed United States emerged directly as a result of a general conviction that societies succeeded when they encouraged localism while at the same time deterring man's individualistic disposition. Storing has explored this strand of Anti-Federalist thought most thoroughly. Anti-Federalism, he wrote, suggested that the communal goodness issuing from shared traditions was cultivated only in "the restricted sphere of the small republic, which offers little inducement or opportunity for the exercise of divisive or corrupting talents and which daily reminds each man of the benefits derived from and the duties owed to his little community."[13] The newly drafted American Constitution denied citizens the continued sense of community that was present under the Articles of Confederation, mainly because it introduced a "new federalism" in which the primary essence of power (and possibly the locus of shared values and beliefs) was grounded at the nation's capital and not at the local or state levels. It wrested the very instruments of political virtue—the identification and simultaneous promotion of common values and traditions—from the local governmental institutions that most needed them. And it placed those critically important instruments, the Anti-Federalists cried, in perpetual jeopardy.

It should now be clear that the intellectual differences between Federalists and Anti-Federalists—like modern liberals and communitarians—actually operate along two intersecting axes: nationalism versus localism, and individualism versus collectivism. Historians and theorists have correctly placed more emphasis on the axis related directly to scale. As has been inferred above, Anti-Federalists are perhaps best remembered for their opposition to the argument articulated by Madison in the 10th *Federalist* that a "well-constructed" polity was one that "extended the sphere." Yet there was much more to the Anti-Federalist philosophy than an awareness of scale. Anti-Federalists were, in fact, anything but one-dimensional. Their opposition to centralized, heterogeneous polities was informed and nourished by a deep commitment to personal connectedness and community spirit. In the minds of many Anti-Federalists, the two could not easily be separated. An impressive devotion to classical republicanism—and more importantly, a conviction that the new text stifled and sacrificed the American tradition in favor of self-interest and individualism—motivated the Anti-Federalist attack on the proposed constitution.

Storing has argued that one of the reasons Anti-Federalism was eventually doomed to failure was that many secretly supported commercial republicanism. Many were, in other words, more closely aligned with Federalist ideology than originally thought. Yet despite this truth, it is hard to deny that the community was of paramount concern in the Anti-Federalist mind. The community was far more critical than the isolated individual because it held transformative power, the power to connect citizens to a common tradition.[14] Barry Alan Shain has recently emphasized this dimension of early American history, suggesting that when one evaluates the perception of politics at the time of the founding, "one finds in the ethnically and religiously exclusive enclaves of the eighteenth century a vision of human virtue that rested on local self-government and an active role for intermediate institutions in the corporate shaping of the individual's moral character."[15] Wilfred McClay also recounts the Anti-Federalist anxiety that there was a "growing tendency [at the founding] to define the individual as a 'self,' a free-standing entity ontologically distinct from the political and social order."[16]

The link between community and civic virtue is an essential component of Anti-Federalist thought. Much of the recent literature on the ratification debate has highlighted the communitarian aspect of the Anti-Federalist position.[17] For many (including some supporters of ratification), designing a republic meant that one should "conceiv[e] of society in organic terms, viewing it as an independent entity distinct from its members. The common good was thus distinct from and paramount to the good of individuals."[18] Anti-Federalists differed from most supporters of the Constitution in that they perceived the text as encouraging self-interest rather than the public good. If not now, many thought, then certainly at some point in the future, the Constitution's liberal and egalitarian priorities would discourage kinship and signal the demise of community. Federalists, on the other hand, assumed that those disconnections that supposedly threatened the viability of the state could be harmonized most effectively through aggregation.[19] Even the Anti-Federalist push for greater protection of individual freedoms in the form of a bill of rights—a noticeably liberal tendency, to be sure—was in part an attempt to liberate individuals so that they could cultivate those constitutive relationships that were most meaningful to them.[20]

When Tocqueville, fewer than sixty years after ratification, commented that America's egalitarian tendencies had, in fact, advanced individualism at the expense of community and that the only way to recover virtue in America was to reframe it in terms of private self-interest, Anti-Federalist fears were finally realized. It was Tocqueville himself who observed that "not only does democracy make men forget their ancestors, but also clouds their view of their descendants and isolates them from their contemporaries. Each man is forever thrown back on himself alone, and there is danger that he may be shut up in the solitude of his own heart."[21] Tocqueville's was a voice that echoed many of the convictions of the Anti-Federalists. The general sentiment among opponents of ratification was that since "everyone in the community was linked organically to everyone else, what was good for the whole community was ultimately good for all the parts."[22] Republicanism, in other words, could also ensure the sense of secular civic virtue that was deemed necessary for effective governance. Passion for the public good could be fostered only by attending to the needs of the community and by resisting the desires of the self. The most powerful tradition brought to the founding, Shain argues, was that "the community was not 'an aggregation of individuals' but 'an organism, functioning for a definite purpose, with all parts subordinate to the whole.'"[23]

Anti-Federalists insisted that local government was *the* crucial intermediate institution to foster consensus and that it provided a key to unlocking man's shared destiny. Private virtue and public good could not be achieved in the isolation of government institutions. The purpose of government was not just bureaucratic supervision but the active pursuit of the common good: "In a republic, the manners, sentiments and interests of the people should be similar. If this be not the case, there will be a constant clashing of opinions; and the representatives of one part will be continuously striving against those of the other. This will retard the operations of government, and prevent such conclusions as will promote the public good."[24] The classical republican thought of Aristotle taught us that government can be an instrument to promote a virtuous citizenry and not simply a means to resolve disputes based on private self-interest. Government can be a force, Aristotle said, to achieve ends that are substantive and not merely procedural, aspirational and not merely bureaucratic. Joseph Lathrop, a pastor in West Springfield, Massachusetts, at the time of the founding, echoed these sentiments when he maintained that "government is a combination of the whole community against the vices of each particular member. [It] should exercise a controul over each member, to restrain him from wrong and compel him to right."[25] Moreover, the Anti-Federalist known as Brutus went so far as to suggest that the "happiness of the people depends" on the government's ability to ensure "internal peace and good order."[26] In order for a people to defend a government, Brutus insisted, it ought to be designed in such a way as to identify particular values that will foster a widespread belief that the crucial principles of collectivity and virtue are themselves valuable.

Sometimes the common good actively pursued involved secular interests, but equally often the shared conception of the good in eighteenth-century America was based on religious faith. Communities founded on particular religious beliefs inculcated the shared traditions and communal attachments necessary for competent government. "Religion was the strongest promoter of virtue, the most important ally of a well-constituted republic,"[27] according to historian Gordon S. Wood. The state of Massachusetts, in fact, grounded the importance of religion in Article III of its constitution: " 'As the happiness of a people, and the good order and preservation of civil government, essentially depend upon piety, religion and morality,' the legislature has the right to establish and promote public worship and religious training."[28]

Religious faith also provided the community with a purpose—a teleological end that prescribed a structured and particular way of life. The newly proposed constitutional text, seen by many Anti-Federalists as an irreversible usurpation of all the community's moral and substantive authority into the hands of the individual, neither commanded a similar value-laden purpose nor explicitly granted to the local and state communities the means to sponsor religious orthodoxy. Through its inherent ambiguity, the constitutional text permitted each individual citizen to determine what was in his best interest and what was the appropriate mode of existence. For the Anti-Federalists, such a constitutional mandate was deeply troubling, for some form of theological (albeit nondenominational) commonality was believed to be essential to promoting moral stability within the local community.

It was the perceived loss of republican or civic virtue that compelled the Anti-Federalist movement to oppose the ratification of the proposed Constitution. It was, in fact, this loss that they feared most from the newly formed union of independent states. A centralized government suggested the end of a longstanding commitment in America to localized political control—a right Americans secured at Yorktown. The Anti-Federalists argued that concentrated power implied the erosion of a communal tradition dating back to the time of the earliest colonial settlers. Recovery of that tradition could be assured only through the embrace of small, independent territorial units and the revitalization of civic virtue. Since the fledgling polity rejected the theory of simple federalism, problems of national as well as individual identity would surely arise. Homogeneity, the Anti-Federalists thought, nurtured familiarity, a familiarity with neighbors and customs that led directly to the realization of one's character. A majority of Anti-Federalist supporters thus concluded that severing those clearly defined and visible bonds would result in an irrevocable loss of the American's identity.

The Anti-Federalism of Modern Communitarians

The anxiety of losing one's identity and separating from one's community are certainly universal fears, and they are in no way unique to the debate between Federalists and Anti-Federalists even if they were particularly acute at the founding moment. In fact, those same fears are often raised today, couched in much the same manner that provoked the Anti-Federalists to resist ratification. In such a large and diverse nation as ours, can we locate and recover a common or shared identity? How is it that a liberal-democratic polity can be attentive to the principles of individualism and, at the same time, fully constituted? How, in other words, can we maintain a predominantly neutral state whereby no single way of life is favored, yet still encourage a strong sense of grounding and attachment among citizens?

This book contemplates the strong theoretical and constitutional challenge posed by one member of that recent critical community—the communitarians. It recognizes that, unlike policy changes that are automatically introduced with each successive ideological administration, the communitarians are calling for fundamental change at the very foundation of our political system. Indeed, the arguments constructed by the modern descendants of the Anti-Federalist doctrine parallel the earlier movement in more ways than simply attempting to recover the principles of communal autonomy and civic virtue. The contemporary communitarian challenge to the American political structure is, like the Federalist/Anti-Federalist debate, centered squarely on the ideal. Communitarians, in confronting the current liberal-democratic order, have elevated to the political fore the profound issue of constitutional change. Are the aspirations set out in the Preamble to the United States Constitution the ones most appealing and indispensable to contemporary American citizens? If so, what is the best way to arrange the institutions of this polity in order to achieve those particular goals? If not, what constitutional changes should be considered to ensure that other goals are actively pursued?

Modern communitarians share a number of qualities with Anti-Federalists.

They are, for the most part, heterogeneous. The diversity of their positions can best be comprehended when one juxtaposes the thoughts of certain radical communitarians with the more conservative wing of the movement. On the one hand, radical communitarians like Michael Walzer, Charles Taylor, and William Galston often have more in common with liberals than they do with their more conservative counterparts. They insist that individualism and rights are a necessary component of any modern political regime and that one of the aims of political and social institutions is to promote freedom. Conservative and more moderate communitarians, on the other hand, are less enamored with the liberal notion that freedom is the primary objective of most governments. They insist instead that virtue and the promotion of the good ought to be the top priority of any regime and that individual freedom can only truly be realized within a virtuous polity.

What links the radical and conservative communitarians, however, is the fact that along with their embrace of community in general, they dismiss the liberal notion that one can conceive of oneself outside of the communities we inhabit. In other words, all communitarians—both radical and conservative— believe that a conception of the self is impossible without a corresponding recognition, and indeed an endorsement, of the communities that order our individual lives. From the largest political regime to the smallest, communitarians proclaim—in contradistinction to the liberal ideal—that it is the institutions of the family, the schools, the churches and synagogues, the governments, and so forth that make us who we are. Modern communitarians, therefore, largely mirror the Anti-Federalists in that their arguments also rest along intersecting axes. The radical wing of communitarian thought is primarily, although not exclusively, interested in the balance between the community and the individual, while the conservative wing is principally focused on a variation of the issue related to political scale. As with the Anti-Federalists, however, these differences should not overshadow the fact that the axes do intersect, and it is the intersection between them that is most interesting.

From a more theoretical perspective, modern American communitarians also share with Anti-Federalists a critical mission. In their ongoing dispute with liberals, communitarians have resurrected a uniquely American phenomenon—the ability to question peacefully the merits of the political system at the constitutional level.[29] They have utilized some of the main tenets of the current Constitution—liberalism and freedom of thought—to counter the existing text itself. And in so doing, they have introduced one of the most prominent intellectual attempts at constitutional revision in this country since the mid-nineteenth-century Civil War.

Yet it is very apparent and somewhat ironic that communitarians have operated within a too-narrow understanding of constitutionalism.[30] And this is where they diverge most obviously from Anti-Federalists. Many contemporary communitarians have overlooked, or at least forgotten, the fact that their clash with liberalism is not specifically about policy preferences, but rather is a dispute about regime change. The implication of their movement goes far beyond simple political and ideological differences: it involves the very nature of politics itself, the very foundation of all political communities. Diverging most unmistakably from their Anti-Federalist ancestors, contemporary American communitarians regularly speak of "shared identities" or "constituted selves" without fully considering the meaning of constitution. They often defend their antiliberal position by exhorting a need for common roots and virtues, while at the same time refusing to acknowledge the overall strategic order that must accompany their communitarian principles. In its most intense form, what community-centered thinkers propose is not minor changes to a stable and attractive constitutional design, but rather the systematic reconfiguration of the current liberal-democratic polity. Less radical communitarians seek to shift emphases within the liberal tradition, while others call for a greater understanding of our most basic social and political relationships. All, however, imagine a polity that takes some features of communitarianism for granted. Indeed, a shift to a primarily community-centered polity—however radical—would represent a departure from our current political scheme that for better or worse is dominated by an individualistic agenda.

By altering the fundamental design of the polity's institutions, American communitarians are ultimately suggesting a reordering—or a replacement—of the current liberal regime and the introduction, in its stead, of a more community-based constitutional strategy. The argument that greater allegiance to community can be realized through attitudinal (and not exclusively institutional) change is simply a further indication of the obliviousness of most communitarians to the constitutional ramifications of their project. For the central communitarian critique of liberalism is an implicit repudiation of any constitutionalist regime that engenders liberalist principles. Similar to the most ardent Anti-Federalists, communitarians are, in short, calling for the

community allegence represents the institution

repudiation of the dominant political order, the hegemonic constitutional design. But unlike their forebears, they appear to be mostly indifferent to the deeper, more critical constitutional issues.

Thus, it may be time to capture their attention. By focusing on the constitutional component of communitarian theory, the participants of that movement will be called to account for the significant implications of their alternative position. On an intellectual level, it must be conceded that communitarianism represents one side of an expanding constitutional battle over the appropriate political order for the United States. The first goal of this project, therefore, is to remind the participants of this popular movement of the seriousness of their enterprise. But this book certainly has higher aspirations. It will directly challenge the communitarians from a constitutional level.

Before embarking on the traditional debate over the merits of competing political ideologies like communitarianism and liberalism, it seems necessary to consider the feasibility of such constitutional designs. What will a communitarian order look like? Will it have the necessary constitutional ingredients to make it a practical political experiment? The communitarian position doubtless presents an opportunity for contemporary students of constitutional theory to evaluate seriously the nature of alternative political orders. It may be the case that not every political theory is translatable into real constitutional politics; maybe the current conception of communitarianism simply does not have all the required constitutional elements to make it a viable political endeavor. Perhaps, then, the communitarian position, with its emphasis on community values, shared identities, and local sovereignty, is not as politically appealing as is currently assumed.

Constitutional Themes Past and Present

The issues of identity and community are part of an ongoing attempt to understand the nature of political systems, to come to grips with competing political structures. More specifically, they are part of a continuing dialogue that surrounds the pursuit of the ideally constituted polity.[31] In the example of the U.S. constitutional founding, the Federalists and Anti-Federalists were not only debating the merits of the proposed charter, but as an important part of that overarching conflict, they were also contemplating the deeper issue of political modeling. How should we organize and ultimately constrain the institutions of American government so that they are capable of promoting one particular vision of the ideal polity? We must somehow empower governmental bodies while simultaneously controlling them, thought the founding generation, so that they can fulfill their constitutionally designed mandate. Each side of the ratification debate had an important opinion on the quality of the newly created document, but the exchange involved much more than the simple endorsement or rejection of the text: it involved the pursuit of constitutional excellence.[32]

The Anti-Federalist known as "the Impartial Examiner" repeated many of these same themes in a February 20, 1788, editorial describing the defects of a primarily centralized government. He began by drawing a distinction between "arbitrary" and "free" governments, noting that "in the former the governors are invested with powers of acting according to their own wills, without any other limits than what they themselves may understand to be necessary for the general good; whereas in the latter they are entrusted with no such unlimited authority, but are restrained in their operations to conform to certain fundamental principles, the preservation whereof is expressly stipulated for in the civil compact."[33] Beyond identifying limits, however, the Impartial Examiner also proclaimed that the purpose of a constitution is to "create a covenant between each with all" so that the entire community is "constituted" and "obliged to obedience."[34] A constitution, he wrote, can and should be an anchor for all members of the community, providing them with a common or shared political identity. Moreover, a constitution should also reflect the political ideal. The primary task of the framer, according to the Impartial Examiner, is to draft a constitutional text that attempts to organize institutions in a way that maximizes the public good:

> It may not be improper to remark that persons forming a social community cannot take too much precaution when they are about to establish the plan of their government. They ought to construct it in such a manner as to procure the best possible security for their rights—in doing this they ought to give up no greater share than what is understood to be absolutely necessary—and they should endeavor so to organize, arrange and connect its several branches, that when duly exercised it may tend to promote the common good of all, and contribute as many advantages, as the civil institution is capable of.[35]

On its highest level, then, a constitution is the polity's substantive and procedural model; it is the attempt at political perfection. By ordering the institutions of the society in a particular way, the polity creates a normative design that reveals its priorities. That is, constitutions mandate a specific vision, typically based on a particular ideology that is said to be, at least for that individual political society, the best vision possible. As Albert Blaustein and Jay Sigler have suggested, a constitution will "reduce the abstractions of the political ideology of its age into a concrete reality."[36] Either by force or compromise, framers aspire to textualize the essential qualities of a regime in constitutional form. These qualities can reveal themselves in the preferences of the leaders/citizens or in the history of the nation, but in the end they are chosen self-consciously and placed within the constitutional text both for posterity and for the added security that accompanies a nation's most important document. Revolution, like that recently in the former Soviet bloc, occurs when the institutions of the crumbling regime can no longer sustain the means to achieve its constitutionally endorsed goals. It is at that point that alternative political schemes and designs—or constitutions—can be considered.

Put another way, constitutions are believed to be of such importance and are given such reverence mainly because they structure the entire polity in order to achieve certain clearly defined goals and ends—ends that (in the U.S. example at least) are articulated in the text's Preamble. A quick survey of constitutions around the world reveals that most articulate some version of a regime's ideological preferences. For example, the newly minted South African constitution begins by announcing that the Republic is a "sovereign, democratic state founded on the following values:

> (1) Human dignity, the achievement of equality and the advancement of human rights and freedoms.
> (2) Non-racialism and non-sexism.
> (3) Supremacy of the constitution and the rule of law.
> (4) Universal adult suffrage, a national common voters roll, regular elections and a multi-party system of democratic government, to ensure accountability, responsiveness and openness."[37]

No doubt much of what prompted the framers of the South African constitution to endorse these particular values was the country's enduring legacy of oppression and racial inequality. But the point should not be lost that the principles of human dignity, equality, freedom, and democracy were chosen carefully and deliberately. They were selected with an eye toward what a new, post-apartheid South Africa should look like, and they were arranged in such a way that the structure of South Africa's new government could maximize their possible impact. The combination of the ideological priorities and the design of a nation's public institutions, therefore, creates a distinct constitutional mandate.

There are few, if any, modest constitutions. Even the ones that do not specifically embrace those principles we normally attribute to modern constitutions—liberty, equality, sovereignty, democracy, and so forth—can be said to endorse *some* values. The absence of lofty aspirations, in other words, is itself a statement of preferences.[38] Certain constitutions simply set out the rules of the game and do not also include substantive declarations like a bill of rights or a pledge of equality. For example, consider the British North America Act of 1867—Canada's principal constitution—prior to the 1982 ratification of the Canadian Charter of Rights and Freedoms. The Constitution Act, 1867 (as it has come to be known) is virtually devoid of aspirational language.[39] Yet that too is by design. The document is based entirely on the British image of ~~colonialism~~ and thus the constitutional principles that might accompany a population that enjoys self-rule—freedom, equality, and so forth—are largely absent. Part of the constitution's character derives from its peculiar form and its technical rigidity, but another defining feature is the fact that it exclusively reflects British hegemony. It is, according to three members of Canada's founding generation, a constitution that does not "derive from the people," but rather has been "provided by the Imperial Parliament" in England.[40] The constitution does not, in other words, originate with the consent of the citizens in the way most other modern regimes have. Instead, the 1867 Canadian constitution has been imposed on the people by an extrinsic source, and is largely consistent with a regime engaged in extensive colonial governance. It made little sense at the time to promote universal freedom or equality, for to do so would be to acknowledge, in direct contrast to the object of colonialism itself, that other cultures were parallel to the British way of life. The critical constitutional point is not so much that colonialism was wrong, but that the British Parliament deliberately chose a constitutional framework for Canada that reflected very specific and very imperialistic values. *freedoms not valued*

In eighteenth-century America, Federalists and Anti-Federalists were embroiled in a similar constitutional exchange, even if the specifics of each constitutional dialogue were somewhat unique. Each side believed in its own political vision for America, and thus each advocated what it thought was the correct constitutional model, the ideal political order. For the Federalists, that order was manifest in the 1787 constitutional text, but for the Anti-Federalists, the more appropriate structure was one that left greater authority in the hands of the local and state governments. Broadly defined, the goals or ends sought by the Anti-Federalist "constitution" involved some form of communal autonomy and the pursuit of civic or republican virtue. The 1787 Federalist text, while perhaps slightly less transparent about the specific means to achieve its objectives, nonetheless also supported a particular set of normative goals. These goals focused primarily on the national government and its procedural ability to set the country's substantive agenda. Even the ultimate ratification and acceptance of the Federalist-sponsored Constitution did not resolve the deeper question, for it remained at the nucleus of American politics during most of the eighteenth and nineteenth centuries.[41]

Today, perhaps unknowingly, the issue of political modeling and the pursuit of the ideal has seen something of a renaissance as many once again reexamine the nature of constitutional alternatives while specifically questioning the excellence of a liberal-democratic order.[42] Contemporary critiques of the dominant constitutional order are again emerging, and this time they appear to be gaining significant popularity. It may be fair to say that we are presently engaged in an ongoing conversation about first principles—freedom, equality, democracy, sovereignty—even if we do not always recognize that the stakes are so high. ✳ patriot Act? terrorism

For some time we have automatically assumed that any serious talk about political change must come first from our governmental institutions, that it is our representatives who somehow know when the time is ripe to question our most basic values. But debate about change can take many forms, and questions of constitutional importance are in no way reserved exclusively for politicians and jurists. Instead, they are broached whenever we are willing to consider a fundamental shift in political climate. Our methods may be comparatively informal, but like the Federalist/Anti-Federalist debate, we are constantly striving to improve our political environment. Whether we like it or not, many critics of the American political scheme are currently asking whether the United States should modify (or perhaps even abandon) its present liberal-democratic design in favor of a fundamentally different political order, one that places greater emphasis on full and active political participation.[43] ✳

Domestic violence, greed, and political apathy, some are quick to point out, are on the rise, while literacy, honorable or ethical conduct, and benevolence are simultaneously dropping. And what is more, traditional institutions that in the past had gone a long way toward successfully countering the country's major problems have recently lost much of their transformative import. Is it time, then, for constitutional revolution in this country? Is the U.S. Constitution, with its liberal vision and democratic design, still the most appropriate model to ensure that all its citizens are fully constituted? Or, many contemporary critics are wondering, is there an alternative constitutional strategy that is perhaps more desirable for the continually changing American polity?

Modern American Communitarianism

For the past twenty years communitarians have waged a two-front war: against liberal theory in general, and, more recently, against the American embodiment of that idea. Mainly in response to the rise of neo-Kantian liberalism, early American communitarianism focused primarily on the theoretical or abstract principles of each ideology. Prominent political commentators like Michael Sandel, Charles Taylor, and Michael Walzer pointed to a few of the apparent faults—extreme personal autonomy, hyperindividualism, and loss of communal identity, among others—often associated with liberal politics. In doing so, they began to construct a modern theoretical agenda that stressed the community over the individual, the good over the right, and the public over the private. While they have never fully accepted the label of communitarians, these thinkers are viewed by most as encompassing the theoretical foundation of the recent communitarian movement. Their widely read works have influenced the nature of political theory; some have even referred to their ongoing debate with liberal theorists as "central to the discipline" of modern political philosophy.[44]

Reminiscent of a Western tradition replete with influential political theory, the writings of Walzer, Sandel, Taylor, and Alasdair MacIntyre are profound commentaries on the state of contemporary politics. Each, in a slightly different manner, is critical of the dominance of liberalist ideology. MacIntyre, for instance, condemns modern liberal society for its propensity to encourage "emotivist" personalities. He insists that "we have—very largely, if not entirely —lost our comprehension, both theoretical and practical, of morality."[45] Taylor refers to modern society as "atomistic," maintaining that the term is used "loosely to characterize the doctrines of social contract theory which arose in the seventeenth century and also successor doctrines . . . which inherited a vision of society as in some sense constituted by individuals for the fulfillment of ends which were primarily individual."[46] Sandel further posits that modern culture is dominated by the notion of "deontological liberalism," the claim that society is governed best when it is "arranged by principles that do not presuppose any particular conception of the good."[47]

Yet despite the subtle differences and the distinct terminological preferences, what makes these theorists so compelling is that when combined, their work creates a distinct and, in places, revolutionary political design based on the community. In attempting to destroy (or at least refashion) the principles of liberalism, theoretical communitarians have proposed a unique political order for modern society. They have engineered a community-based theoretical model that now exists as a genuine counter to the liberal paradigm.[48]

An important component of the theoretical debate between liberals and communitarians, and one that should be introduced here, is manifest in the more moderate or conservative approach first advanced by Alasdair MacIntyre. A Thomist by reputation, MacIntyre represents a departure from the more radical wing of the communitarian movement. He is more fiercely antiliberal than, say, Michael Sandel, and he is seemingly more devoted to the principles of truth and virtue than is Michael Walzer. He nonetheless remains a true communitarian insofar as the central aim of his writings is to highlight both the vices of the liberal individual and the frailties of the unbound community. He shares much in common with other communitarians, including a perception that the communities we inhabit are often discouraged from acting as moral compasses; they are in essence discarded as institutions without any binding authority. MacIntyre laments the post-Enlightenment philosophy that encourages the individual to be the captain of his own destiny without any acknowledgment of the relationships and the organizations that shape us.

Yet MacIntyre's writings are important for other reasons as well. In trying to organize the sequence of communitarian thinkers, MacIntyre occupies a pivotal position. He is at once aligned with the original communitarian critics like Walzer, Taylor, and Sandel who view extreme individualism as corrosive of the modern polity. But his work has also spawned a new generation of *conservative* communitarians led by George Carey, Bruce Frohnen, Norman Barry, and Kenneth Grasso. A conservative voice, in other words, has entered the dialogue over the value of community in recent years, owing in large part to the intellectual impact of MacIntyre's work. These conservatives argue not only that the core principles of liberalism are faulty but also that the radical community-centered theorists like Walzer and William Galston are simply liberals masquerading as communitarians. For example, Barry has described Taylor's overall

homogeneous

philosophical project as one that tries to "reconcile two apparently conflicting doctrines: liberalism, with its stress on formal (or substantive) equality, universal and nondiscriminatory law, and communitarianism, which emphasizes the distinctive properties of identifiable groups and demands that the law recognize them and, indeed, privilege them if the remorseless progress of a free and open society threatens their integrity."[49] Barry's conclusion, consistent with those of other conservative communitarians, is that Taylor's attempt is both unsuccessful and disingenuous.

Over the past decade communitarians, while certainly building on the earlier theoretical work, have shifted their focus away from abstract thinking in favor of a more policy-oriented approach. In accord with the traditional—and theoretical—community-centered writings, the recent *prescriptive movement* suggests as problematic the overall moral deterioration and loss of constitutive values that has accompanied a modern liberal (or, in the more specific case, American) state. Indeed, the new prescriptive defense of communitarianism takes as its launching point the arguments of prior theorists who contended that liberal society consists largely of "atomistic" souls devoid of tradition and commonality, yet it manages simultaneously to broaden and apply those ideas by (1) introducing into the debate specific proposals for political change, and (2) relating their normative findings specifically to the American political experiment.[50] Scholars and practitioners such as Amitai Etzioni, Benjamin Barber, Mary Ann Glendon, and William Galston have translated many provisions of the ongoing liberal-communitarian debate into ideas that they insist will improve this nation's public policy. Etzioni, for example, is not only concerned that liberal America tends to encourage severe personal autonomy and political apathy but also that individual citizens have in the past been too preoccupied with the protection of their private rights and liberties. He thus suggests, as necessary for America's future, "a moratorium on the minting of most, if not all, new rights."[51] Benjamin Barber supports Etzioni's prescriptive crusade, yet his interest lies, not in the reinterpretation of the Bill of Rights, but in altering America's participatory system. He calls for the advent of a national community through a more involved, deeply active populace. To be fully constituted, he argues, requires both an understanding of the citizen's place in the polity and a commitment to genuine "civic activity."[52] Consistent with the new prescriptive branch of communitarianism, Barber and others combine

ppl. need to get involved w/ govt

elements of the rigorous abstract thinking introduced by the earlier theoretical communitarians with a strong penchant for specific, more policy-oriented change.

These two distinct "periods" of American communitarianism—the theoretical and the prescriptive—provide the general backdrop of this book. In Part I, I focus on the schematic challenge to the vision of communitarian politics that emerges from a comprehensive fusion of the earlier theoretical writings and the later prescriptive teachings. It is important to consider the viability of a general communitarian design before turning directly to the question of a communitarian America; therefore, the initial section will preface the theoretical compatibility of communitarianism and constitutionalism. In chapter 2, I set up the argument by examining the nature of the still-contentious liberal-communitarian debate, with an eye toward the stalemate that has been reached in the last few years between proponents of both positions. Both radical and conservative communitarians regularly fault liberalism for encouraging rabid individualism and extreme personal autonomy. They further argue that such a promise leads directly to an unconstituted or "rootless" citizenry, one that has no conception of the society as a whole or the community that is inhabited. Accordingly, communitarians posit that an alternative to the liberal paradigm, one based more prominently on the community, should be embraced.

Liberals, on the other hand, maintain that their communitarian adversaries tend to characterize liberal politics as, among other things, too extreme — either an individual is thoroughly independent of community influences, or that same individual is totally constituted by communal values—there appears to be no middle ground.[53] Liberals suggest that such communitarian extremism is unfounded. Citizens of a liberal political order are neither unconstituted nor fully affected by shared principles; instead, they locate some median between complete personal autonomy and pure group solidarity.

Chapter 2 continues by focusing directly on the recent prescriptive branch of the communitarian position. How is the new breed of communitarian different from the traditional theoretical group? Is the communitarian call for sweeping policy change in the United States tantamount to a verbal constitutional revolution? This section analyzes the specifics of the American communitarian position from a primarily structuralist perspective, with a critical eye toward the vision of what the country would look like under such a political regime. It further explores the principles defended by the recently formed communitarian social movement. Headed by the likes of Etzioni, Galston, and

Glendon, the movement is attempting to gather support for the communitarian position by appealing to both political leaders and everyday citizens. Its platform begins:

> American men, women, and children are members of many communities—families; neighborhoods; innumerable social, religious, ethnic, workplace, and professional associations; and the body politic itself. Neither human existence nor individual liberty can be sustained for long outside the interdependent and overlapping communities to which we all belong. Nor can any community long survive unless its members dedicate some of their attention, energy, and resources to shared projects. The exclusive pursuit of private interest erodes the network of social environments on which we all depend, and is destructive to our shared experiment in democratic self-government. For these reasons, we hold that the rights of individuals cannot long be preserved without a communitarian perspective. A communitarian perspective recognizes both individual human dignity and the social dimension of human existence.[54]

It continues by defining communitarianism as a political ideology that strives to "restore the moral voice" of American society. Commencing with the family and continuing through the school and the community, the "Responsive Communitarian Platform" seeks to alter fundamentally the "institutions of civil society" in an attempt to return some degree of moral consensus to the general American polity.

As the debate rages on, neither side is willing to concede even the slightest advantage, and the opposition of liberal and communitarian claims has reached something of an impasse.[55] Hence, the introduction of an alternative perspective like that of constitutional theory appears to be warranted. The infusion of constitutional theory into the core of the liberal-communitarian debate is made even more germane by the propensity on the part of both sides to speak in the language of constituted individuals and constituted regimes without being fully cognizant of the larger constitutional principles. The final five chapters, therefore, continue the intellectual course begun by Stephen Macedo, whose *Liberal Virtues: Citizenship, Virtue, and Community in Liberal Constitutionalism* was the first to defend a "thicker" conception of liberalism based on the idea that liberalism itself is a "public morality."[56] Macedo recognizes that both liberals and communitarians are engaged in the most crucial of public projects—the constitutional project. Both, he insists, are asking the same critical question: "What is the right way for us to live?"[57] According to

Macedo, the answer, when looking at the American polity, is unabashed liberalism. His unique insight into the realm of modern political thought is that the American style of liberalism is a conscious choice and not, as communitarians would want us to believe, the default of a largely rudderless population. My work differs from Macedo's in that I do not propose to support liberalism directly, nor am I entirely convinced that America's embrace of liberalism can be defended so easily. If anything, I am neither a liberal nor a communitarian but rather an unapologetic constitutionalist. My intention, therefore, is to focus entirely on the constitutional defects of the communitarian framework. Macedo does a bit of this in his book, but I propose to go further.

Chapter 3 thus begins the constitutionalist inquiry by envisioning a functioning communitarian design. Through the union of theoretical writings and prescriptive proposals, and by using the works of communitarian sympathizers, we can piece together the most obvious ingredients of a communitarian political construction. What will a communitarian polity look like? Which decision-rule will most likely be employed? How will the regime identify and foster collective and communal values? What will it do with those shared values once they have been identified?

The construction of a hypothetical communitarian polity is both essential and dangerous.[58] It is necessary to design a communitarian polity so that one may have a working model with which to ultimately juxtapose constitutionalist maxims. Claiming that communitarian theory is inattentive to constitutionalist principles would be simple if one merely isolated particular communitarian ideas and visions for scrutiny. But by conceiving of an entire (albeit conjectural) communitarian regime, the central task of this project is made significantly more challenging, not to mention more legitimate. At the same time, however, the construction of a communitarian polity is deeply perilous precisely because it runs the risk of producing a mere shadow of a thriving, fully developed communitarian regime. Because (as has been admitted by most communitarians) there are few clearly defined examples to consult, one must speculate on the extent of a working communitarian polity—and speculation can often be misleading. Yet if it is done responsibly by using the most accurate descriptions of communitarian thinking and by situating community values historically and contextually, a useful model of communitarian politics should come into focus.

Having erected the frame of a contemporary communitarian polity, Part II of this study begins the heart of the project. Chapter 4 will begin the constitutionalist assault on communitarianism as I review the first principle of constitutionalism—limitation of political power—and apply it to the previously constructed communitarian regime. A modern constitutionalist polity is one that at the very least recognizes and articulates a meaningful constraint on public power, the objective limitation of governmental authority. Predominantly liberal polities have, for the most part, been attentive to this first principle of modern constitutionalism. They have tended to place certain powers and privileges beyond the reach of those who occupy positions of authority, thereby precluding the possibility of tyrannical rule. Bills of rights and political systems that grant minority protection[59] have provided objective means for citizen safeguards against complete and unfettered governmental authority. Many semi-liberal regimes have also managed to foster constitutionalist maxims. Primarily religious states, like Ireland and post-Communist Poland, have, for example, composed political systems that include measures to ensure meaningful limited rule. In contrast, however, communitarian polities as they are currently imagined fail in their attempt to impose significant objective limits on political power. Substantive authority is not placed beyond the reach of those occupying political office but rather is fully determined by the "shared understandings or values" manifest within the boundaries of the communitarian polity. Citizens, therefore, have no recourse from the apparently unfettered grip of the community. They must either abide by the one prescribed course or run the risk of becoming unconstituted or unbounded—clearly the worst fate for the true communitarian.

It may be useful to recall our discussion in the preface about Lincoln's suspension of habeas corpus since it illustrates most vividly the problems associated with constitutional restraints and communitarian theory. As I noted, Lincoln's interpretation of Article I, Section 9, was logically motivated by a belief that the well-being of the overall polity would be jeopardized by inactivity. Had he not taken action on behalf of the community, there might have been no community left to lead when all was said and done. But again, that understanding of unfettered power contrasts directly with the principal intention of constitutionalism. Indeed, the limits imposed by a constitutional document must have force if that document is to perform its many functions. Even the community's most ardent wishes cannot prevail over the provisions of the constitutional text. On occasions when a community's desires conflict with a constitution's mandate, Chief Justice Taney proclaimed, the constitution must triumph. Otherwise, the whole notion of constitutional government collapses.

The examination of constitutional restraint is the perfect preamble to a larger discussion of communitarian democracy. Full and active participation in the political process lies at the core of the communitarian creed. Indeed, aside from a vague notion of "community," some form of political self-determination stands as the most crucial component of a communitarian political regime. Without a firm commitment to democratic or republican theory, in other words, communitarianism cannot fully be realized. But when juxtaposed alongside the idea of pure constitutionalism, democracy can be viewed with significant disfavor. With the communitarian stance in mind, chapter 5 thus explores the fundamental tension between constitutionalism and democracy.

The objective limitation of government authority is, nonetheless, only the first of the required components of constitutionalism. In chapter 5, I also take up the equally critical and deeply related constitutionalist principle described as the authorization or creation of political power. Aside from its function as an objective limit on unfettered public authority, a constitution must also grant political power; it must invest authority in the hands of particular institutions so as to infuse those institutions (and the commands that may emanate from them) with legitimacy. In the same way representatives are required to act in direct accordance with the interests of their constituents, institutions of government maintain legitimacy only through the clear distribution of objectively constitutional authority. Current communitarian theory, however, confounds this central constitutionalist maxim by blurring the distinction between the people as founders and the people as political decision makers, between those who are engaged in the necessary (but singular) process of creation and empowerment, and the political representatives who are charged with the ongoing responsibility of furthering the constitution's central mission. In so doing, the proponents of the modern communitarian movement renounce the fundamentals of constitutionalism itself.

In chapter 6, I attempt to locate the theoretical discussion involving constitutionalism and communitarianism within the context of the real nation-state. Specifically, I identify two regimes whose "constitutional" structure does not exactly resemble those that inform either the American polity or similar liberal-democratic regimes. Israel and Germany, as examples of alternative constitutional designs, offer insight into the nature of constitutional organization and the contrast between classical and modern notions of constitutionalism. Since these two countries have adopted significantly different models of constitutionalism, by considering their differences, we are better able to solidify our broader understanding of constitutional theory.

First, I consider the character of Israel's governing charter. Israel's unwritten "constitution" contrasts nicely with more liberal documents in that it reinforces the most profound example of a contemporary communitarian polity currently known. The country, as it is currently configured, is fully dedicated to the idea of Jewish self-determination and, pragmatically speaking, to the protection of the Jewish people. As a result, it supports a particularistic, or singularly substantive, constitutional agenda, an agenda that is not at all neutral to competing conceptions of the good. Individual rights are valued in Israel, but they are not paramount and are often suppressed when they pose a threat to the continued existence of the nation's primary mission. Similarly, the principle of equality differs from that found in more liberal constitutions. Non-Jews cannot in any way be considered equal to their Jewish neighbors in their comparative ability to advance the common good. If Israel is to remain a state informed principally by the teachings of Judaism, it must listen only to the words and ideas of those who are dedicated to that mission. What differentiates Israel's approach with regard to competing ethnic and religious groups is not that some positions are favored, while others are not; indeed, that sort of inequity occurs in virtually every polity that subscribes to even the most rudimentary democratic rules. Rather, what distinguishes Israel is the fact that its particularist—or communitarian—foundation is fully state-sponsored. Israel's highest institutions and its most fundamental documents celebrate above all else the notion that all public policies must in some way be compatible with the principles espoused in the *Torah*. There is no deviation from that course, for to do so would place the entire experiment of Jewish statehood in jeopardy.

Chapter 6 then turns to the less contentious but equally compelling issue of bonding communitarian and liberal provisions into one constitutional text. By considering the semi-liberal constitutional model offered by the German Basic Law, this section addresses the question of whether the United States could sustain even a partial communitarian overhaul. For some communitarians, the difference between a liberal polity and a communitarian one is subtle, requiring only slight (albeit important) political changes. The "Responsive Communitarian Platform" asks that we, as citizens of the United States, consider the possibility of refining particular elements of the liberal-democratic text to reveal certain communitarian principles. It seeks to integrate aspects of the liberal American Constitution with parts of the community-based agenda in an attempt to redefine fundamentally the existent nature of American politics. But such a proposed endeavor raises important foundational questions: Is it possible to realize the style of mixed constitution envisioned by most contemporary communitarians? Does the American text have the flexibility to embrace alternative constitutional principles? The theory of constitutionalism provides some answers to these questions, and it is the goal of this project to bring those answers—as well as the animating questions—to the political fore.

The constitutionalist challenge to recent American communitarianism is not just an exercise in rhetoric. Communitarianism in this country is currently in vogue as some of the most influential political actors are beginning to take the movement seriously. Consider the fact that the sitting president and vice president have, at various times, indicated their strong affinity for some of the ideas espoused by the prescriptive thinkers.[60] Consider also the fact that the communitarian movement has shifted from one based predominantly on theory, to one focused squarely on the possibilities for real and fundamental change. Clearly, the communitarian position is one that Americans must seriously review.

Liberals and other ideological thinkers have begun to do so.[61] But, perhaps because they are too embroiled in the traditional liberal-communitarian rivalry, their arguments have gone largely unnoticed by their communitarian opponents. Now it is time to move beyond the liberal-communitarian impasse —to transcend the current stalemate—by challenging the new prescriptive communitarian position on its own terms. If communitarians desire actual and fundamental change in this (and presumably other liberal-democratic) societies, they must contend with the larger, deeper issue of political modeling. As both the Federalists and Anti-Federalists did to each other more than two hundred years ago, contemporary communitarians must be reminded that they are not simply tinkering with previously established rules, procedures, and norms, but rather with the very foundation of politics itself. They are asking themselves: What is the appropriate political order for a country like the United States? How can Americans achieve constitutional excellence? And because the communitarians have begun to ask these deeply profound questions, we must begin to supply them with answers—some of which they may not want to hear.

Part I / Toward a Vision of Communitarian Politics

CHAPTER TWO

Theoretical and Prescriptive Foundations

The Liberal-Communitarian Debate

The communitarian movement in America has a long and staggered history. Beginning with the Anti-Federalists, communitarianism has come in and out of vogue at regular intervals. Michael Walzer, himself a noted contemporary communitarian, remarks that the movement "is like pleated trousers: transient but certain to return."[1] Over the past two decades, communitarianism has been resurgent, once again resurfacing to challenge the dominant political ideology—liberalism. That, however, is not to suggest that proponents of modern American communitarianism represent a uniform, fully consistent position. In fact, recent American communitarianism is quite divergent, with three distinct branches and multiple normative agendas. Some community-centered thinkers look to the past, particularly to the ancients, for a model of the good polity; others attempt to combine elements of a community-based enterprise with more contemporary "liberal" provisions. Still others tend to use the earlier theoretical communitarianism as a springboard for proposing specific, and possibly radical, policy changes.

Adding another dimension to an already complicated puzzle, within the variety of communitarianism lies a group that is at least partially sympathetic to the ideal of liberalism. Certain communitarians—most noticeably Michael Walzer and William Galston—see the freedom explicit in liberal ideology as the fulfillment of the state's central aspirations. They argue that true freedom is an ideal worthy of our deepest affection. What makes them communitarians and not liberals is their belief that liberty can be achieved solely through the strengthening of community, that it is possible to be free only when we have fortified the communities that energize and surround us. As Walzer notes throughout *Radical Principles*, true liberation can only come once the individual acknowledges the importance of his collective relationships and then acts in such a way as to regularly remind the community that he has accepted responsibility for membership. True liberty, Walzer seems to be saying, cannot come from a liberal society constituted by isolated beings but must instead be cultivated on the foundation of collective action.

Notwithstanding their apparent moderation, virtually all community-centered thinkers who retain some affinity for liberalism (including Walzer and Galston) also subscribe to most of the central propositions adopted by more extreme communitarians. Reflecting the thoughts of Alasdair MacIntyre and Charles Taylor, they are deeply troubled by the notion of the self existing in physical and metaphorical isolation. Similarly, they—like Michael Sandel—are unimpressed by the image of the polity that emerges from a largely egotistical, self-interested citizenry. They further posit that neither the liberal conception of the self nor the corresponding vision of the polity makes much sense outside the realm of communal attachments. And finally, they contend that the neutral state is not sustainable over time; it will disappear into irrelevancy just as soon as individual citizens recognize that it cannot provide them with meaningful bonds. For those reasons, they stand firmly inside the communitarian camp.

Thus, despite its many apparent iterations, contemporary American communitarianism can be said to represent one, albeit broadly defined, line of thought. As the patrons of a characteristic political design sharing a number of meaningful themes in common, present-day communitarians can be loosely grouped together to form a consolidated union. That is, insofar as they continue to challenge the dominant theoretical paradigms, they are the modern equivalent of the Anti-Federalist movement—not a fully homogeneous band, but certainly representative of a generally consistent argument. Most political commentators identify a few essential principles typically attributed to all communitarians. Those principles often include a call for the "constituted," or "encumbered," self; the attempt to reestablish within the polity some sense of "civic or communal virtue;" and the insistence that an individual's identity is realized only through the various relationships one fosters within diverse and numerous community structures.

Like no other movement in this country since the Anti-Federalists two hundred years ago, American communitarians have created a political project centered almost entirely on the constitutive nature of the community. What distinguishes these thinkers and gives them genuine solidarity is that they share a deep interest in an alternative to the hegemonic political order, to the dominant normative design. They share a burning conviction that the current political strategy suffers from seriously debilitating flaws. Indeed, they protest, it is neither a fully effective method to organize the institutions of the polity nor the most alluring political design available; another political scheme, one that places more emphasis on the community, might be more appropriate for many of the world's political societies. Stephen Holmes nicely captures this dynamic: "Antiliberalism is a resilient, diverse, fairly consistent, unbroken— but theoretically understudied—intellectual tradition. Its unity does not consist in uniformity, to be sure, but in a handful of basic assumptions plus, above all, a common enemy."[2]

That enemy, of course, is the liberal ideal, the system of morality ordered by the major liberal propositions. But as a necessary consequence of that broad opposition, the enemy must also be the manifestation of that moral theory in what can be described as the liberal *constitutional* polity. Beyond the particularities of a liberal regime, communitarians are lashing out at the liberal project itself. In criticizing the liberalist agenda, they are condemning any constitutional design that predominantly embraces liberal principles. Hence, what unites the communitarian crusade is not only "the view that liberalism does not sufficiently take into account the importance of community for personal identity, moral and political thinking, and judgments about our well being in the contemporary world,"[3] but also the notion that a political community constitutionally structured around the principles of liberalism is a flawed and unwelcome society. It is a society marred and splintered by extreme selfishness and autonomy, its institutions promoting citizen apathy and general detachment. Liberal principles, communitarians allege, do not organize a society of rooted, contented individuals working together to effect certain collective goals and aspirations, but rather, a community of avaricious egoists all seemingly fixated on their own personal interests. Thus, even if the supporters of the communitarian position do not always use the same language or advocate the same policy proposals, they almost invariably stand by the premise that liberal politics can be improved and that political communities should be strengthened.

Theoretical Communitarianism

Contemporary communitarians concentrate their assault on the liberal project in the liberal belief in the primacy of state neutrality and the corresponding conception of the autonomous individual. Whereas the liberal envisions the individual self as the authoritative moral agent in questions as to the good, communitarians see the community as contributing to the realization of that end. Justice, they contend, is not meant to be exclusively procedural, but rather it must have a substantive component; some ways of life are simply better than others.

Indeed, the communitarian critique of the theory of liberalism is squarely focused on two fundamental political inquiries—questions about the self, and questions about the structure of the overall polity. Contemporary community-centered thinkers concentrate on attempting to derail, first, the liberal understanding of the self as autonomously constituted, and then, second, the parallel conception of liberal society that is largely impartial or neutral to competing visions of the good life. Furthermore, communitarians tend to attack these liberal views from two critical perspectives: a pragmatic perspective, and a normative one. The pragmatic attack on liberalism attempts to probe the overall credibility of the liberal project. It asks whether the liberal view of the self or the theory's related notion of the polity are tenable—whether they are even conceivable. And the response most often heard by communitarian thinkers is that they are not.

The normative communitarian impulse, on the other hand, is subtly, and importantly, distinct. For different reasons, communitarians believe that a neutral society composed of independent, insular individuals is both unappealing and undesirable. Communitarians who subscribe to this line of reasoning are not so much interested in the *possibility* of realizing, in political form, the liberal agenda, but rather in the *desirability* or *appeal* of a society organized around liberal values. They might concede the existence of the rootless self or the neutral polity, but they almost unanimously assert that "the premises of individualism give rise to morally unsatisfactory consequences."[4] Even if it is possible to organize individuals around private interests and then provide them with no means to promote communal bonds, communitarians ask, who would want to live in such a society? Why would we self-consciously choose to inhabit a polity where there is little hope of sharing anything meaningful in common? Central to this communitarian complaint, then, is the claim that even if the liberal vision of the individual and the society is accurate, it is odious, and that a polity governed by communitarian rules would be more suitable to any constituted citizenry.

To be sure, almost all communitarians make both pragmatic and normative arguments at one time or another. It is exceedingly difficult to distinguish one's critique of liberal society by insisting that it rests on unstable foundations without also arguing that its premises are less appealing than any number of alternatives. Sandel, for example, travels back and forth regularly between the pragmatic and normative realms while condemning the neo-Kantian image of the ideal polity. On the one hand, he suggests that Rawls' assumptions lead to a portrait of the self that is impossible to imagine; on the other, he argues that a polity built on liberal presuppositions "creates a moral void that opens the way for narrow, intolerant moralisms . . . [while failing] to cultivate the qualities of character that equip citizens to share in self-rule."[5] Yet separating the pragmatic from the normative can be highly useful when describing the breadth of communitarian scholarship. They are, in the end, distinct areas of inquiry. They seek to answer fundamentally different questions by addressing different concerns. In some respects they are predicated on each other. But overall, distinguishing the normative from the pragmatic enables us to visualize more clearly the subtleties of the community-centered position. For the sake of that clarity, I divide them below.

Questions of the Self

Pragmatic Problems

The self exists as the true symbol of liberal theory; it is the primary political unit as well as the initial focus of all foundational political inquiry. Accordingly, the self is the first principle thrust directly into the middle of the contemporary liberal-communitarian debate. Modern liberals like John Rawls and Ronald Dworkin postulate that the individual is antecedent to the formation of the political community and, as such, should be viewed as an autonomous being capable of independent reflection and self-conscious definition. One is free to make one's own life choices, both good and bad; and because those decisions constitute who one is, there must be a conception of the self as existing prior to, and, to a certain extent, independent from, the larger political universe. It is this autonomy or freedom of choice that most liberals claim gives essential import to our understanding of personhood. Without such liberty, they say, one cannot comprehend the true meaning of life, nor can one distinguish oneself from others who may be similarly situated. The inherent value of being human, that is, resides specifically in the principle of self-determination.

As a result of the primacy of the self, liberal thinkers can assert that the individual also exists prior to any particular conception of the good—or substantive telos—that may emanate from a political society. The liberal understanding of the self supports the notion that persons are able to choose among many competing visions of the good life without being completely controlled or manipulated by external factors. They can, as part of being human, decide to ignore all communal or particularistic influences in favor of strictly personal ones. Of course, those same citizens may elect to follow a specific community-centered vision of the good—in fact, religious, ethnic, and other collective visions are frequently followed—but restrictions on the individual's *capacity* or *freedom* to choose among those differing views of the good are deemed by most liberal theorists as substantially illegitimate. In fact, the notion of freedom is inviolate to the liberal advocate. For example, Rawls writes:

> As free persons, citizens recognize one another as having the moral power to have a conception of the good. This means that they do not view themselves as inevitably tied to the pursuit of the particular conception of the good and its final ends which they espouse at any given time. Instead, as citizens, they are regarded as, in general, capable of revising and changing this conception on reasonable and rational grounds. Thus it is permissible for citizens to stand apart from conceptions of the good and to survey and assess their various final ends.[6]

Liberals, therefore, defend the claim that personal identity is formed and determined, not from primarily environmental forces, but instead from internal ones. No one other than the individual knows better what may be right for one's self, and thus no one can rightly discern what is in one's best interest. Such profoundly important decisions can and should only come from within one's soul.[7]

In distinction to this individualistic stance, communitarians argue that the community plays a much larger role—indeed, the largest role—in the shaping of personal identity. Communitarians ask: What is the self? What constitutes a human identity? And furthermore, which principles or stimuli will determine what choices an individual makes? Communitarian advocates believe an individual's choices are deeply, if not totally, constrained by his relationships with other members of the communities that nourish him. An individual cannot escape the control of his culture, heritage, and surroundings. Volunteering to join an association, communitarians point out, is a sign of the individual's need to form relationships and find support from various communities. Liberals, on the other hand, shun complete community authority, claiming instead that the individual has freedom from those relationships to choose among competing interests. Stephen Mulhall and Adam Swift write: "The debate . . . between the liberal and the communitarian concerns itself with the importance of the individual's right to choose her own way of life and to express herself freely, even where this conflicts with the values and commitments of the community or society of which she is a member."[8]

Michael Sandel defends the pragmatists' argument when he takes on Rawls' theory of the "antecedently individuated" person. He first suggests that the liberal idea of the self as unencumbered is impossible to conceive: an individual is not a transcendent personality, nor is he divorced from attachments, aims, assets, and so forth. He is a person who is constituted by his character, his surroundings, and his community. An individual cannot ignore his social situation in much the same way as he cannot flatly reject his social position; he simply must accept that he is part of numerous interconnected communities.

Sandel's aim in uncovering the inherent flaws associated with Rawls' neo-Kantian liberalism is to portray the liberal individual as essentially empty of substance. To do that, he initially sketches an image of Rawls' theory that highlights the antecedent nature of modern liberal society. He points to Rawls' "original position"—the imaginary locale in which we are invited to debate, without knowledge of our particular assets and liabilities, those principles that we would select to govern our society—and suggests that its central premise is defective. The principal defect of the original position, Sandel argues, is that it presupposes an image of the individual as being somehow detached from his goals or aims. The individual in Rawls' calculus is asked to choose a conception of justice without any knowledge of his capabilities or influences; he has no knowledge, in other words, of his own purposes or ends. Yet an awareness of one's abilities, interests, values, and goals, Sandel says, is precisely what allows us to conceive of *any* principles of justice. Without an appreciation of our identity, we can't hope to do much at all. We may be free to make choices, but those choices will be mostly hollow.

Rawls' self, Sandel insists, is the epitome of the unencumbered self: "For the unencumbered self, what matters above all, what is most essential to our personhood, are not the ends we choose but our capacity to choose them."[10] Rawls claims that "it is not our aims that primarily reveal our nature but rather the principles that we would acknowledge to govern the background conditions under which these aims are to be formed and the manner in which they are to be pursued. . . . We should therefore reverse the relation between the right and the good proposed by teleological doctrines and view the right as prior."[11] In Sandel's estimation, a sense of identity can never be fully recognized unless we first acknowledge our position within our varied social settings. Any comprehension of the self, he argues, is impossible without a corresponding conception of the society in which we live; for identity is formed by those exact associations and commitments that an individual makes as part of a political community. Writes Sandel: "To have character is to know that I move in a history I neither summon nor command, which carries consequences nonetheless for my choices and conduct."[12]

The image of Sandel's communitarian theory is most vividly portrayed in his latest book, *Democracy's Discontent*. Here he directs his attention beyond the abstract theories of Kant and Rawls to American society more generally. Drawing on his earlier works, Sandel begins by tracing the loss of classical republicanism back to the American founding. There was a time, he insists, when American society was not so enamored of individualism and private self-interest. Gradually, however, a robust public philosophy characterized by a need to "debate the common good" in order to "shape the destiny of the political community" gave way to a rival philosophical ideal that favored freedom and egalitarianism above all else. The result has been the replacement of a public ethos developed from classical republicanism and, in its place, the emergence of an ethos resting on the principles of modern liberalism. Such a change has had consequences for the reflection of the self we now favor.

"Despite its powerful appeal," Sandel writes, "the image of the unencumbered self is flawed. It cannot make sense of our moral experience, because it cannot account for certain moral and political obligations that we commonly recognize, even prize."[13] The obligations to which Sandel refers are the ones that help sustain us as humans. Religious or familial obligations, for example, provide us with a moral grounding independent of, and antecedent to, individual choice. The patriotic call to arms, he notes, is another example of a moral obligation that exists outside the realm of personal sensibilities. The stories of individuals conflicted by a personal distaste for combat who have nonetheless enlisted in the armed services are too numerous to count. What accounts for such actions, Sandel asks, if not a greater call to duty? How can we reconcile the individual's private choices when his actions seem to contradict his very preferences? For Sandel, the liberal notion of the self is simply "too thin" to explain these contradictions. In fact, he contends that the liberal conception of the self "may even be too weak to support the less strenuous communal obligations expected of citizens in the modern welfare state. Some stronger conception of community may be required, not only to make sense of tragic-heroic dilemmas . . . but even to sustain the rights that many liberals defend."[14]

Replicating Sandel's major themes, Charles Taylor similarly claims that the principles of community and identity are inseparable. He argues that "our identity is always partly defined in conversation with others or through the common understanding which underlies the practice of our society."[15] But, he notes, contemporary liberal society has suppressed this simple truth. Today's fetishistic conception of individualism—or what he calls "atomism"—is unintelligible because it disavows—has no room for—any recognition of the collective element in political society. Like Sandel, Taylor faults liberal society for seeming to grant individuals the opportunity to articulate a conception of the good that is independent of any communal understanding. The claim that decisions about ends or goals are always voluntaristic, arbitrary, and continually isolated from any similarly conceived communal teleology is quite simply false, he says. Even the liberal conception of freedom, or of self-sufficiency apart from society, Taylor suggests, cannot come from each individual autonomously, but rather comes from a shared understanding of a heritage that transmits those liberal principles. Emphasis should be placed on the word "shared" and not, as all liberals seem to prefer, on the principles of freedom and liberty. The liberal ideal known broadly as "individualism" is solely the product of a *common* tradition that emphasizes free will and autonomy.

Alasdair MacIntyre also reiterates Sandel's sentiments: "I understand the story of my life in such a way that it is part of the history of my family or of this farm or of this university or of this countryside; and I understand the story of the lives of other individuals around me as embedded in the same larger stories, so that I and they share a common stake in the outcome of that story and in what sort of story it both is and is to be."[16] One knows one's self only through one's religious, ethnic, or even class convictions; and to self-consciously ignore those fundamental beliefs when reviewing one's most important personal decisions is, at best, dubious.[17] We cannot define ourselves as detached individuals, communitarians proclaim. We are an intricate part of the fabric that makes up our communities, and as part of that fabric we come to realize our distinctiveness only through the varying relationships we make with others.

Embedded in much of the discussion about the meaning of individual identity and personhood is the communitarian implication that liberals keenly misunderstand certain crucial questions about the self. Will Kymlicka describes this basic communitarian observation as the difference between "practical reason as judgment" and "practical reason as self-discovery."[18] In brief, the suggestion is that liberals, when deciding upon an individualistic, autonomous conception of the good, ask themselves, What sort of person do I want to become? Judgment combined with independence, they say, dictates that the self alone ascertains what is a proper life course, an appropriate good. Self-determination allows one continually to question where he is going and where he has been; but more importantly, it grants him the freedom of choice necessary for meaningful self-reflection. Communitarian ideology, however, teaches that such a general inquiry is illogical. Sandel writes: "The self 'comes by' its ends not 'by choice' but 'by discovery,' not 'by choosing that which is already given (this would be unintelligible) but by reflecting on itself and inquiring into its constituent nature, discerning its laws and imperatives, and acknowledging its purposes as its own.'"[19] Because a citizen of a particular polity is constituted by the substantive good professed in that political community, the question is not Who do I want to be? but rather Who am I already? Identity, communitarians insist, is discovered, not determined.

For the communitarian theorist, personal character is discovered inside the group setting mainly because it is there that constituents are able to visualize a clear conception of the good. In describing the Rawlsian nature of individualism, Sandel notes: "The antecedent unity of the self means that the subject, however heavily conditioned by his surroundings, is always, irreducibly, prior to his values and ends, and never fully constituted by them."[20] No individual, in other words, can be a full member of the liberal polity because none can ever define himself by the substantive principles and rules that might govern the individualistic community. But how can that be? communitarians often ask. Community-centered theorists who point to the alleged conceptual inconsistencies of liberal politics argue that the current understanding of identity in a liberal society is largely erroneous. Surely an individual cannot know who he is unless he also knows what is important to him, and those critical inquiries cannot be adequately addressed without first knowing what position he occupies within a given community. As MacIntyre notes in his essay "Is Patriotism a Virtue?" humans are born into particular situations—particular families, towns, nations—and they cannot easily escape these ties.

Contemporary communitarianism rests initially on the recognition that identity, as a meaningful characteristic of the individual, is embedded in the very relations one has, in the very commitments to a substantive notion of the good that emanates directly from the social community. Freedom and self-determination are not what give a political citizen import; instead, it is the sense of being a constituted member of something that communitarians say lends meaningfulness to a life.

Normative Issues

Despite the apparent persuasiveness of the pragmatic attack on the liberal view of the self, certain communitarian theorists will, for the sake of argument, concede that particular portion of the debate in order to offer a greater normative challenge to the liberal idea. Two of those communitarian thinkers are Alasdair MacIntyre and Charles Taylor.[21] Like so many other theorists engaged by the thought of the community, Taylor and MacIntyre fervently believe that the liberal conception of the self is empty or devoid of expressive character. Our ability to lead a fulfilling life depends, not on the degree of our isolation from each other, nor on the extent of our personal rights and liberties, but precisely on the meaningful commitments and relationships we make with our family and friends. Being surrounded by a culture and a heritage, they say, is what imparts value and purpose into our lives. The liberal perception of the self as antecedently individuated, in contrast, discounts the very importance of a communal setting in the overall development of the individual. Communitarian thinkers like Taylor and MacIntyre assert that by refusing to recognize a collective conception of the good, liberal politics strips the individual of a vital component of his identity. Hence, even if we were to accept as true the conception of the self articulated by such liberals as Rawls and Dworkin, normative communitarian theory maintains that we ought to reject that understanding in favor of one that recognizes a more substantial communal purpose.

The normative communitarian argument, for Taylor, begins in the seventeenth century because it was during this period of human history that the quest for the good became largely a private endeavor. Specifically, he blames the seventeenth-century social contract theorists for introducing the concept of "atomism"—a movement "whose vision of society is in some sense constituted by individuals for the fulfillment of ends which were primarily individual."[22] He cites Hobbes and Locke as the most obvious culprits, but he also argues that other social contract theorists "have left us a legacy of political thinking in which the notion of rights plays a central part in the justification of political structures and action."[23] The rootless, isolated conception of the self that emerged from that era now reigns as the prevailing tenet of contemporary public life.

For Taylor, community itself is a condition of selfhood. "We are only selves," he notes, "insofar as we move in a certain space of questions, as we seek and find an orientation to the good."[24] We should always consider primary the importance of collective action or communal habitation because without these fundamentally governing principles, we cannot regard ourselves as human in any real sense. Persons are self-interpreting beings, he continues: we understand ourselves only within certain defined parameters, and those parameters are set for us solely by the extent of our language, by the degree of our shared comprehension of a human tradition.[25] To Taylor, self-interpretation is only possible if we have access to a language that enables us to place meaning on our feelings and emotions. Membership in a language community, therefore, is a necessary prerequisite for identity; for without it, the self is hard-pressed to become a fully moral agent. Without the ability to communicate to other persons, we cannot hope to understand ourselves and our lives. Yet for the atomistic individual who is principally ruled by his own self-interest, any community—language or otherwise—is irrelevant. He can presumably find all he needs for self-definition and self-interpretation in complete isolation from other citizen actors. For Taylor this raises fundamental normative questions: What sort of person will that isolated individual be? Will he understand the extent of his human capacity? Will he be any different than an animal, or even a rock? It is the community that provides us with the necessary environment to communicate with others, to see and hear real people working and playing, and, most importantly, to pursue our full human potential. A defined community, Taylor argues, allows us to fully understand ourselves as humans.

Taylor furthers his thesis by suggesting that the atomistic self, as defined in liberal scholarship, cannot feel any significant obligation to the larger political community. A liberal individual's only connection to the community "is seen as derivative, as laid on us conditionally, through our consent, or through its being to our advantage."[26] In other words, as liberal individuals governed by a social contract, our commitment to a political community exists only insofar as the polity is working for us; it ends when we no longer see any advantage (security or otherwise) in staying in the community. Such a vision of the self as only minimally related to the community is, for Taylor, seriously disturbing. The result of this relationship is a modern society that wallows in a state of general "malaise."[27] In describing society's current condition, Taylor's immedi- *we are* ate worry is that "the very things which define our break with earlier 'tradi- *destroying* tional' societies—our affirmation of freedom, equality, radical new beginnings, control over nature, democratic self-rule—will somehow be carried beyond *natural* feasible limits and will undo us."[28] The way out of this predicament is, once *communities* again, to recognize the community as an important variable in the overall construction of our identities.

Despite compelling arguments about the language community and the relationship between liberal selfhood and the polity, Taylor is most explicitly normative when referring to the atomistic or unencumbered liberal self as "devoid" of meaning. To claim, as liberals do, that the very nature or value of "humanness" involves the freedom to construct and modify personal goals is disconcerting. "The self which has arrived at freedom by setting aside all external obstacles and impingements," Taylor notes, "is characterless, and hence without defined purpose."[29] In many ways the liberal self, as Taylor envisions him, wanders aimlessly, lacking function and plan. He rejects any communal conception of the good—or what Taylor calls "authoritative horizons"—and instead, imposes one upon himself. That is, he refuses to acknowledge authority from any substantive source—familial, religious, ethnic—outside himself. But accompanying the rejection of all "authoritative horizons" comes the probability that society will eventually endorse Nietzschean nihilism, or no values at all. In other words, the atomistic rule that places the good in a subordinate position to the right leads directly to an understanding of community values and cultural guidelines as ultimately arbitrary. The disastrous conclusion? "Only the will to power remains."[30]

MacIntyre's concern is similar to Taylor's. He too contends that liberal individuals have come to accept and even celebrate the contemporary notion of complete personal autonomy. Because persons are now able to develop their identities apart from the societies they inhabit, they can no longer be viewed as social beings in the Aristotelian sense. Pure liberty and freedom are not valued in themselves; they are only prized because the liberal community places independent importance on them. Yet MacIntyre is an altogether different type of communitarian than both Taylor and Sandel.[31] From *After Virtue*, where the author attempts to debunk the modern "emotivist" individual, to *Whose Justice? Which Rationality?* where he steps beyond the purely descriptive attack to introduce a normative edge, MacIntyre has constructed a coherent thesis that undertakes to restore a forgotten sense of virtue and morality to modern politics. His work, unlike some other communitarian scholarship, is not specifically directed at modern liberal theory but rather focuses on the general demise of political civilization since man's embrace of the liberal project. Indeed, his strategy in describing the development of moral theory from the ancients to the present is ultimately to show why the recovery of a pre-Enlightenment definition of virtue and morality is needed, why a cure for society's ailments is required. In that respect, the work is expressly normative.

Deeply troubling, says MacIntyre, is modern society's inclination toward emotivism that began as a result of the Enlightenment rejection of virtue.[32] According to both MacIntyre and Taylor, the emotivist or atomistic self is ruled by his passions and feelings and not by objective moral standards and virtues that once governed political society. Modern man, as a result, has left behind all remnants of an identity constituted by the good. "The peculiarly modern self, the emotivist self, in acquiring sovereignty in its own realm lost its traditional boundaries provided by a social identity and a view of human life as ordered to a given end,"[33] writes MacIntyre. That individual should be seen as artificial because personal character and identity can only be acknowledged in specific reference to the individual's culture and tradition. But, more critically, MacIntyre insists that the individual must also be defined as morally hollow. He lacks the objective moral tools that, prior to the Enlightenment, were found in communal authorities like the family, the church, and the polity. Modern man, he writes, is no longer able to locate any real source of moral and ethical authority.

By shifting moral responsibility from communal bodies to the individual, the liberal self is discouraged from appealing directly to any objective moral rules and norms. An individual knows of nothing outside of himself that will help guide his decision making or will identify a distinction between what is right and what is wrong. Accordingly, he is alienated. "Such a person cannot be said to have a history; there is no way of telling an intelligible story of her movements through moral positions and through life—no narrative thread concerning the development or refinement of her self-understanding," say Mulhall and Swift.[34] The "narrative thread" so central to MacIntyre's position is the common root that binds individuals in a society to each other and to the larger polity. He insists that it is an essential part of the makeup of the self; for without it, an individual's life has no grand purpose, no telos. All he has is an arbitrary private will that bases its most important decisions solely on personal interests and private values—or worse, on his appetites and impulses.

In unconventional communitarian language, MacIntyre notes that we have entered an era of selfishness and isolation—a "new dark age"—where rootlessness is celebrated and alienation abounds. Current society is so grossly disorganized that "we have—very largely, if not entirely—lost our comprehension, both theoretical and practical, of morality."[35] Still, he, like so many communitarians, talks of present culture being plagued by inexorable individualism. Like Taylor, MacIntyre remarks that polities of the past were solidary and unified, but modern society is just the opposite—frayed and fragmented. As a result, modern man is fragmented: "[The] type of self which has too many half-convictions and too few settled coherent convictions, too many partly formulated alternatives and too few opportunities to evaluate them systematically, brings to its encounters with the claims of rival traditions a fundamental incoherence which is too disturbing to be admitted to self-conscious awareness except on the rarest of occasions."[36] The conception of the modern liberal self as fragmented, unencumbered, atomistic, or emotivist, MacIntyre asserts, needs to be recognized. Moreover, that conception ought to be corrected.

Michael Walzer paints a more or less corresponding picture of the liberal self in *Radical Principles*. More moderate than MacIntyre in his critique of liberalism, Walzer is no less troubled, however, by the idea that liberal political theory has produced a shallow, "featureless" self. Modern liberalism, he says, creates a "bleak vision" of the self, where men and women are not liberated, freethinking souls but selfish and unhappy beings. They seek individualism because they think it will give them the best chance at happiness. Yet they may not even be fully aware of their own predicament. Modern liberals, Walzer says, are willing to eschew community because they have been so affected by the apparent lure of a life spent free of constraint. The problem is that such a life does not look so pleasant when examined closely. The liberal individual, he argues, can only be described as "dissociated, passive, and lonely"[37] He is largely uninterested in his state, his community, or his neighbor. He does not participate in the political process because he does not see how participation benefits him directly. He is far too absorbed with personal financial gain and far too apathetic about those things that affect us collectively. He is, according to Walzer, not someone we should be proud of—especially when we stop to think that he is us.

Continuing his argument, Walzer points to recent judicial trends—the redefinition of striptease as a form of free speech, or the use of equal protection as a means for children to divorce their parents—as indicative of our infatuation with individual liberty and our willingness to use the law to promote mostly liberal beliefs. But Walzer warns that such an infatuation comes at a tremendous cost both to the conception of the self and to the organization of the polity. He describes the end result of the liberal ideal as promoting "individualism with a vengeance."[38] Perhaps a bit tongue-in-cheek, he imagines the liberal self as "being thoroughly divorced, freed of parents, spouse, and children, watching pornographic performances in some dark theater, joining (it may be his only membership) this or that odd cult, which he will probably leave in a month or two for another still odder."[39]

The path to true liberation, Walzer says, can only be traversed if we first acknowledge our responsibilities to each other; only together will we shape our common experience. Interestingly, Walzer's conclusions about the self and his place in the larger political world suggest that beyond some vague notion of community, the real beneficiaries of the social democratic revolution he longs for will be those who cry out for more independence. Freedom and liberty, he argues, require a greater awareness of the importance of community; they simply cannot perpetuate themselves without the mainstay of community structures.

All three communitarian theorists—Taylor, MacIntyre, and Walzer—approach the topic from fundamentally different ideological perspectives, yet each considers the profile of the self created by a liberal political ethos to be disturbing. Moreover, the image of the liberal self constructed by each is remarkably similar. Characteristic of communitarian scholarship more generally, more extreme thinkers such as Taylor and MacIntyre share with the more democratically minded Walzer a belief that the liberal self is not someone we should strive to replicate. He is empty of any meaning, rootless in his existence, and altogether devoid of any real substantive qualities. Even Walzer, the most sympathetic of the three to the liberal cause, is hard-pressed to embrace a liberal agenda if it refuses to acknowledge the primary place of community in the formation of personal identity. We don't need political communities filled with individuals who have no common bonds, he argues. We should avoid sustaining polities that do not encourage citizens to identify and share their deepest connections. This is not because we desire warmth and camaraderie—these are all fine but are largely secondary to the bigger concern. Rather, we should discourage succumbing to the liberal ethos because it does not produce liberated beings; it does not inspire us to be better in our political and social relationships. Societies made up of liberal souls tend to promote disconnection, he says; and for that reason they should never be the yardsticks by which we measure ourselves.

Questions of the Polity

Pragmatic Problems

In leaving behind the communitarian dispute with the liberal vision of the self and taking up the issue of the polity itself, we see many of the same pragmatic questions and normative issues resurfacing. Conceptually, the communitarian challenge to the modern liberal notion of the polity resembles its attack on the earlier definition of the individualistic self. Consistent with the argument against the unencumbered, alienated self, communitarian thinking faults liberalism for constructing—or at least envisioning—a collective society that is virtually impossible to define. Communitarian advocates insist the liberal understanding of a political community constituted by an aggregation of isolated individuals is incoherent. It cannot be said to be a community in any real sense if there is nothing to bind the citizens together beyond a common desire for safety; there must be more to it than that. Although many of the same conflicts that motivated theorists to question the liberal notion of the self are once again present, a more accurate depiction of the communitarian opposition to the liberal conception of a polity reveals that the current attack is more of an expansion than a replication of the earlier assault on liberal selfhood.

The communitarian discussion surrounding the concept of the polity builds on the previous debate about the self by initially focusing on how and why individuals come together to form societies. Social contract theorists like Hobbes, Locke, and Rawls enjoy a particular view of politics which suggests that moral beings assemble mostly for procedural reasons (security or justice), with questions about substantive values and interests remaining largely private. As such, liberals posit that the state, once the social contract has been ratified, should only minimally interfere in the life of the individual. Whether it be for the purposes of security, as Locke suggests, or for security and limited distributive considerations, as Rawls proposes, the state is best when it does not infringe on the freedom of its citizens, particularly when it refuses to disturb those deeply held personal decisions about the good.

Sandel refers to this liberal construction of the state as the "procedural republic." Because of the absence of any shared conception of the good in a neutral regime, the best we can hope for is a collective ratification of the *process* by which we govern ourselves and the *rules* that regulate our behavior. We cannot agree on a substantive life, but we can agree to leave each other alone to pursue our own individual lives. The law, with its emphasis on process and control, then becomes the institution most responsible for refereeing our public and private relationships.

From the communitarian viewpoint, such an image of the polity is problematic. It presupposes the possibility of constituting a political society from generally self-interested, autonomous selves—a possibility that many contend is difficult to achieve. The communitarian impulse points out that liberal political societies are composed of collections of individuals hoping to gain "benefits through common action." Yet, as Taylor indicates, "The action [may be] collective, but the point of it remains individual."[40] In describing the Rawlsian self as conceptually erroneous, Sandel explicitly argues that a collection of isolated agents in a single geographical location can never form "a community in the constitutive sense."[41] In fact, the liberal propensity to define isolation and autonomy as primary governing principles "carries consequences for the kind of community of which we are capable." Sandel continues:

> Understood as unencumbered selves, we are of course free to join in voluntary association with others, and so are capable of community in the cooperative sense. What is denied to the unencumbered self is the possibility of membership in any community bound by moral ties antecedent to choice; he cannot belong to any community where the self *itself* is at stake. Such a community—call it constitutive as against merely cooperative—would engage the identity as well as the interests of the participants, and so implicate its members in a citizenship more thoroughgoing than the unencumbered self can know.[42]

Liberal society, Sandel declares, discourages citizens from organizing their communities around any maxim more tangible or substantive than a procedural notion of autonomy or independence. There is nothing to bind people in a liberal polity—no "moral ties," no objective ethical rules—other than the low commonality of mutual advantage. Substantive guidelines like religious and other moral teachings are relegated to subordinate status. They are permitted, through private choice, to interfere in the life of a single individual, but they are prohibited from gaining sovereignty over any collection or congregation of those individuals. Membership and citizenship, as meaningful terms, thus have no real significance.

As Sandel sees it, identity and character play little or no role in the individual's attachment to a liberal community, yet because it is the very perception of inseparability between identity and community that allows an individual to feel he is a member of some group, a liberal polity made up of isolated, unencumbered selves does not qualify as a truly constitutive society. A constituted self, Sandel continues, is unable to distinguish his identity from his community; he finds it impossible to classify himself and his ends in terms different from those of the community. A liberal self, in contrast, actively seeks to define himself as distinct from both his goals and his community. He cannot belong to any community where the "self *itself* is at stake" because membership requires the type of commitment that goes to the very core of the being, that gives the individual some sense of who he is. For example, Sandel was disappointed (but not surprised) that the U.S. Supreme Court reinforced this blank-slate notion of personhood by refusing to overturn a U.S. Air Force decree that yarmulkes could not be worn on duty. Captain Simcha Goldman, an Orthodox Jew, petitioned the military to wear what he defined as an item that is critical to his character. The air force refused, and the Supreme Court affirmed that ruling, citing a need to "defer to the 'professional judgment of military authorities' on the importance of uniform dress."[43] In Sandel's opinion, the actions of Goldman were decidedly antiliberal: he was attempting to establish his identity as an Orthodox Jew *outside* of his personal or private realm, within the larger public domain. And yet the institutions of American society would not permit him to do so. They would not allow him to see himself as distinct from a community that neither embraced Orthodox Judaism nor welcomed any other substantive conception of the good. According to Sandel, the type of liberal theory adopted by the air force and the Supreme Court is, at best, one that hastily or thinly defines the overall organization of its institutions in terms of real political societies. All a liberal "society" can thus hope to be, he concludes, is a cooperative agency.

Sandel's primary concern is that the tools an individual acquires while living in a predominantly liberal polity are not capable of addressing our

because we are not trying to be "good citizens" → no concern for common good

deepest troubles. More specifically, he argues that we cannot fully capture and embrace the meaning of self-government; it is illusory precisely because it requires something a liberal cannot provide: "a concern for the whole, an orientation to the common good."[44] The principle of self-government has no depth because the very discussions about shared values and common goals that citizens ought to be having are off-limits in a liberal regime. They are marginalized so as not to offend anyone's private sensibilities. Liberals, he insists, are ill-equipped to respond to the moral decay that surrounds them because the liberal political philosophy that animates our lives provides no internal mechanism to teach us right from wrong. We are directed by our private self-interest and not by a deeper allegiance to each other; thus, misunderstood notions of privacy or material welfare dominate our contemporary politics. *People want space and equality*

Consequently, the concept of liberal citizenship, for communitarians, is difficult to define. When a society consciously represses its conception(s) of the good, and hence provides nothing with which a constituent can substantively identify, citizenship becomes a trivial issue. Communitarians often question what the term "citizenship" really means if it does not include some form of responsibility or obligation to the polity. Can there really be an understanding of liberalism and citizenship together? Sandel argues that Rawlsian theory disavows such a possibility, alleging that an individual who is guided solely by his own private choices can feel little obligation to a community that does not similarly govern his identity. He feels responsibility only to himself, and as a result, is an active participant in the polity only when it may be personally beneficial. By divorcing identity and community, Sandel seems to be suggesting that liberalism makes citizenship a voluntary endeavor. As such, he contends, a liberal "polity" is not really a society at all.

MacIntyre is equally pessimistic about the quality of citizenship in a liberal polity, even if his assessment of one's obligation to the state does not exactly mirror Sandel's. According to MacIntyre, citizenship, like patriotism, requires an awareness of one's social particulars and an acceptance of their authority. Membership in a community, he contends, cannot be based on "impersonal" principles whereby each is "left free to pursue in his or her own way that way of life which he or she judges to be best."[45] Rather, "it is in general only within a community that individuals become capable of morality, are sustained in their morality, and are constituted as moral agents by the way in which other people regard them and what is owed to and by them as well as by the way in which they regard themselves."[46] Liberal beliefs, according to MacIntyre, demand that individuals constantly reflect on the polity's most basic institutions, including the institution of citizenship. And yet citizenship itself—defined as the quality of owing allegiance to a particular state—requires just the opposite. We would not expect family ties to be regulated entirely by self-interest; nor would we expect patriots to be inspired by selfishness. Similarly, if membership in a nation were "governed only by reciprocal self-interest," it would not be much of a nation at all.

Interestingly, Michael Walzer's earlier writings reveal a divide with MacIntyre over the issue of obligation. Specifically, Walzer sees an individual's obligation to the state as being determined by something more than mere natural allegiance.[47] A necessary component of citizenship, in his estimation, is consent—the willfulness on the part of the citizen to engage actively in the pursuit of the ideal. The state provides security, and in exchange the citizen agrees to live by its rules and, if the need arises, die defending its principles.

In later writings, however, Walzer's conception of obligation moves more in line with MacIntyre's naturalist position, even if he never fully embraces MacIntyre's premises. Walzer first contends that citizenship in liberal polities is a passive exercise: the extent of citizen involvement in the political process is exhausted by the vote. Then he writes, "But in the associational network of civil society—in unions, parties, movements, interest groups, and so on—these same [citizens] make many smaller decisions and shape to some degree the more distant determinations of state and economy."[48] That is to say, our path into politics has shifted lately, with less-traditional institutions now playing the role of enabler. The stated purpose of these and many other similar associations is to influence politics. Thus, Walzer's conclusion is that citizenship has meaning if one looks beyond the thin act of voting. Insofar as one's identity is predetermined by one's communal relationships and shared understandings—a theme Walzer regularly repeats—citizenship becomes largely a natural phenomenon. We naturally gravitate to these associations, and thus, by default, we are thrust into the public sphere.

Sandel, MacIntyre, and Walzer are certainly not alone in their preoccupation with the conceptual faults of the liberal enterprise; Taylor, too, takes up the methodological charge. "Functioning republics," Taylor contends, "are like conversations and families" in that they cannot be understood without a corresponding conception of "us"—a conception of collective action.[49] It does not make sense to think of a conversation between a single, isolated person in much the same way as it does not make sense to think of a polity being constituted by atomistic, isolated individuals. Again, the society constructed from autonomous selves is not a society in any real sense; it is merely an aggregation of separate, self-interested identities. "The very definition of a republican regime as classically understood requires an ontology different from atomism, and which falls outside atomism-infected common sense."[50] It requires a thinking that is largely foreign to liberal ideology—an admittance that identity, community, membership, and citizenship are principles that are so critically important that they require a full and robust conceptualization.

For communitarian theorists, in short, there is a crucial difference between the good espoused by a liberal society—a "convergent good"—and the good that comes from recognizing identity and community as interrelated.[51] The latter is not convergent, or in Sandel's words, "cooperative," but instead is described as "common," and represents a deeper, more thoroughgoing understanding of the good. A convergent good is one that communitarians insist can only be found in modern liberal polities, and although it may be shared by all constituents, its primary purpose is based on "enlightened self-interest."[52] To use the example provided by Taylor, persons may collectively desire security and thus support some form of official police protection. Yet that endorsement is not completely altruistic. In reality, we share no common penchant for police protection—we are not nobly concerned with the welfare of others—we can only locate and express our own individual desire for security. But the aggregation of those many individual needs forms a single, collective (but not common) preference.

A common good, in contrast, is collective action aimed at a larger purpose: the community itself. Instead of contracting a police force for the protection of the community, the common good might endorse a "Neighborhood Watch," where the citizens themselves voluntarily patrol their surroundings. The purpose is still security, but the focus has changed. Instead of private self-interest being the driving force behind security patrols, the new Neighborhood Watch is intended to protect first and foremost the community at large. Liberals might suggest that community-driven initiatives like Neighborhood Watch are instituted primarily in response to the inadequacies of the paid police force, but communitarians would surely counter by arguing that they also serve important bonding functions. Indeed, communitarians assert that liberal polities, with incoherent conceptions of societies and implausible understandings of the self, simply cannot admit that "the bond of solidarity with my compatriots in a functioning republic is based on a sense of shared fate, where the sharing itself is of value."[53]

Normative Issues

The attempt to recapture a belief in the common good is the basis for the normative communitarian assault on the liberal polity. At the core of the normative debate is the question of the community's value. Communitarians, whether interpreting liberal theory correctly or not, contend that in the modern era of rabid hyperindividualism, community is valued or prized only insofar as it is seen as an instrument for the promotion of self-interest and collective security. Beyond that, the community has minimal function or pragmatic import. The community-centered position insists that society should be valued regardless of the benefits it may provide to its inhabitants individually. It has independent merit because it supports a distinct, commonly sanctioned "way of life" (i.e., religious, moral, ethnic) that is constitutively authoritative. In fact, all other ways of life, communitarians assert, ought to be examined in specific reference to the common good endorsed by the state. Accordingly, the communitarian polity is defined as a "perfectionist" or particularistic state.[54]

Proposing that the community ought to be valued independently of its function, however, is but the first part of the communitarian's normative position. There remains the issue of what form or theory of justice is most appropriate in modern politics. Is the liberal conception of justice—and thus the liberal order of public institutions—the optimal strategy for modern political organization? It might be valuable to recall at this point that Rawls' theory of justice combines liberal freedom with minimal state intervention in the distribution of goods. Moreover, his theory, with its appeal to human reason and rationality, is meant to be broadly universal.[55] Presumably, all persons, whether rich or poor, educated or uneducated, black or white would, if placed in the original position and under the veil of ignorance, subscribe to the theory of "justice as fairness." Hence, Rawls logically must claim, all societies, if aiming to achieve the highest level of justice, would adopt "justice as fairness" as the prevailing model. Communitarian and social democrat Michael Walzer thinks this is a mistaken assumption. But even more importantly, he believes that any notion of justice that outwardly eschews the particularistic factors distinct to a given community is not one we want to embrace. In fact, in

Spheres of Justice, Walzer argues that we should actively work to support an alternative theory of justice that is not meant to be universal. And herein lies the second element of the normative communitarian argument.

When conceiving of a coherent theory of justice, one should consider the specific context of the community in question. In much the same way that Montesquieu spoke of unique climatic, environmental, and moral characteristics of different polities,[56] Walzer insists that each community carries with it a distinct history and tradition. He calls these unique characteristics "shared understandings" and "shared social meanings," and claims they must be acknowledged when deciding on an appropriate societal system of justice. Specifically, Walzer posits that communities share conceptions of social goods—education, money, honors—and that an appropriate system of political justice requires an adherence to the shared or common definitions of those goods. Distribution of each individual good occurs in its own autonomous "sphere" and follows its own shared understanding, and as long as goods are not transferred from one sphere to another, a degree of social equality is realized.

For example, there is a common understanding of health care in America that follows a distributive model based on the concept of need. To misinterpret that shared understanding of health care and thus to introduce education, prestige, money, or influence into the independent sphere is to violate the principles of distributive justice. Because each sphere has its own shared meaning or understanding, the transfer of goods from one sphere to another is patently unfair. Americans are troubled when an individual is able to use personal financial resources to obtain medical attention and in the process bypass other patients who have greater needs. A patient requiring an organ transplant is not supposed to move up or down the waiting list because he or she has a greater or lesser capacity to pay for services. Decisions about organ transplantation, it is thought, should be based entirely on the comparative health of the patients.

Walzer contends that our discomfort when we hear stories about the influence of such goods as money and prestige can be attributed to our inherent belief that the entire arena of health care should be dictated by a shared understanding based exclusively on need. Maximizing the sense of fairness explicit in a particular system of distributive justice requires a more community-based mentality. To understand and accept the theory of autonomous spheres, says Walzer, is to recognize that each community shares in a common substantive life. "Justice," he concludes, "is relative to social meanings. . . . A given society is just if its substantive life is lived in a certain way—that is, in a way faithful to the shared understandings of its members."[57] Justice, therefore, cannot follow the model proposed by Rawls but must adhere to a more community-specific strategy. America's uneasiness about its social and political institutions, Walzer suggests, is tied directly to the liberal inclination to ignore a community-based notion of justice.

In later writings, Walzer is even more explicitly normative, although no more conventional.[58] He transfers his preoccupation with the shared meanings of a community to a discussion of the neutral state. He argues that a non-neutral state "is solider and more coherent" than a liberal polity bent on impartiality. Indeed, the state should act as an instrument to foster certain associations that encourage "the development and display of civic virtue in a pluralist variety of social settings."[59] "The Idea of Civil Society: A Path to Reconstruction" is Walzer's defense of a plan meant to alter our current understanding of civil society and answer the question: What is the preferred setting, the most supportive environment, for the good life?[60] The answer he provides centers on what he refers to as "critical associationalism," a conception of civil society that stresses "inclusiveness." For a better future—or at least to encourage a "supportive environment" for one—Walzer suggests: "(1) decentralizing the state so that there are more opportunities for citizens to take responsibility for (some of) its activities; (2) socializing the economy so that there is a greater diversity of market agents, communal as well as private; and (3) pluralizing and domesticating nationalism, on the religious model, so that there are different ways to realize and sustain historical identities."[61] But what is most interesting, and what makes Walzer a communitarian in the truest sense, is his plan to implement critical associationalism by "using political power to redistribute resources *and to underwrite and subsidize the most desirable associational activities.*"[62]

By suggesting that the state should endorse certain actions and thus support particular "ways of life," Walzer raises the broad normative question most evident in the contemporary liberal-communitarian debate: What sort of political order do we, as political animals, truly desire? Should we permit each individual to decide for him- or herself what is a proper life, or should we give some authority to resolve those fundamental questions to the community? Surely a life spent in the video arcade is in some way less valuable than a life spent pursuing the arts. And if that is indeed the case, don't we, as a political community, have a responsibility to discourage people from wasting their lives in front of the video screen? Isn't it permissible, then, to cultivate, through state sponsorship, those activities we collectively deem to be most worthy? Liberal theory flatly rejects the notion of state sponsorship of particularistic goods. Either we cannot objectively determine which activity is inherently more valuable, or, even if we could, the state has no place in dictating for us what sort of life we should lead.[63] The self is still the primary political object and as such must be viewed as morally competent to make critically important life choices. Communitarians, not surprisingly, are more receptive to the possibility of state promotion of the good. Our identities are constituted by the good articulated by the community, and thus to grant moral sovereignty to the state is not to give up personal freedom but rather to ratify those values already defined collectively as paramount.

Communitarians are opposed to the idea of the neutral state, which is to say they object to the absence of any substantive governing principles. To most of them, liberal theory imagines a society that is both difficult to conceptualize and generally unappealing once it has been realized. The community is not an instrument to be used by each member as a means to gain personal advantage but an independent political force charged with the responsibility of articulating a substantive and authoritative conception of the good. Because we seek a full and robust existence, communitarians proclaim we ought to dilute the pure freedom of choice associated with liberal individualism and, in its stead, celebrate the principles—both concrete and abstract—we share in common. The only way to do that, according to communitarian thinking, is to abandon the liberal conception of the polity and of justice, and introduce a purely communitarian project.

In the end, Sandel is the most explicit about the flaws of American liberalism and the need to recapture a political ideology based on the collective good. "The priority of individual rights, the ideal of neutrality, and the conception of persons as freely choosing, unencumbered selves, taken together," he writes, "form the public philosophy of the procedural republic. These three connected notions inform [America's] present constitutional practice. They do not, however, characterize our tradition as a whole."[64] The answer, for Sandel, is to recapture the classical republican ethos that at one time dominated public life. A republican polity is one that promotes a collective good for the benefit of the citizens. Self-rule is not appealing, he says, without "cultivating in citizens the qualities of character necessary to the common good of self-government. Insofar as certain dispositions, attachments, and commitments are essential to the realization of self-government, republican politics regards moral character as a public, not merely private, concern." In this sense, Sandel concludes, "it attends to the identity, not just the interests, of its citizens."[65]

Conservative Communitarianism

Emerging most notably out of the antiliberal ideas of Alasdair MacIntyre, an interesting new strain of theoretical communitarianism has surfaced in recent years. This particular group is known widely for its more conservative approach to modern society and for the fact that its members take issue with traditional liberals and mainstream communitarians alike. They insist, in other words, that modern politics has not only surrendered to the ideals of individualism but that even communitarian critiques of liberalism now show signs of being co-opted by liberal forces. The communitarianism of Sandel, Galston, and Taylor, conservatives proclaim, is not grounded in an appreciation for the merits of public virtue, nor does it recognize the importance of traditional institutions such as the church and the family that historically furnished citizens with some sort of moral compass. Instead, egalitarian varieties of communitarianism defended mainly by social democrats are really just amended forms of liberalism disguised by their affinity for group cooperation. The most prominent communitarian supporters, conservatives remark, are masquerading as defenders of community; the true champions of community acknowledge the inherent difficulty in sponsoring both traditions simultaneously.

On this point, Kenneth Grasso admires an article written by Michael Walzer that expresses what Grasso sees as the central defect of the broader communitarian perspective.[66] In "The Communitarian Critique of Liberalism," Walzer suggests that particular conceptions of communitarianism—those not fortified by social democratic principles—are better understood as "corrections" of liberal ideology than as outright challenges to the dominant moral theory. Walzer insists that conventional communitarian scholarship is none other than a distinctive form of liberalism, a separate branch of the intellectual tradition that maintains a prominent place for community within a mostly individualistic framework. He claims that communitarians are most accurate when assuming that humans come to know themselves as "social beings," but they remain dangerously naïve when insisting that we can replace a liberal political construction with a nonliberal one.

Grasso, a leading conservative communitarian, concurs. He too asserts that the convictions of the major community-centered thinkers represent only a slight modification of liberalism. The communitarian thinking of Michael Sandel or William Sullivan is not all that dissimilar from a liberal line of thought that stresses autonomous choice or individual egotism and may in fact be "virtually indistinguishable from that which informs egalitarian liberalism," according to Grasso.[67] He refers to these communitarian theorists as "timid" because they refuse to leave behind the major liberal propositions and devise a new political strategy based entirely on the idea of community engagement. In the end, Grasso even derides the likes of Sandel and Sullivan for consulting the liberal canon—Locke, Madison, Hamilton, Mill—for inspiration. They cannot hope to escape the shadow of liberalism, he says, if they continue to draw on the theory's most persuasive sponsors.

Echoing the uneasiness of Grasso, Bruce Frohnen is even more damning in his overall critique of mainstream communitarianism. He posits that communitarians like Sandel and Galston "share the liberal vision of the good life" insofar as they seek to promote individual advancement rather than collective development. In fact, Frohnen contends that "communitarians are in the awkward position of decrying liberalism's actual effects while lauding its theoretical goals."[68] They criticize the polity constructed from liberal principles, and yet they refuse to condemn the foundation on which liberalism rests. Both liberal and communitarian scholarship, Frohnen argues, assert that "each individual 'flourishes' by pursuing goals he has chosen for himself on the basis of his own independently constructed moral code." The two intellectual traditions are therefore cut from the same cloth in that they both believe that personal satisfaction comes not from collective action, but from individual choice. "Communitarians," Frohnen concludes, "do not seek to replace liberalism but to save it."[69]

Frohnen and Grasso's criticism of communitarianism in general is aimed at those—ironically, like Walzer—who insist that the ideas of liberation and equality express a partial truth. That is to say, conservative communitarians attack liberals and antiliberals alike for attempting to salvage components of the individualistic agenda, including those instruments of the state that secure personal freedom and equal treatment. For example, Frohnen insists that the communitarianism of William Galston leads inevitably to a decidedly liberal conclusion: Galston would like to permit debate concerning proper moral decisions, but certain topics, he says, should not be allowed to derail the dialogue, no matter how persuasive they may be. Frohnen maintains that the subjects Galston is referring to are the ones, like those espoused by certain religious faiths, that do not square with the first principles of toleration and equality. Particular topics are prohibited, in other words, unless they contribute to the realization of individual autonomy and personal growth; certain positions are precluded from entering the marketplace if they in some way close off individually generated debate. Frohnen thus goes so far as to suggest that "the new communitarians cannot achieve, construct, or even maintain true community" as long as they "demand material equality" and protect above all else the principle of tolerance. "Given their commitment to individual autonomy [and tangible egalitarianism]," he argues, "it seems unlikely that they really want strong communities at all."[70]

A difficulty for most conservative communitarians relates to our heavy reliance on individual rights as a prescription for personal success and happiness. Like MacIntyre, conservative communitarians do not recognize individual freedom as definitive. Civic virtue, moral goodness, patriotism—these are the ends that people should aim to achieve. Liberal societies, say conservative communitarians, tend to encourage the use of rights as weapons by promoting universal freedoms in the first place. In fact, contemporary liberal politics often promises that individual rights will trump all other interests. Redefining striptease shows as falling within the protective confines of free speech (using Walzer's example) illustrates the problem. Instead of considering whether we truly want strip clubs in our communities, we allow proprietors and patrons of these establishments to use the right to free speech to cut off all discussion. The fact that a right lies at the base of *any* discussion means that the inevitable debate that accompanies it is automatically one-sided. More to the point, a polity designed around the maximization of individual rights is the enemy of one that places virtue as its highest priority. The liberal propensity to prioritize individual freedoms is, of course, a modern trend conservative communitarians refuse to endorse. And yet our contemporary culture knows no other way, they argue. Selfish individuals uninterested in civic responsibility are all around us. We cannot escape.

In many respects, conservative communitarianism is rightly recognized as a departure from the communitarian thoughts of more familiar theorists. Yet on further examination, the differences between conservative communitarians and other proponents of community become a bit blurred. Although I am painting their political ideology with admittedly broad strokes, I think it is clear that both Frohnen and Grasso share with other communitarians an attraction to many of the major themes associated with the movement. Their anxiety concerning the dominion of self-interest over individual lives, for example, is quite familiar. "The moral vacuousness of liberal politics," Frohnen writes, "invades our communities, replacing the moral and institutional ties that bind a people together with a destructive glorification of selfishness."[71] Moreover, they, like so many communitarians, chastise liberal theory for placing the right prior to the good and refusing to acknowledge that certain ways of life are simply more valuable than others. A life in which we listen to our own moral voices and learn from our most basic social and political institutions is far worthier of our collective approval than is one based entirely on hedonistic instincts. In fact, Frohnen contends, the state's primary responsibility is to encourage local associations like the church and the schools to instill a sense of morality in their followers. Absent a program to protect the moral authority of intermediate institutions, the state's influence is only marginal.

If there is one defining feature of conservative communitarianism, it is a radical faith in the power of a polity's intermediate political and social institutions.[72] The local organizations that surround us, that we regularly contribute to, and that directly give back to us are the ones that provide meaning, both individually and collectively, to our lives. Believing that the ties that bind us are national—that we somehow relate to our neighbors because we share a common citizenship or a common passport—is, according to Frohnen, absurd. We first relate to our families and then to our neighborhoods, schools, churches, synagogues, little league teams, rotary clubs, unions, and so forth. It is through these intermediate institutions—institutions that act as formal and informal conduits between the individual and the government—that we come to know who we are and begin to form a personal identity that is largely inspired by the local organizations themselves. On this point, Frohnen insists that "to allow a highly centralized government to replace or to undercut subsidiary groups and associations is to cut off prospects for individuals to fulfill themselves as human beings and to reach their potential as productive and responsible citizens."[73] We cannot hope to be moral beings if we constantly ignore our local attachments; our awareness of virtue and responsibility is tied too closely to our natural inclination to participate primarily in local rather than national affairs.

Troubling for most conservative communitarians is the notion that the sort of moral timidity we presently embrace somehow descends from our nation's origins. In fact, conservative communitarians consistently maintain that the relationship between local associations and civic virtue can be traced to our deepest roots. Frohnen, for one, argues that early American beliefs on this point were strikingly homogeneous. Individuals may have differed about the specifics of their inspiration—different religions worshipped different conceptions of God—but all Americans understood that "transcendent standards of right and wrong," derived from religious faith, ordered their everyday lives. In Frohnen's words, "[The] Constitution left the bulk of governmental power at the state and local level, where it could be hedged and even taken over by local townships and other associations. The result was a community of communities held together by a Constitution that intentionally failed to provide the moral basis for society—instead protecting such bases as already had been formed in local communities."[74] Moral teachings were deliberately left to the local communities to sort out. That, combined with the fact that people were God-fearing souls who attended to the common good because they were taught that moral character was linked directly to God's will, made public virtue a reality in early America. To think self-interestedly was not only to defy your neighbor and friend but also to insult God.

Following the cue provided by Anti-Federalists, Tocqueville was the first in the nineteenth century to remark that American liberalism would inevitably lead to disassociation.[75] He was convinced that the centralization of power would catapult the principle of equality above all others and create an environment in which individuals had little incentive to interact. As long as the eyes of citizens remain primarily focused on the far-off business of national politics, men and women would not feel as compelled to cultivate local attachments. Recognizing that there is no need to nourish intimate political relationships with those who share only abstract public ties, they would retreat into their own lives without worrying about their neighbors. Because politics at the national level is so general and so distant, Tocqueville said, only a few leading statesmen are responsible for governmental decision making. Consequently, the population at large is not given any meaningful responsibility, and thus there is no chance to generate "lasting bonds" with one another. In the end, citizens of a liberal polity are not required to know each other in a way that allows them to gain respect through familiarity. The notion of obligation—of being obliged to surrender to the needs of the community—is thus absent from everyday liberal politics.[76]

On the flip side, however, Tocqueville also noted that concerns at home inspire cooperation. He understood that mutual aid, if it becomes habitual, has a positive effect on a community's sustainability. People come to know each other as friends rather than simply as neighbors, and they work together to remedy shared problems. A local concern is shared by all in a way that a national concern is experienced by only a few. "When the people who live [together] have to look after the particular affairs of a district, the same people are always meeting and they are forced, in a manner, to know and adapt themselves to one another."[77] Ties are established through the process of collective decision making and through the compromises that inevitably emerge from ongoing deliberations. Real commitments are thus formed.

Barry Alan Shain agrees. His findings reveal that the communities of seventeenth- and eighteenth-century America were not recognized as conglomerations of individuals but were "organisms, functioning for a definite purpose, with all parts subordinate to the whole."[78] They were larger and more important than was any single constituent who might reside within a country's borders or participate in a community's meetings. Consequently, the isolated individual of the colonial and revolutionary periods, according to Shain, would have felt "radically incomplete." If the individual could not easily locate a tangible attachment to the community, he was emotionally and physically doomed. Local associations empowered individuals by giving them a sense of belonging, a sense of connectedness to a fraternity that furnished them with an identity. For most early Americans, therefore, membership in a local community meant that one could maintain some control over one's own life. The relationship between the individual and the community was in some sense reciprocal in that the individual contributed to the moral direction of the particular association at the same time that the association defined the individual.

Government at all levels was also a willing participant in this dialogue. The state promoted virtue by enacting laws (against public displays of indecency, for example) that were derived from religious teachings and that promoted a particular vision of the good life. More to the point, law could provide citizens with a guide as to what constituted proper action, what was acceptable behavior, and what was beyond the pale. Legislative enactments often reflected the tenor of the time, while public institutions like state legislatures were considered by early Americans as a genuine source of support for groups engaged in civic education and socialization. Certainly, public officials did not threaten to marginalize or replace local institutions interested in furnishing a sense of rectitude; the two worked together, according to Frohnen, to provide moral direction for all. And what the law could not accomplish, informal shaming mechanisms did. In Tocqueville's words: "The multitude requires no laws to coerce those who do not think like themselves: public disapprobation is enough; a sense of their loneliness and impotence overtakes them and drives them to despair."[79]

Conservative communitarians now suggest that the attitudes and practices of our ancestors were correct. Indeed, among all communitarians, it is the conservatives who are most likely to resurrect the original themes of the Anti-Federalists. Prominent components of the conservative communitarian argument relate directly to the issues of scale and civic virtue so critical to early Anti-Federalist thought. Grasso, for example, has explicitly stated that contemporary communitarians—or what he calls "liberal communitarians"—fail to recognize that the nation-state is incapable of organizing people in a constitutive manner and that intermediate institutions thus ought to be charged with that responsibility. Similarly, George Carey contends that the federal Constitution should be interpreted in such a way as to allow local associations the necessary "space" or "room" to function properly.[80] The space Carey craves is one that can only come from a decentralized government lacking extensive powers. If a central government is designed only to employ limited supervision and is thus unable to satisfy peoples' interests, says Carey, the local associations will meet the challenge of providing moral and spiritual leadership. To put it another way, a decentralized, limited government is a government that enables local institutions to rectify local problems, including ones related to the questions of civic virtue and responsibility. This, of course, is a decidedly Anti-Federalist position.

From the colonial period until the early twentieth century, Carey continues, government acted with enough self-restraint to provide the requisite space for intermediate institutions to thrive. That empowered local associations to promote virtue on their own terms. Carey describes the founding period as one in which most citizens simply assumed that families, churches, schools, and neighborhoods were the main source of moral inspiration and that the national government played little or no role in that educative process. As further proof, Carey remarks that the argument presented in the *Federalist Papers* assumes a moral and virtuous citizenry. Publius insisted that a virtuous citizenry was indispensable for good government. The core beliefs of early colonists were that government could not cultivate proper citizenship as effectively as could nongovernmental associations. Churches taught American citizens right from wrong much more sensibly and pragmatically than did state or national governmental institutions. And so did families, neighborhood associations, and schools. These were the primary institutions that kept one from defying the basic rules and norms of a community; governmental representatives did not enjoy that same ascendancy.

While the principle of localized self-rule dominated early American society, today, Frohnen and Carey insist, it no longer commands the same level of attention it once did. Americans, they say, have grown accustomed to allowing the national government to perform those functions that at one time were managed on an exclusively local level, including directing the moral dialogue. The dilemma, as both Tocqueville and the modern conservative communitarians see it, is that the only moral agenda that can ever emerge from the nation's capital is one based on a thin, watered-down version of tolerance. In a country like the United States, the responsibility of the national government must be to remain silent on the subject of morality. The size of the country, combined with the variety of specific subcultures, renders the possibility of being anything but neutral toward particular moral preferences all but impossible. Twenty-first-century representatives in America's legislatures, in fact, regularly refuse to condemn specific ways of life, fearing they may come across as intolerant or even authoritarian. Thus, without local organizations providing leadership and moral guidance—a situation that conservative communitarians insist currently plagues us—morality becomes a purely private choice, and the concept of civic virtue is all but forgotten.

The Rise of Prescriptive Communitarianism

"In the fifties we had a clear set of values that spoke to most Americans, most of the time, with a firm voice," says leading prescriptive communitarian Amitai Etzioni.[81] In the nineties that voice, according to Etzioni, has become garbled. No longer do Americans recognize certain values and principles such as authority and obedience that at one time dominated public life. Lost is any notion of a shared or public understanding of moral convention. Gone is the apparent clear line between right and wrong—the "moral voice" that informs us "when certain actions are beyond the pale."[82]

According to the second generation of communitarian scholarship, America is in a precarious position. Its citizens are politically apathetic, increasingly frustrated with government and the public sphere. Crime is still on the rise in some pockets of the country, despite improved crime rates in most areas.

Teenage pregnancy, divorce, and illiteracy are all maladies whose numbers have stabilized, but communitarians are quick to remind us that they are still far too prevalent, particularly when the data are evaluated in historical context. Furthermore, traditional communal institutions like the family and the church have lost much of their authoritative import as they continue to crumble under the weight of American expectations. The country, in short, is teetering on the edge of moral disintegration, and the only way to bring it back from the precipice is to articulate a new "moral voice," one that replaces the recent focus on liberal individualism with a more desirable emphasis on national or subnational communities.

The words and theories of Etzioni are familiar, for he, along with a cadre of prescriptive American communitarians, is expanding the theoretical position that began in the United States with the early Anti-Federalists and has forcefully reemerged over the last three decades in the work of both philosophers and political theorists. Like the more traditional—and theoretical—communitarian writings of MacIntyre, Walzer, Taylor, Sandel, Grasso, Frohnen, and others, the recent prescriptive position decries the general moral decay and loss of shared values that has accompanied the modern liberal (or more specifically, American) polity. Indeed, the new prescriptive defense of communitarianism takes as its launching point the arguments of prior theorists who insist liberal society is constituted by "unencumbered," isolated selves who are devoid of rootedness and commonality. Yet it proceeds to further those ideas by including concrete proposals for institutional change. Etzioni, for example, concurs with Walzer's notion that contemporary liberal society has lost sight of its "shared understandings"—its conventions and moral principles—but in elaborating on the early theoretical point (and ultimately applying it to the American case), he suggests it is time to take practical steps to cure its many ailments. He thus proposes an initial "four-point agenda: a moratorium on the minting of most, if not all, new rights; reestablishing the link between rights and responsibilities; recognizing that some responsibilities do not entail rights; and, most carefully, adjusting some rights to the country's recently changed circumstances."[83]

In addition, Etzioni has founded "The Responsive Community," a public interest group dedicated to furthering the communitarian position. Its platform explicitly calls for the embrace of the communitarian project in this country through the implementation of practical and realistic policy initiatives. The document continues by defining communitarianism as a political ideology and an activist movement attempting to "restore the moral voice" of American society. Commencing with a comprehensive overhaul of the American family, the educational system, and the community structure, the "Responsive Communitarian Platform" seeks to gain enough popular support to fundamentally influence the various "institutions of our civil society."

Etzioni, of course, is not alone. Others have joined the prescriptive communitarian crusade for political change. Mary Ann Glendon and William Galston have both indicated their affinity for practical communitarianism by claiming it represents the best option for recovering American shared values and moral principles. Glendon, whose *Rights Talk* takes direct aim at our contemporary preoccupation with individual and personal liberties, argues that the prominence of rights in American society has contributed significantly to the overall deterioration of what was at one time a clearly defined national community.[84] Because of the nature of absoluteness that accompanies a discourse on rights, she says, the United States is caught in an irreversible cycle of political "disorder," a cycle that cannot be broken without the fundamental transformation of contemporary American culture. Galston, in turn, has described how contemporary liberal theory—from Rawls to Nozick to Ackerman[85]—misunderstands the true essence of the American political experiment. Institutions such as our educational system and our religious community have for two centuries contributed to defining individual citizenship and civic responsibility, but liberal theorists have mistakenly interpreted that reality in a way that is hostile to a conception of community. A correct reading, Galston says, would celebrate the notion of substantive liberalism; and hence we must, as Americans, introduce public policy and other initiatives that strongly encourage a reinterpretation of central political conflicts and essential cultural institutions.[86]

Prescriptive communitarians find further inspiration in the work of their more conservative counterparts. Etzioni, for one, argues that the key to shoring up contemporary American society is to reinvigorate local associations and give them additional authority in relation to national governmental institutions. Similarly, Glendon has revised the conservative distrust of individual rights into a more coherent and more practical discussion centered on the steps necessary to reposition our national dialogue away from individualism and rights. Prescriptive communitarianism thus represents, in short, both a synthesis and a progression in the development of communitarian theory.

Perhaps dissatisfied with the propensity of theoretical communitarians to challenge contemporary liberal politics from a strictly pedantic or academic perspective, the policy-oriented communitarians of the last decade are attempting to move the philosophical debate to a different level. Admittedly not satisfied with engaging liberal thinkers in a war of words, they instead call for direct and swift political action. Their enterprise, in other words, does not end with a concession that liberal theory is somehow flawed, but rather it includes, as part of its overall strategy, viable and potentially dynamic measures for remedying such inaccuracies. The communitarian movement, therefore, strives to give roots to the unencumbered self; to provide identity to the isolated, atomistic individual; and to reclaim a more substantial meaning of citizenship. As a result, the overall prescriptive communitarian project in this country endeavors to be simultaneously provocative and pragmatic.

Like their theoretical predecessors, the recent prescriptive company shares some broad and important beliefs. For all communitarian advocates, the enemy remains the sense of hyperindividualism predominant in modern liberal politics; but for the prescriptive branch of the movement, the similarities in their work run much deeper. Recent communitarians almost unanimously allege that the moral and societal deterioration of the American political order can be attributed to the rising tendency among citizens to think selfishly and act independently. The perception of individualism and freedom prevalent in the United States, they tell us, exists for many as a license to partake in virtually any type of activity. It gives apparent authority for citizens of this country to engage in unconventional (and possibly unethical) behavior, while at the same time acting as a formidable barrier to moral compliance. Moreover, liberal autonomy has recently taught that rights and liberties can be all too readily redeemed; while the responsibilities that accompany our tradition of freedom can be just as easily sidestepped. A troubling paradox has emerged over the past generation. In Etzioni's words, American citizens feel "a strong sense of entitlement—that is, a demand that the community provide more services and strongly uphold rights—[but] a rather weak sense of obligation to the local and national community."[87] Members of the American political system have largely forgotten the words of President Kennedy, who reminded us not so long ago to think first about our responsibilities to country and only secondarily about what personal benefits this nation has to offer us.

To resolve the seeming paradox, prescriptive communitarians favor a three-pronged normative attack on American civil society: "If we are to safeguard and enhance our future," we must first change our "values, habits, and public policies" according to Etzioni.[88] To do so, however, requires first an initial assessment of the specific problems akin to the modern American polity. The prescriptive communitarian movement points to three major political realities that derive from American individualism and that have contributed in the last forty years to the steady demise of the American body politic: (1) our almost exclusive reliance on individual rights and liberties; (2) our refusal to take an active role in the shaping of the public sphere; and (3) our abandonment of traditionally important public institutions. If we can somehow attend to these formative problems and fix what is wrong with each, prescriptive communitarians believe, we will witness a dramatic improvement in the overall progression of our political order. The answers, they tell us, lie in our comprehension of the importance of community.

Inflation of Rights in American Culture

The first problem prescriptive communitarianism points out is this country's overwhelming affinity for individual or personal rights. The conception of individual freedom rampant in American society has so grossly inflated the importance of civil rights and liberties that any corresponding recognition of community or consensus is largely discounted. Since the civil rights movement of the mid-twentieth century, rights have become the most formidable weapons for individuals to pursue their own private needs and interests. Etzioni and others remark that this historical expansion of rights and liberties runs counter to America's longstanding democratic tradition.[89] We no longer seek to resolve controversies collectively or through singularly procedural channels. Instead, when we feel a personal interest is in jeopardy, we simply sit back, claim our rights have been seriously violated, and wait for judicial relief. Prescriptive communitarians insist that rather than convening at a bargaining table and considering the point of view of the opposing party, contemporary Americans prefer to resolve differences privately through legal channels and by utilizing a modern but extensive language based chiefly on rights.

For most prescriptive thinkers the current dilemma surrounding the amplification of rights in the United States comes from the public's propensity to either create new rights or simply to couch all political discussion in terms of competing rights. Policy-centered communitarians are primarily troubled by America's willingness, first, to manufacture rights, and then to use them (and others) to trump all rival interests. Etzioni offers a number of examples of America's tendency to create new rights out of thin air: an activist in California who opposed a state ordinance prohibiting individuals from using opposite sex facilities by arguing in favor of a "woman's right to urinate in any public facility, at any time"; or the supposed right to "future" life invoked by individuals on death row who are concerned about the loss of their lineage. He mentions these eccentric examples to illustrate the point that the creation of additional rights significantly demeans the value of existing ones: "The incessant issuance of new rights, like the wholesale printing of currency, causes a massive inflation of rights that devalues their moral claims." Every time a new right is embraced, Etzioni argues, the old ones—the ones that lie at the center of the American political universe and are arguably critical to the proper functioning of the nation's political system—become less meaningful; their leverage and importance begins to erode.[90]

Rights are further devalued when they become overworked. Mary Ann Glendon is the principal communitarian spokesperson in favor of harnessing the often excessive significance liberal Americans place on individual rights. Like Etzioni, she is troubled by the overextension of individual rights, but primarily as they contribute to the continued deterioration of informed political dialogue. She consistently argues that "the prominence of a certain kind of rights talk in our political discussions is both a symptom of, and a contributing factor to, the disorder in the [American] body politic." Furthermore, she continues, "Rights talk encourages our all-too-human tendency to place the self at the center of our moral universe. In tandem with consumerism and a normal dislike of inconvenience, it regularly promotes the short-run over the long-term, crisis intervention over preventive measures, and particular interests over the common good."[91] According to Glendon, "In its simple American form, the language of rights is the language of no compromise. The winner takes all and the loser has to get out of town. The conversation is over."[92]

The American individual, Glendon concludes, is a "lone rights-bearer." Because our political society supports a tradition based on the liberalism of Locke and the legalism of Blackstone, rights have come to be considered in simultaneously absolute and solitary terms. In the United States one cannot have less of a right, nor can one share part of a right with others. Indeed, a personal right (like that of free speech or privacy) is enjoyed completely and independently by each individual. As such, rights have emerged as the primary symbol of American excessivism and seclusion: they are always invoked privately (or at least not collectively), and they are always deemed absolute. This mentality leads, according to Glendon, to the inability of American citizens to think and talk rationally about "what kind of society we are and what kind of polity we are trying to create."[93] Americans are so concerned with how to get ahead and how to reap the most out of public initiatives that we have forgotten how to relate to each other in pursuit of a shared purpose. "In the common enterprise of ordering our lives together," Glendon writes, "much depends on communication, reason-giving and mutual understanding." Yet, she continues, "the rhetoric of absoluteness [associated with rights] increases the likelihood of conflict and inhibits the sort of dialogue that is increasingly necessary in a pluralistic society."[94]

Here Glendon's communitarian roots are clearly evident. Our tendency to raise the rights banner prohibits us from thinking collectively; it prevents us from considering the importance of others in relation to ourselves. More imperative, however, the starkness of rights language precludes the possibility of Americans' thinking collectively about our *shared future together*, and this thwarts our chances of envisioning, and thus working toward, the ideal political society.

An important caution: Etzioni, Glendon, and the communitarian movement, although raising serious objections to the rising tide of rights in this country, should not be viewed as being averse to the idea of civil and personal liberties. In fact, the movement regularly celebrates the very conception of rights as belonging to individuals and acting as buffers against governmental intervention. Rights, Glendon argues, are necessary: they "can assist citizens in a large heterogeneous country to live together in a reasonably peaceful way."[95] However, for communitarians, rights should never be viewed in isolation, but rather as part of package that includes obligations to the community. "Strong rights," Etzioni says, "presume strong responsibilities."[96] The constitutionally protected right to trial by jury, for example, is one that is held sacred by most Americans. Yet a recent study found that many Americans are reluctant to participate in the realization of that right—they refuse to sit on juries.[97] Such defiance, communitarians insist, symbolizes all that is wrong with the contemporary American polity.

So what can be done? To combat the problems associated with America's affection for rights, prescriptive communitarians suggest refining both the nature and the "rhetoric" of rights. Etzioni proposes his "four-point agenda" to "correct the current imbalance between rights and responsibilities,"[98] while Glendon offers a much more subtle solution. For her, dialogue is both the disease and the antidote. Americans are currently embroiled in a troubling period of "rights talk" that can only be alleviated by embracing the concept of "deliberation."[99] Her style of communitarianism purports to elevate communication from the single-minded egoism that has saturated American politics, to a more deliberative, unified dialect necessary for a shared and peaceful tradition. Of course, Glendon argues that meaningful deliberation requires much more than a willingness to talk; it requires, among other things, "time, information, forums for the exchange of ideas, and vigorous political parties" ready to represent the masses.[100]

But in order to determine collectively what type of society we desire, Glendon and other sympathetic communitarians insist that we must first commence a renewed conversation based on common purposes and shared understandings. We must (consistent with the three-pronged attack on American liberalism) alter our deeply ingrained attitudes, "our values and habits." Otherwise, we may never succeed in realizing any of these political necessities, and we may never achieve the fundamental transformation of American politics.

Political Apathy   *✕common goals*

What is missing from contemporary American society, prescriptive communitarians tell us, is an essential desire to work together to shape our common public lives. Etzioni and Glendon assert that American individualism (as manifest in the prevalence of rights and liberties) precludes the possibility of attaining the degree of deliberation and cooperation necessary for us to envision a collective or common good. As a liberal inhabiting the United States, one thinks of oneself and one's private interests first, and only secondarily about what might be best for the community at large. Prescriptive communitarians maintain that such an attitude leads directly to an almost inescapable egoism among American citizens. Moreover, recent community-centered advocates suggest that the liberal canons of independence and autonomy have begun to infect our entire political consciousness. American individualism has, in the past two decades, been interpreted in such a way as to seemingly authorize or condone the widespread apathy that currently plagues our political system. We are no longer merely discouraged (by the powerful principles and maxims of liberal theory) from proposing a common way of life; we have now become almost indifferent to the very *possibility* of a shared, collective future.[101]

That profound lethargy, Benjamin Barber notes, stems from the fact that politics in twenty-first-century America is "nothing more than the chambermaid of private interests."[102] Our political society, he argues, suffers from an "excess of liberalism" that has largely "undone democratic institutions," so much so that "liberalism [now] serves democracy badly if at all." The sense of individualism displayed by the liberal paradigm contributes to the perception that the political importance of a single American voter is negligible, that one's vote is not pivotal enough to make an impact in the direction of our public policy.[103] Moreover, liberal individualism also encourages the belief that citizens can all but abandon their political and electoral responsibilities without suffering serious repercussions. Modern liberalism, according to Barber, "does not so much provide a justification for politics as it offers a politics that justifies individual rights. It is concerned more to promote individual liberty than to secure public justice, to advance interests rather than to discover goods, and to keep men safely apart rather than to bring them fruitfully together."[104] What Barber proposes is a reevaluation of America's public disposition: remediation, he says, will come from a reworking of our political awareness, of our political way of life.

In contrast to Etzioni and Glendon, Barber is strikingly less concerned about how individual freedoms stifle a collective existence. Instead, he suggests that in order to embrace real change there must be a systemic overhaul of the American political regime in favor of a more participatory system, with all citizens acting together to resolve public controversies. Accordingly, he creates a political design—"strong democracy"—that reflects his firm commitment to the principles of self-government, citizenship in the true sense of the word, and community. "Strong democracy in the participatory mode," he writes, "resolves conflicts in the absence of an independent ground through a participatory process of ongoing, proximate self-legislation and the creation of a political community capable of transforming dependent private individuals into free citizens and partial and private interests into public goods."[105] Liberal or weak democracy, on the other hand, erects too many participatory hurdles for citizens to feel they have a stake in the shaping of the general polity. It "is a 'thin' theory of democracy, one whose democratic values are prudential and thus provisional, optional and conditional—means to exclusively individualistic and private ends. From this precarious foundation, no firm theory of citizenship, participation, public goods, or civic virtue can be expected to arise."[106] Liberal democracy, that is, tends to encourage apathy and laziness while helping to create an uninformed, uninspired populace.

Barber's normative proposition begins and ends with the concept of self-government. In the tradition set forth by the theoretical communitarians, the goal is to shape our common lives collectively and cooperatively. In a strong democratic world, citizens have a responsibility to be serious political actors, to become fully involved in all aspects of the political experience—from the setting of an agenda, to the deliberation and decision, and finally to the implementation of the sanctioned policy. They cannot drop in and out of the political equation whenever it suits them, for their lives, according to Barber, are intertwined with both the process and the result of the community's democratic action. In Barber's mind, representation as we currently know it must be reconsidered. Participants cannot be removed from the political process as the theory of representation mandates but must have a tangible, firsthand relationship to politics itself.

Citizenship as a robust concept is thus central to Barber's construction. Reminiscent of the theoretical communitarian complaint expressed by Sandel and Taylor, Barber insists that our current liberal or "thin" theory of democracy carries with it a mistaken notion of citizenship. For the prescriptive communitarian, citizenship in the true sense of the word has to include some notion of political action or participation. Thin or liberal democracy eschews the principle of political participation by an engaged populace; and in turn, it settles for, at best, mass gesturing. "To be a citizen *is* to participate in a certain conscious fashion that presumes awareness and engagement in activity with others," Barber writes. "This consciousness alters attitudes and lends to participation that sense of the *we* I have associated with community. To participate *is* to create a community that governs itself, and to create a self-governing community *is* to participate."[107] Citizenship is a "way of living"; it is as much social as it is political. Strong democracy demands that subjects of the polity work in unison, under the same rules and guidelines, to devise a similar teleological strategy. It provides inhabitants with the necessary tools to engage actively and vigorously in the shaping of the political order, and it allows them, as a result, to proudly carry the emblem of citizenship.

Finally, the principles of self-government and citizenship are meaningless without a corresponding image of community. Politics, Barber notes, is a collective enterprise. Strong democracy seeks to recognize and celebrate its cooperative nature, whereas liberal or thin democracy either fails to recognize it or outwardly shuns it. According to Barber and other communitarian thinkers, politics can not be conceived of as an isolated, singular endeavor. When an individual undertakes an activity, that action may be private; but when an action is private, it is not political. Writes Barber: "Politics describes a realm of action . . . that is both undertaken by a public and intended to have public consequences."[108] As such, politics has to include a grounded conception of community.

For this modern-day Rousseauian, the key to a complete revitalization of the American polity is to welcome the communitarian spirit where each individual makes decisions, not for personal or private benefit, but for the good of the entire group, and to further translate that spirit into an attitude about politics that encourages intense collective action. In fact, Barber suggests a number of specific policies that he believes will significantly contribute to the ultimate realization of strong democracy. Among his many suggestions are ones that reform the postal service and the communication system in order to broaden access to vital public information. In addition, he proposes a restructuring of our election and balloting system in an attempt to achieve a higher degree of electoral fairness as well as a greater diversity of interests.[109] Altering America's attitude toward politics will dismantle the country's troubling devotion to individualism, claims Barber. It will transform politics from an occasional, often tedious duty into an irresistible, vibrant "way of living." Strong democracy therefore becomes both the remedy and the objective. A theory of active politics can thus both rescue us from our current political apathy and provide us with a comprehensive model of future political behavior.

America's Abandonment of Critical Public Institutions

Success for the communitarian movement would mean an ultimate "restoration of America's moral voice," Etzioni tells us. In the 1950s American values were presumed, they were clearly articulated, and furthermore, they were almost universally observed: "When your doctor told you that you needed surgery, you did not even think of asking for a second opinion. When your boss ordered you around at work, you did not mention that the Japanese invite their workers to participate in decision making. When your priest, labor leader, or father spoke, he spoke with authority."[110]

The point Etzioni is trying to make by recalling the 1950s is not that America ought to recover the values that governed society in the mid-twentieth century, but rather that the network of values that once ordered our shared way of life has vanished and has not been replaced with a contemporary one. The 1960s, he points out approvingly, was the era in recent American history in which our shared beliefs and moral values were profoundly challenged. Indeed, such a challenge was healthy and exciting. But what was deeply troubling about the countercultural movement was that the confrontation between sixties activists and fifties traditions produced no fresh—or seventies—values. Consequently, the communitarian movement claims that without any governing and authoritative principles, we are now caught in a web of "social and moral anarchy." *is this true though? have moral values only dramatically shifted?*

Strikingly similar to the ideas advocated by conservatives, prescriptive communitarians insist that any attempt to "restore America's moral voice" originates with institutions. "To rebuild America's moral foundations, to bring our regard for individuals and their rights into a better relationship with our sense of personal and collective responsibility," the Responsive Communitarian Platform pleads, "we must begin with the institutions of civil society." Institutions like the church, the synagogue, the family, and the schools are critical to any community in which they operate. They provide much-needed social services to the residents, but even beyond that, they instill a sense of identity and distinctiveness to the community as a whole. To put it differently, the institutions of civil society simultaneously furnish individuals with the physical and emotional goods necessary to survive while also acting as a visible beacon for community spirit. Communitarians regularly remind us that people often rally behind a school's athletic team or look forward to coming together on the day of Sabbath. Many even use the supermarket or the local VFW to air their ideas or grievances in an informal, city-council-like meeting. Communal institutions, therefore, must be given our utmost attention; they must be seriously attended to.

For the communitarian supporter, institutional reform centers primarily around moral and civic education. In fact, the Responsive Communitarian Platform places enormous confidence in the transformative capacity of education, claiming early on that "moral voices achieve their effect mainly through education and persuasion." The school, therefore, is the first public institution to come under communitarian scrutiny. America's educational system is, according to prescriptive communitarians, simply broken. It has failed to impart to students the character traits and moral foundation that underpin self-government and cultivate responsible and constituted members of the polity. William Galston insists that schooling in liberal democratic America has abandoned teaching "civic education" and has turned its attention to the so-called truth claims associated with the natural and social sciences.[111] "Civic education differs from philosophical education in all respects. Its purpose is not the pursuit and acquisition of truth but, rather, the formation of individuals who can conduct their lives within, and support, their political community."[112] Defined broadly as "a core of civic commitments and competences the broad acceptance of which undergirds a well-ordered liberal polity,"[113] civic education is meant to cultivate in students the essential doctrine of citizenship. Galston is suggesting that if properly administered, civic education will prepare students for the realization that sometime in the future they will actively shape America's public existence. Accordingly, he argues that such education ought to be sanctioned directly by the state.[114]

Etzioni similarly claims that our educational structure should concentrate less on inane, often useless facts and devote more resources to the morals and values that we as a national community share. Etzioni and his communitarian following suggest educating America's youth in the principles of dignity, tolerance, and hard work, while downplaying the realities of discrimination and exclusion. They insist that students must be made aware of the differences between democracy and totalitarianism and must be given the political tools required to actively participate in the public process. Finally, prescriptive communitarians believe contemporary schooling is too often ineffectual in preparing students for the professional world outside the classroom.[115] We cannot educate pupils in morality and responsibility and then allow them to go off to work in establishments that refuse to continue the lesson. Teaching our youth the shared values and principles lying at the core of the American political experience, they say, is an ongoing task that requires a permanent and thorough effort.

The failure to educate our children in the ways of citizenship and moral responsibility also falls on the shoulders of the American family. Character formation and personality development begin at home, prescriptive communitarians assert. Traditionally, says Etzioni, "the family was always entrusted with laying the foundations of moral education."[116] Parents, not babysitters or childcare centers, are charged with the responsibility of raising their children; furthermore, it is a full-time occupation that requires exhaustive and complete attention. Prescriptive communitarians insist that Americans must reorder their priorities and place more importance on the discipline of parenting. There must be a "change in orientation" where staying home to nurture a child is once again viewed as a noble and honorable career choice. Of course, such a change in consciousness includes a dramatic adjustment on the part of employers. The Responsive Communitarian Platform suggests that "*workplaces*

✕ the role of parents

should provide maximum flexible opportunities to parents to preserve an important part of their time and their energy, of their life, to attend to their educational-moral duties, for the sake of the next generation, its civic and moral character, and its capacity to contribute economically and socially to the commonweal" (emphasis theirs). Both the employers and the employees must work together to achieve a new understanding of parenthood. Like so many other proposals from the antiliberal front, the duty to educate the youth of America in the ways of morality and citizenship is viewed as a community endeavor.

To put pragmatic force behind the movement's normative strategy, both Etzioni and Galston propose extensive reform of America's major institutions. The family, along with the educational system, the economic structure, and the political realm, must all be reevaluated to correspond with the communitarian agenda. Parents, for example, have a responsibility to instruct their children as to the moral values required for a functioning American polity. This requires caregivers in some cases to sacrifice the upward progression of their careers in favor of the continued development of their offspring. Similarly, our religious communities, although constitutionally limited in certain areas, are charged with the task of instilling in those who voluntarily solicit their services, broad-based notions of morality and commitment.[117] Lastly, our educational system should not be satisfied with merely transferring skills to students but must strive to teach them the shared values necessary to preserving a national community. Stress must be placed on civic education in order to prepare students for the rigors and challenges of a shared public life.

CHAPTER THREE

Participation, Consensus, and the Common Good

Constructing a Communitarian Polity

What does a society look like if it is governed by contemporary communitarian institutions and values? Will it resemble its now discredited distant cousin, the communist regime, or does it more closely mirror the small, often-admired, New England town? Or perhaps even more plausibly, is the portrait of a modern communitarian polity conceptually different from that of any ordered political society we have yet encountered? Beyond the particulars of the theoretical and prescriptive movement, the practical construction or vision of the entire communitarian project is important in order to appraise the merits of its fully realized form. If we are seriously to consider adopting parts or the whole of the communitarian plan, we must first visualize it. Where is sovereignty located in the communitarian scheme? How will the institutions of the polity be organized effectively? What values and principles will be given priority? Only with the immediate evaluation and resolution of these and other questions will we be in a position to adequately assess the possibility of a predominantly communitarian America.

Attempting to envision a working communitarian polity is hazardous because few advocates focus directly on the structural framework of real politics.[1]

There is no modern communitarian equivalent to the *Federalist Papers*, no impressively detailed and definitive description of the mechanics of a newly proposed constitutional charter. Most communitarians are content to view human nature from a grassroots perspective. Their criticism of liberal theory centers on questions of the self and the relationship of selves and only rarely on the pragmatic issue of structural organization. Furthermore, communitarians readily admit that there is no clear example of a fully functioning modern communitarian system.[2] Communitarian scholarship, in short, has not evolved beyond the question of what needs to be changed about contemporary politics, to the more pragmatic inquiry about how to systematically organize those changes.[3]

As part of any effort to construct a fully developed political community, there exists the real possibility of building a communitarian straw man. One student of communitarianism remarks that supporters of the communitarian impulse "have been criticized for failing to develop a theory of community."[4] It is a delicate enterprise, therefore, to visualize a communitarian polity out of the often subtly connected writings of particular theorists, then to challenge that construction as problematic. Such a strategy (on both sides) is part of what currently inhibits the present liberal-communitarian debate. If falling into a similar trap, one will undoubtedly tend to conceive of the proposed political system in extreme or highly dubious terms so as to allow a challenge more maneuverability, and perhaps lend it additional credibility. Surely, it is easy to criticize a biased or incomplete image of the communitarian polity; it is infinitely more difficult to conceptualize and then critique a comprehensive and fully coherent account of such an important theory.

Difficult, however, does not mean impossible. To avoid the many pitfalls of imagining a functioning communitarian polity, we must access at least two critical resources—the writings of communitarian sympathizers, and the Platform of the Responsive Communitarian Movement. Sympathetic accounts of the main theoretical communitarian advocates are highly useful in that they are not primarily distracted by particulars beyond the communitarian enterprise. Their agenda is strictly supportive of communitarianism, and as such, they provide, as much as possible, an unbiased and exhaustive account of the communitarian project. Authors such as Robert Bellah, Daniel Bell, William Sullivan, and Ronald Beiner have stripped community theory of its more antagonistic elements and have, in a speculative manner, highlighted (as much as possible) the precise vision of communitarian politics.[5] The Responsive

Communitarian Platform is equally helpful in that it is the single most comprehensive design for a communitarian polity. In a concrete way, the Platform reveals the communitarian movement's preliminary strategy. Together, these sources of community theory provide an important glimpse into the proposed pragmatic future of communitarian politics.

Another difficulty in conceiving of a communitarian polity is to identify the common thread that runs through all communitarian scholarship. As I suggested earlier, modern communitarian thought is highly divergent, particularly when one compares the beliefs of certain conservative communitarians with the ideas of their more liberal cousins. The specific polity envisioned by MacIntyre, Carey, Grasso, and Frohnen, in short, might not fully resemble the one imagined by, say, Walzer, Barber, and Galston. MacIntyre, for example, advocates a *thick* conception of the good where members of the collective are obliged to live their lives under comparatively strict moral guidelines. Thus, a community, in MacIntyre's mind, requires more than just a mechanism to identify the collective will; it requires a substantive moral belief powerful enough to inspire the citizenry. Walzer, in contrast, discounts such a perfectionist doctrine, preferring instead to organize the polity around mostly procedural norms. His understanding of community might be characterized (particularly by conservatives) as a *thin* conception of the good. There is little substance behind Walzer's vision of community, claim conservative communitarians, and thus his portrait of the polity more closely aligns with the features of liberalism than with communitarianism. Such a claim is debatable, of course, but it is fair to say that at a minimum, the conservative image of community often includes a substantive or moral component that many liberal communitarians do not always embrace.

Constructing a single communitarian polity, therefore, is a precarious undertaking: too much emphasis on either the conservative or liberal writings will no doubt skew our vision of a working communitarian regime. The distinctions, however, are not irreconcilable; they are grounded in a set of common principles. Both liberal and conservative communitarians consent to the belief that the interests of the community supersede the particular desires of the individual. That is to say, they each agree that the community's values exist prior to, and are more critical than, the wants of any single resident of the polity. Some communitarians describe this position in terms of the relationship between the right and the good; others view it as derivative of the larger debate surrounding the notion of the self. But all communitarians, in one form or another, defend it.

I would further suggest that the *practical* differences between the thick and thin conceptions of the good are not as dramatic as some have implied. Conservative communitarians are indeed more vocal about the need to recapture a sense of morality—a substantive telos—at the communal level, but even they must defend some decidedly liberal ideals. The principle of localized control— one of the mainstays of conservative communitarian thought—can only work if one subscribes to a pluralist formula at the national level. In other words, the idea that we can sustain local communities and permit them to identify and subsequently foster their own conceptions of the good is possible only if we adopt the principle of neutrality—a thin conception of the good—at the national level. Conveniently, this is done by all but ignoring the nation-state. The conservative communitarianism of MacIntyre, Frohnen, Carey, and Grasso requires that the nation-state be viewed as something distinct and altogether noncommunitarian; it is an afterthought for most conservative communitarians.[6] Brad Lowell Stone writes that "traditional communitarians recognized the existence of nations but did not regard them as communities."[7] They are not communities, say conservatives, because they cannot cultivate meaningful bonds among diverse populations. The reaction by conservative voices to the deficiencies of the nation-state is not to reconstruct them in the communitarian image but rather to redefine them as somehow outside the arena altogether. In the end, what the division between the nation-state and the local polity accomplishes for conservatives is the ability to maintain a certain fidelity to the principle of community while avoiding the label of intolerance.

Conversely, however, liberal communitarians are not always so enamored with the pragmatic result of the thin conception of the good. Sandel is a critical figure here. Often linked with the liberal communitarians as one who favors a more or less free society where constitutive ties are based largely on nothing more than a set of procedural rules, Sandel yet seems to reflect the ideas of most communitarians: his work transcends both liberal and conservative foundations. In his later writings especially, he has been more vocal in supporting conservative values. *Democracy's Discontent* presents Sandel's critique of an American society that has, over the past few generations, erected numerous barriers to the realization of a shared moral value system. "In recent decades," he writes, "the civic or formative aspect of our politics has largely given way to the liberalism that conceives persons as free and independent selves, unencumbered by moral or civic ties they have not chosen." "This shift," he then concludes, "sheds light on our present political predicament."[8]

Accordingly, Sandel is quick to move beyond a simple critique of liberalism based entirely on procedural norms. He claims that the institutions of a modern liberal state fail to take morality seriously. As an example, he argues that the Supreme Court's recent decisions regarding religious conscience signal a disturbing lack of attention to those principles and policies that might encourage universally shared values. In the domain of religion, the Court has confused two unrelated notions lately—freedom of conscience and freedom of choice—and has consequently refused to recognize that the freedom to worship without "suffering civil penalties or incapacities" is not the same as the "right to choose one's beliefs." Freedom of conscience, Sandel asserts, has traditionally meant that citizens could decide the extent of their commitment to a particular religious belief, but not the substance of that belief. That, he insists, is beyond individual capacity. Citing Madison and Jefferson, he contends that religious liberty "relies heavily on the assumption that beliefs are not a matter of choice." They are not a matter of will; they exist apart from any single member of the community, and they are largely based on moral or substantive teachings. What disturbs Sandel most acutely is the idea that liberalism, and the institutions like the Supreme Court that have adopted primarily liberal influences, cannot account for this distinction. "For procedural liberalism the case for religious liberty derives not from the moral importance of religion but from the need to protect individual autonomy." We need to alter our vision, he says, to embrace the communitarian ideal that shared moral values can be both binding and transformative.[9] Indeed, the liberal communitarian sounds like a conservative here.

Even Benjamin Barber sounds remarkably conservative at times. In fact, Barber has noted with considerable excitement that the civic republican perspective championed by so many conservative communitarians is the close "cousin" of his strong democratic position.[10] He tells of his admiration for Sandel, claiming that the theorist's more recent writings incorporate both his desire for a robust political process *and* the need to expose the common good. This, of course, is an important admission in that it helps draw Barber's liberal communitarianism a bit closer to his more conservative counterparts. But that is not all. In *A Place for Us: How to Make Society Civil and Democracy Strong*, Barber introduces a new concept—"strong democratic civil society." Actually, the term is taken from two of Barber's most intense passions: a full and healthy democratic existence, combined with a blending of the public and the private realms. Yet the concept accurately reflects Barber's communitarian vision. Sounding strikingly similar to some conservative communitarians, Barber writes: "Strong democratic civil society, like Tocqueville's civic republican civil society, shares with government a sense of publicity and a regard for the public good and the common weal. . . . [I]t is a voluntary and in this sense "private" realm devoted to public goods."[11] Institutions like the family, the church, and the school become "training grounds" for public action; they mediate between the individual and the state in ways that allow us to experience the feeling of collective engagement. Moreover, they give us practice in the art of politics, says Barber. And yet they are just as critical to the development of personal character as they are to the continued vitality of the state. They form us in ways that permit us to live a common life. Accordingly, local communities of all shapes and sizes are indispensable, he argues, and they ought to be left alone to develop their own conceptions of the good.

Finally, all communitarians promote the principle of discussion as a means of identifying the common good. As often as Barber defends the need to implement measures aimed at securing democratic principles on a national scale, conservative communitarians opine that a local community's substantive telos is uncovered primarily through intimate dialogue. MacIntyre, for one, argues that one comes to know the good life only as an integrated member of the polity, and not as an independent, isolated being. In fact, MacIntyre notes that it is precisely one's isolation from others that renders the modern liberal incapable of creating and sustaining the bonds necessary to realize the good. A constituted being carries on a conversation—a narrative—with members of the community that implicates the past and sets the agenda for the future. In MacIntyre's words, when an "institution—a university, say, or a farm or a hospital—is the bearer of a tradition of practice or practices, its common life will be partly, but in a centrally important way, constituted by a continuous argument as to what a university is and ought to be or what good farming is or what good medicine is."[12]

Frohnen is even more closely aligned with Barber on the issue of political deliberation and consensus. In a lengthy passage aimed at describing the importance of civic participation, he writes:

> Political life is central to communitarians because it forms the nexus within which we create and order our values. Just as we require common values to hold our society together, so we require society to help us form common values. . . . For communitarians we need symbols and ideals that transcend the particular interests of particular actors—we require common values that apply to everyone in our society. But we also require politics; we require a mechanism by which to motivate the people and put our ideals into action.[13]

The attempt to locate the good is thus undertaken as an ongoing, deliberative exercise. Mankind is inherently flawed and is unable to know the good without the help of others. The good may be preconceived, as MacIntyre argues, but the discovery of that good takes place within the tangible world of real politics. He and other conservative communitarians therefore conclude that "the good life for man is the life spent in seeking for the good life for man,"[14] and the way to realize that good life is through continuous and collective reflection. The same is true for communities.

The metaphor of the journey may prove useful here. The division in communitarian literature between the liberal communitarians and the conservatives—between the participatory democrats and the republicans more specifically—roughly corresponds to the distinction between the journey and the end. Participatory democrats like Barber suggest that the journey is the critical factor, that participating in the political process, regardless of the outcome, somehow transforms egoistic individuals into actively engaged citizens. Republicans, in contrast, are said to value the destination more than the journey. MacIntyre speaks of the blessings that accompany man's arrival at the end, at the moment in which he discovers the good life. Nonetheless, it is important to remember that a journey makes little sense without a destination, and a destination is not possible without a journey. To infer that MacIntyre is somehow uninterested in the journey because he de-emphasizes the process is to acknowledge only a portion of his grand theory. Conservative communitarians are acutely attentive to the journey in that the discovery of the good for them requires a "continuous argument" about the good itself. Individuals do not instinctively know how to achieve the good life, and thus they must repeatedly engage in a conversation aimed at revealing its many facets. Norman Barry, a conservative communitarian, refers to this broad communitarian characteristic as giving "voice" to a community.[15]

Conversely, liberal communitarians are equally focused on the end. Both Sandel and Barber have at different times demonstrated their affinity for the type of civic republican values conservative communitarians so eagerly defend. Both have advanced the principle that one's love for the community ought to be cultivated and that a polity requires "a continuous preference of the public interest over one's own."[16] Sandel is certainly more explicit in his promotion of virtue, but even Barber's version of republicanism resembles portions of the conservative argument. His republicanism is decidedly Rousseauian in that he envisions the representatives of the republic transforming "each individual who by himself is a perfect and solitary whole, into a part of a larger whole from which this individual receives, in a sense, his life and his being."[17] Individuals are converted into citizens precisely by their passion for the polity and their willingness to participate in charting its collective future. Above all, then, communitarians of all species advocate the need to uncover the pulse of the community. Even MacIntyre, who argues that the principles of virtue predate the birth of the political community, implies that a political order is necessary to discover and promote morality. Critical to that order is the process of communal dialogue.

Taken together, these are powerful intellectual ties that bind all communitarians; they are communitarianism's first principles. Furthermore, they are not so abstract and intangible that they cannot be conceived of in terms of real politics. When communitarians speak of the priority of the community over the individual, they are suggesting, for example, that policy (on abortion, race relations, religion, rights, responsibilities, and so on) reflect the collective and shared will of the community. Those policies should be based entirely on the interests of the collective whole; there simply can be no other influencing factor for communitarians. A conservative communitarian who advocates a thick notion of the good, therefore, will still consult the community's inter- *queueing* pretation of tradition and virtue for practical guidance. Similarly, a liberal communitarian will adopt the same approach even if he does not fully agree that the aim of the community should be some substantive aspiration. Whether local communities or national, perfectionist polities or merely procedural, all communitarians—from MacIntyre to Walzer—defend the principle that the community's values supersede all competing noncommunal interests. To suggest otherwise is to suggest that the intellectual leaders of the communitarian movement are impostors.   *✱ community interest is #1 always*

Imagining a Communitarian Polity

If enhanced community is the goal of any communitarian polity, then commonality is the means to achieve that goal. Rather than nourishing the individual and his interests, communitarian polities celebrate the collective— the community of individuals—as the primary moral and political value.[18] Because it is believed to be the correct path to moral and political "flourishing," what any communitarian society principally aspires to promote is a feeling of cooperation and mutuality, a spirit of sharing in the resolution of its collective problems.[19] "Many of our problems are truly common," says Bellah. "We all breathe the same air. We all are vulnerable to the same lethal rays of the sun coming through an ozone-depleted atmosphere. It is not only the poor inhabitants of decayed inner cities who suffer from their civic decline but the inhabitants of expensive town houses and suburban homes when no one dares to go out on the street at night or even feels safe in his own home."[20] Together we feel the effects of society's shortcomings, and together, Bellah seems to be saying, we must work to overcome them.

It stands to reason, therefore, that the construction of a communitarian polity begins and ends with some notion of solidarity. In the political process, as in the realm of public discourse and the private sphere, a communitarian regime succeeds or fails by the degree to which it can foster a sense of togetherness and a perception of unified action. David Miller describes the "promise of overall community" as "allow[ing] people to regard themselves as active subjects shaping the world according to their will."[21]

The crucial theoretical claim that identities are constituted precisely by their relationships and shared experiences within the community further suggests that communitarianism places significant authoritative weight on the concept of cohesion. Alasdair MacIntyre remarks that "we live out our lives, both individually and in our relationships with each other, in the light of certain conceptions of a possible *shared* future, a future in which certain possibilities beckon us forward and others repel us, some seem already foreclosed and others perhaps inevitable."[22] Robert Bellah and his coauthors echo these sentiments. In both *Habits of the Heart* and *The Good Society*, they assert that modern liberal regimes like the United States have a tendency to discount the very institutions best equipped to bind us together. The hyperindividualism that pervades American society, says Bellah, invariably leads to the inhabitant's retreat from the public realm into his own private world. Moreover, liberal societies have no means to retard such an inevitability.

In order to capture, embrace, and preserve the notion of shared cooperation, communitarians must therefore be committed to certain specific institutional realities. To begin with, communitarian politics must be principally arranged in direct reference to the "shared and common understandings" of its inhabitants. All communitarian politics, Daniel Bell indicates, in some way concerns the society's common or collective heritage: "The whole point of communitarian politics is to structure society in accordance with people's deepest shared understandings."[23] This is no abstract, intangible point. Many past and present political commentators, including Rousseau, Montesquieu, Publius, Sunstein, and others have thought it important enough to first isolate the "common character" or identity of a nation when envisioning a working political order.[24] In fact, from the profound theoretical arguments of these thinkers, we can imagine a number of possible shared traditions that form the foundation of hypothetical communitarian and semi-communitarian polities. Anti-Federalists, for example, sought to organize their vision for American politics around procedural republicanism and substantive and religious conservatism. Similarly, the former socialist states of Eastern Europe, although considered semi-communitarian at best, attempted (unsuccessfully) to structure their regimes around the perceived interests of the proletariat, the majority working class. Israel, perhaps the closest example of a modern regime founded on communitarian ideals, organizes its polity around some broad conception of Judaism. One could continue. The point is not to locate a single substantive vision for all communitarian regimes—indeed, communitarians often remind us that the preferences of any given community will be unique— but rather to focus on the collective or communal nature of the vision itself. Individual welfare and even aggregate interests take a back seat to the priorities of the community.

Communitarianism's first concern is thus to identify and define the collective social goals and "shared understandings" of the group. Since they will eventually form the organizational principles for the entire polity, it is essential that any strategy to construct a working communitarian polity originate with those values and traditions that have bound, or will bind, constituents to each other and to the polity in general. The major disease that plagues liberal politics, communitarians assert, is that it produces largely unencumbered, rootless individuals whose identities are not constituted by the community's collective values. Accordingly, liberal society is an unconstituted society. A communitarian society, in contrast, recognizes and celebrates those ideas, principles, and cultural habits that most people share in common, and it endeavors to use those identifiable institutions for the purpose of organizing the polity around the beliefs of the citizens.

Communitarian life, then, focuses centrally on the values its citizens share, and it attempts to employ those values simultaneously as a means to substantially improve the lives of its citizens as well as to guide the polity to some desired end. For mainstream conservative communitarians the aim will likely be teleological or substantive, whereas the end proposed by liberal advocates of community is more apt to reflect a heightened procedural component. Collectively, however, the objective for all communitarians (in contrast to liberals) is one based on the supremacy of the community's wishes in relation to the individual. Reform of liberalism's unhealthy institutions will come, Bellah and other communitarians argue, from attending to people's attitudes toward others and beliefs about cooperation. Success, and the eventual realization of a functioning communitarian society, will result from combining a sharp recognition that life is a shared experience with the specific procedural mechanisms required to isolate the values and principles that inform a collective existence.

Locating a central political principle or organizational doctrine begins for Daniel Bell and other sympathizers of the communitarian enterprise with some notion of a shared understanding or tradition, but obviously it does not end there. The common heritage of the community finds tangible form in the conception of the good, a "belief" (or way of life) that is shared by members of the community and goes far beyond the mere utilitarian aggregation of private interests. Those specific and palpable principles that dictate a collective "way of life" for the citizens of a communitarian polity are often the ones theoretical communitarians describe as informing the societal good, the basis of all communitarian politics. Communitarianism "posits a need to experience our lives as bound up with the good of the communities out of which our identity has been constituted," writes Bell.[25] The understanding of a communal good regulates our behavior in much the same way a religious teaching operates over its followers. This moral and political consensus, which Bell and other communitarians argue forms our collective identities, guides us and our actions in an organizational, sovereign, and authoritative manner. Because the good organizes and animates what is most valuable in our lives—our "constitutive attachments"—it will manage and direct us as a collective, communal unit.[26]

One of the major controversies surrounding the liberal-communitarian debate centers on the belief, held by advocates of community, that liberals mistakenly dismiss the possibility of a cooperative good, and instead maintain the importance of personal autonomy and private choice in the good's ultimate formulation. Sandel, Taylor, and MacIntyre are particularly averse to this line of liberal thinking. The political manifestation of that individualistic principle is the conceptualization and endorsement of a neutral state. But to them, if personal identity is tied up so tightly in the collective community vision— if individual character is directly formed by the social settings we find ourselves in—then persons could not conceivably possess a telos that is independent of the one identified and followed by the community. Hence, the notion of a purely neutral state is erroneous. The very definition of the state as being constituted by those citizens sharing a concrete conception of the good precludes the possibility of state neutrality. Indeed, political society, the communitarian theorists ultimately conclude, is inherently and unmistakably nonneutral.[27]

Similar reasoning pervades Bell's recent view of politics. In his mind, communitarian politics subscribes to the Aristotelian notion of man as a social being. Thus, institutions of the communitarian polity, including a system of distributive justice, should be structured in such a way as to recognize the traditions and cultural boundaries that form the basis of the social, or in his mind, substantive, conception of the good. To dismiss or merely overlook this political reality, Bell argues, is unscrupulous: The "social world . . . sets the authoritative moral horizons within which we determine 'what's worth doing, achieving, or being.' We cannot make sense of our moral experience unless we situate ourselves within this 'given' moral space."[28] The result of everyone's being situated is a society that is both fully constituted and, more importantly, governed by a constitutive moral and ethical doctrine. His ideal communitarian polity is constructed from, and hinges upon, some clearly articulated substantive "commitment to the good of the nation."

Despite coming from an altogether different position, liberal communitarians like Barber and Walzer ultimately arrive at a similar conclusion. Barber, for example, differs from MacIntyre and the conservative communitarians in that he sees no "preconceptual" framework for politics. Instead, the democratic process itself legitimates beliefs that arise from universalistic doctrines. This does not mean that values and ideas will not be drawn from religious and metaphysical systems of the kind offered by Christians or liberals. Rather, it means that such values will acquire their legitimacy from their political fecundity—from their acceptance into and transformation through the democratic political process."[29] A small segment or the entire population of a particular community may bring religious teachings to bear on the collective choices of the polity. All are welcome, says Barber. But the process is only the first step. Once the process has revealed a collective decision, it becomes the responsibility of the government to sponsor policies that reinforce the will of the community. That is to say, the state must now protect the good (the substantive result) that emerges from participatory deliberation; the end, in short, must be subsidized. To focus only on the process is to miss the point of politics altogether. Things must get done and decisions must be made. Our "common lives" are intimately tied up with the process, to be sure; but the "strong democrat," Barber writes, "understands that while politics begins with conflict and uncertainty, it always ends with what we may call the consensus of action. . . . Out of the diversity of the process comes the unity of the deed."[30] The consequence of strong democracy, therefore, is a polity that values the process and then cherishes the result.

In the end, it does not get us very far to claim that communitarian polities must be structured and organized so as to further some nebulous understanding of the good. In fact, it is certainly conceivable that critics of communitarianism, if not already concerned with other issues addressed, might raise a serious objection to the apparent conjectural or amorphous nature of the communitarian argument thus far explored. For the sake of our immediate position, though, let us assume that a conception of the good—say, one (in the conservative tradition) that preaches a religious, yet pluralist, doctrine—has been identified as paramount in a particular political society, and that it is generally affirmed by the population that the state should promote that religious way of life.[31] How are we to realize, in political form, the endorsed community vision? Moreover, how are we to ensure that the collective religious vision is preserved? Where should we look for help, and what should we do when an aggregate image of the good is acknowledged?

Once we admit that the crux of communitarian politics centers on the community's particular conception of the good, the construction of a working communitarian polity becomes a bit simpler. Communitarian theory notes that the conceptualization of a political regime based on the principles of community requires that we attend to three critical tasks: the introduction of a form of governance that is compatible with communitarian principles; the shoring up of institutions; and the implementation of a system of state sponsorship of certain ways of life.

First, we must determine what form of governance is necessarily suited to identifying the collective conception of the good. For most communitarians, the appropriate political system required to isolate the communal good takes the form of "participatory democracy," or what I will call "communitarian republicanism."[32] Correspondingly, they also indicate that the decision-rule that best complements communitarian republicanism is democratic consensualism. Barber addresses the need for democratic principles directly, but even MacIntyre and the conservative communitarians advocate a form of dialogue/ debate that resembles republican government as necessary for the realization of communitarian policy. Combined, republicanism and democratic consensualism allow citizens of the community to adhere closely to the first principle of communitarianism—acting together to shape the collective environment.[33]

Before proceeding, a slight digression is in order. I refer to a republican style of government as one where the people are sovereign and where the polity itself is governed by the will of the populace manifested in some particular form. This definition is wide enough to encompass both the Madisonian version that characterizes republican government as "representative" and classical conceptions of republicanism that promote notions of *res publica*.[34] My initial inspiration for using it in this broad context derives from Publius, who in *Federalist* 39 (among other places) defined a republic as "a government which derives all its powers directly or indirectly from the great body of the people."[35] Steven Kautz's provocative book, *Liberalism and Community* is also influential in that he refuses to draw major political distinctions between participatory democrats and those who advocate the type of republicanism typically associated only with a certain zeal for the public good. The broad notion of republicanism embraced here is useful—in contrast to a thinner conception that merely identifies a distinction between civic virtue and liberal self-interest—because it can account equally for the type of communitarian framework promised by Barber on the one hand, and the more conservative proponents of community theory on the other.

Returning to the task at hand, the ultimate construction of a viable communitarian project also requires us to address the question of how the conception of the good is to be authoritatively enforced. Sympathetic accounts of communitarian theory point to institutions—including the family, schools, law, language, cultural habits, and other physical organizations—as the principal means to educate and sanction citizens of the community-centered polity. Institutions, of course, must be tailored to meet and endorse the community's shared understanding or collective conception of the good, but as such, they also function as a necessary moral guide to individual action. They inform individuals as to what conduct may be interpreted as faithful to the community good as well as prohibit behavior that is inconsistent with the collective will. The institutions of a polity should foster the vision of the good life and forbid morally incongruous activities.

Once the shared conception of the good has been identified and institutions have been attended to, the final job in the development of a working communitarian polity is to institute a style of political practice that preserves and safeguards the identified conception of the good. For many liberal critics of communitarianism, the practice favored by advocates of community—one that promotes state-sponsorship of certain ways of life—is deeply troubling. It is discomforting because it disavows the notion that individuals have a capacity for self-determination, while simultaneously renouncing the traditional liberal definition of equality. Yet the communitarian state, described by Kymlicka as "perfectionist," is not neutral to competing notions of the good life: "A communitarian state can and should encourage people to adopt conceptions of the good that conform to the community's way of life, while discouraging conceptions of the good that conflict with it."[36] The institutions, along with the endorsed practice of communitarian politics, allow the communitarian state to accomplish that fundamental goal.

Republican Government and the Democratic Decision-rule

Perhaps the most significant endeavor in the ultimate framing of a functioning communitarian polity is the adoption of a viable form of governance. How are we to realize, through political channels, a collective good beyond the simple "utilitarian sum of individual satisfactions"? What sort of systematic arrangement is required to tap into the unified thoughts and ideas of a community's citizenry? Of course, whichever mechanism of political decision making is finally employed by communitarian theorists, its first priority is to capture, identify, and ultimately implement an authoritative collective conception of the good. But it also has additional, less obvious tasks. The communitarian style of government must also, as part of its promise to constitute and give roots to the entire polity, encourage citizens to take an active role in the shaping of the public sphere.[37] It cannot force its constituents to partake in political activities; instead, it must show them that political participation is not just a means to an end but is an end or a good in itself. More to the point, the political scheme ratified by communitarian architects is not simply a mechanism for the protection of interests; it is also and importantly a medium for residents of a community to acquire a sense of solidarity, "a spirit of community." In Barber's normative view of politics, it is vigorous and energetic social action by citizens of a community that will eventually transform persons from mere agents or clients of the state to masters or champions of their own political realm.[38]

In communitarian theory, the form of political governance most often mentioned as befitting the ideology is participatory democracy or communitarian republicanism, while the decision-rule that most appropriately complements community theory is some form of democratic consensualism.[39] Defined best by Barber, participatory democracy (or, using his phraseology, "strong democracy") is "politics in the participatory mode where conflict is resolved in the absence of an independent ground through a participatory process of ongoing, proximate self-legislation and the creation of a political community capable of transforming dependent, private individuals into free citizens and partial and private interests into public goods."[40] The main benefit of participatory democracy is that it accomplishes the two tasks communitarians ask of political schemes: it can locate and identify the community's conception or understanding of the good; and, more importantly, it carries with it a strong sense of inclusion. Communitarian republicanism, it is said, ensures a full understanding of human dignity by abandoning private interest protection and adopting as paramount the principle of collective decision making. It transforms political conduct from a procedural activity into a "way of living."

The idea that politics and the participation of citizens therein should be viewed as a "way of living" rather than a mere "part of living" is fundamental to the communitarian impulse. At the core of communitarian theory is the premise that residents of a community ought to work together to shape their public lives in a particular image. Politics ought to be an instrument to achieve certain policy initiatives, but it should also be a tool to develop individual personalities and craft a shared public existence. In attempting to deter persons from accepting the liberal tendency to favor a utilitarian calculus of private interests, certain communitarians stress the need to emphasize the process and practice of decision making, rather than simply the final decision. The journey itself is an indispensable part of the final result. That participatory journey is part of what constitutes a good life. "The individual's true good must consist not in attaining a sum of satisfactions but in showing in himself, and sharing as a participant, an admirable and worthwhile form of life" wrote William Sullivan.[41] Here, John Dewey is perhaps additionally instructive, as he noted in 1927 that certain types of politics inform "the idea of community life itself."[42] Among the forms Dewey singled out as particularly effective was participatory democracy.

In light of their concern for citizen action, it is not altogether surprising that Barber and other communitarians condemn the practice of representation as one of the great weaknesses of liberal democracy. "Representation is incompatible with freedom," Barber writes, "because it delegates and thus alienates political will at the cost of genuine self-government and autonomy."[43] Citizens who do not have a *direct* say in the policies that shape their everyday lives, who assign responsibility for substantive decisions about the polity to others, are not truly free. He would like to do away with the practice of representation and demand that each citizen participate in common to craft a mutual existence. It is important to underscore this point now because it will resurface below: the communitarian difficulty with representative government leaves the collective citizenry—indeed, the entire voting population—completely responsible for most political decisions. The sovereign people, in other words, are themselves the decision-making institutions of government. There is no need for legislative bodies made up of designated agents of the people because the people themselves directly control their own destiny. Practical reflections of the sovereign in the form of political spokespersons or representatives would thus represent a failure in Barber's mind. His ideal communitarian vision has no room for representation.

In *Reconstructing Public Philosophy*, William Sullivan enthusiastically embraces the participatory or republican form of politics as a way to foster "civic virtue" and identify a collective moral consensus. A staunch communitarian advocate, Sullivan argues that the best way to "shore up morality" is to remodel our sense of "civic virtue"—"loosely translated as a near instinctive concern for the common weal"—away from the egoism associated with modern individualism, and toward a new "public philosophy" that encourages the collective good. According to his interpretation, the rise of liberal individualism in the modern period led to the demise of what he calls the "public philosophy of the revolutionary era." Unlike the current absence of an organizational moral principle, the philosophy of the American Revolution sought to recognize and promote the "shared understanding" of the nation chiefly by stressing the good over the right and the public over the private. Further, it realized the value, later adopted by modern communitarians, of group participation toward a unified goal.[44]

The idea of civic republicanism, Sullivan believes, descended from the teachings of Plato and Aristotle and animated the writings surrounding the founding of the American republic. What is required in order to save us from the malaise of modern egoism, he notes, is a new public philosophy that can once again locate and preserve a collective vision of the moral good. "A public philosophy is an expression and vehicle of practical reason in its classical sense, embodied in the life of a people and bound up with that people's reflection upon itself and its project."[45] The communitarian affinity for connectedness and rootedness is evident in this quote, but what is more interesting is how Sullivan suggests that persons will come to comprehend and extol the public philosophy. For the communitarian supporter, liberalism is not a public project in the sense that it admires and values the individual as an isolated, autonomously constituted agent. Participatory republicanism, on the other hand, is instinctively a public strategy. In contradistinction to the liberal propensity to view the human self as an unencumbered, autonomous being, Sullivan notes that republicanism "address[es] directly the craving of the human self for a life of inclusion in a community of mutual concern."[46]

Since communitarianism stands solidly behind the notion of political power vested in the people, are we to assume that majoritarianism is the decision-rule most frequently cited as politically warranted? Is majority rule the political principle that can most effectively isolate the common good and satisfy the theory of participatory democracy? Although occasionally championing majority rule, communitarians more often fault democratic majoritarianism for being one of the main defects of liberal politics. Writes Barber: "Majoritarianism is a tribute to the failure of democracy: to our inability to create a politics of mutualism that can overcome private interests. It is thus finally the democracy of desperation, an attempt to salvage decision-making from the anarchy of adversary politics."[47] Without reflection, majoritarianism accepts all the tenets of liberal theory to which communitarians are so strongly opposed. It reduces citizens to mere individuals and politics to the simple aggregation of individual choices, while eliminating virtually all possibility of collective and energetic political conduct. Barber unself-consciously describes democratic "mutualism" or "consensuality" as the decision-rule that most appropriately accompanies participatory or republican democracy. Fusing democracy with a fervent desire to reach consensus, communitarian politics shuns most of the traditionally more efficient forms of decision making in favor of one that is perhaps extremely laborious (and even unworkable) but that furthers the essential principle of collectivity. "Strong democracy," says

Barber, "offers an alternative model [to democratic majoritarianism] that incorporates certain of the virtues of liberal democracy's view of decision as choice in the face of necessity, but promotes a richer, more mutualistic understanding of what it means to develop political judgment and to exercise political will."[48]

Throughout the entire construction of a communitarian form of political governance, one theme constantly emerges as the centerpiece of communitarian politics: participation. Active involvement by the population, writes Sullivan, "is a form of personal development, a process of enlarging personal horizons to include other generations and different kinds of people and of expanding the ability to respond with care in an interdependent life."[49] Communitarian republicanism and democratic consensualism are styles of political governance and decision making that ensure dynamic and spirited involvement within the public sphere. As such, they form the basic mechanism of government chosen by communitarian theorists to organize the envisioned community-centered design. Together, they are the first among many political institutions in the communitarian polity that seek to accomplish multiple foundational goals. Of course, as a system designed to initiate policy, their first purpose is to recognize and solidify a sometimes substantive, but always collective, principle. Their second purpose is to demonstrate through example the need to act together when fashioning a mutual existence.

The Importance of Institutions in Communitarian Politics

In *The Good Society* Robert Bellah and his coauthors subscribe to a line of thinking that places institutions at the base of communitarian reform. "We need to understand how much of our lives is lived in and through institutions, and how better institutions are essential if we are to lead better lives."[50] By defining institutions as "the patterned ways [persons] have developed for living together" Bellah is proposing that all institutions, including republicanism and participatory democracy, are inherently communal.[51] That is, they are intrinsically or naturally social. Furthermore, he adds, an institution is a "pattern of expected action of individuals or groups enforced by social sanctions, both positive and negative. For example, institutions may be such simple customs as the confirming handshake in a social situation, where the refusal to respond to an outstretched hand might cause embarrassment and some need for an explanation; or they may be highly formal institutions such as taxation upon which social services depend, where refusal to pay may be punished by fines and imprisonment."[52] Institutions may also be what he describes as "organizations," even more formal physical entities like the agencies of the state, religious bodies, corporations, or schools. In Bellah's mind, all institutions are "normative patterns embedded in and enforced by laws and mores (informal customs and practices)" that provide the community with tangible guides for moral and political action.[53]

Note that there are two critical prongs to this definition of institutions—sociality and sanction. According to Bellah, institutions are innately social; they are definitively communal in that they require, for their existence, the action of more than a single individual. In addition, however, Bellah's explanation of institutions also includes a strong element of command. Institutions teach us (by confirming certain activities and proscribing others) the difference between right and wrong. They inform us of the parameters or boundaries of our actions—what is socially acceptable and what is, in Etzioni's words, "beyond the pale." "Institutions," Bellah explains, "always have a moral element"; they "form individuals by making possible or impossible certain ways of behaving and relating to others. They shape character by assigning responsibility, demanding accountability, and providing the standards in terms of which each person recognizes the excellence of his or her achievements."[54] Consistent with Bellah's description, Daniel Bell refers to institutions as "social practices" that we, as members of the community, have neither a capacity to ignore nor an ability to escape.[55] And while both authors must, of course, admit that liberal institutions also have the capability to "shape character," a major portion of their critique of hyperindividualism is that liberal institutions (like those in America) have been so roundly ignored and dismissed in the recent past that they have lost much of their transformative power.[56]

Institutions, therefore, have a robust and active dual role in the communitarian political design. The authors of *The Good Society* note that for most anticommunitarians, institutions have predominantly functional importance in that their main purpose is to maintain state security and social efficiency. But for communitarians, those same institutional traditions and agencies are interpreted as having both practical and normative functions. Unlike liberal states, where institutions are often simply a pragmatic means to ensure personal autonomy, communitarian polities attempt to tap directly into the normative element and use it specifically for the collective advantage of the citizenry. Institutions show us exactly who we are and how we should properly live our common lives together. We are reflections of the institutions of our society in the same way those institutions are reflections of us, and thus we ought to use them as substantive expressions meant to further the subscribed way of life.

Bellah insists that all institutions shape values: "At every level, new forms of citizen involvement [in institutions] should transform the very conception of interests. The fundamental flaw in the notion that government exists to maximize the satisfaction of individual interests is that what people value is itself shaped by their institutional experience. Thus our public institutions shape the very possibility of public values."[57] It is the communitarian view that all institutions—from the tradition of a handshake to the occasional omnipresence of the state—can and should be used as tools for disseminating, protecting, and nurturing the collective conception of the good. Consider religion: Churches, synagogues, mosques, and other spiritual houses are among the more critical organizations in the communitarian imagination. Etzioni speaks regularly of the need to fortify places of worship so that they are properly equipped to provide inhabitants with a degree of moral education not readily found in the secular world. He argues that religious institutions shape our ways of living in a manner that other institutions cannot match. For that reason, they deserve our attention.

Conservative communitarians are even more assertive in their defense of religion as the key to moral and spiritual development. Prepolitical in nature, religious faith is one of the three main pillars that fortify the conservative communitarian agenda. The "church, the family, and local associations," Frohnen argues, represent the best hope for members of the polity to find common ground and stake out a shared moral existence. Moreover, they perform the dual function that Bellah notes is so essential of institutions: they are social in nature and educative in function. If we do not attend to these institutions, Frohnen continues, not only will they "fall into disorder," but "our society and our very souls also will become disordered."[58] Our lives are so intimately tied up with the institution of the family and the church that it becomes virtually impossible to survive in this world without their influence. With this in mind, Frohnen's idyllic polity combines civic participation with a sharp attention to the moral teachings that accompany religious worship. He writes longingly of eighteenth-century America:

> Men on both sides of the constitutional debates shared with their American
> predecessors a commitment to the way of life that had become traditional in

their land. This way of life consisted of participation in various local associations, bound together by a commitment to well-ordered liberty, and to the system of manners and morals taught through public worship and private habituation. Most important, it was a way of life in which virtue was the goal and was defined as adherence to universal religious standards of piety and morality.[59]

The conformative power of language makes it an important institution in the communitarian world. In fact, language, like few other cultural traditions, guarantees a sense of community by facilitating identity formation and providing a concrete symbol with which to identify others who share a unified experience. It helps distinguish who we collectively are. Writes Bell: "The expressive theory of language is that particular languages embody distinctive ways of experiencing the world, of defining what we are. That is, we not only speak in particular languages, but more fundamentally become the persons we become because of the particular language community in which we grew up— language, above all else, shapes our distinctive ways of being in the world."[60] Bell's point is clear: Language as a political institution helps to frame us in a particular image. As such, it can be a formidable tool in the continued expression of the endorsed community good. That is, if language has the quality of aiding character formation, it also has the capacity to impede those who do not subscribe to the community's shared tradition or conception of the good. Critical to the communitarian construction, the institution of language can be as much of a deterrent on particular conduct as other community agencies and cultural habits; it is a crucial means of ensuring the dissemination of the identified good.[61]

Indeed, institutions, communitarians assert, should be viewed as the principal beacons of the communal good. Because they are the manifestation of the community's conception of the good in practical form, they must be given serious and constant attention. True to its calling, then, the institutions of the communitarian regime all work together to foster the endorsed way of life. They enforce a moral vision so that, within the communitarian political universe, all organizations, cultural habits, and individuals understand and share a single conception of the good life. In other words, organizational institutions of the communitarian polity—government, businesses, schools, and churches —will, as part of their mandate, maintain some level of fidelity to the group's shared understanding. But also the citizens of that polity will presumably dress and speak and carry on their lives in rough accordance with the dictates of the community-endorsed good. For advocates of community, it must be remembered, this is both a sociological reality (in that individuals cannot escape their societal ties) and a normative aspiration. It is a cultural truth that as embedded agents of a particular community our identities are deeply impressed by society's institutions, but it is also a normative proposition that society is considerably rewarded by strongly felt moral and political connections among constituents.

State Sponsorship of the Good Life

The communitarian exploration of cultural institutions and political forms —and the way they isolate and teach the community's conception of the good —is instructive in that it depicts an initial vision of the communitarian polity that features the principles of unity, solidarity, and "rootedness." It is also revealing because it introduces us to the overall strategy of communitarian politics. We now know that all aspects of communitarian politics somehow revolve around the community's identified conception of the good life. The mechanism of political decision making is set up to recognize and distinguish the good, while the institutions of the polity are arranged in such a way as to foster the shared idea. Indeed, the comprehension of the good, being clearly the focus of all communitarian politics, remains key to every part of the final construction of a communitarian political society. Yet once the institutions are in place and the conception of the good has been identified, one additional responsibility is left to the community's political leaders. As part of their pledge to maintain constituted identities, communitarian polities must employ a strategy of politics that maintains support for the original constitutive or organizational principle(s). That is, the builders of a communitarian polity must somehow preserve and protect the agreed-upon "moral or political voice," or else risk uprooting and disengaging the citizenry.

The way they accomplish this all-important political task is by introducing governmental policies that cultivate certain ways of life and discourage others. State sponsorship of certain activities, they claim, is essential to the development and nourishment of the community's conception of the good. Although a liberal in his sensibilities, Kymlicka describes this line of communitarian political thinking best when he imagines that under a communitarian regime, "[the] common good, rather than adjusting itself to the pattern of people's preferences, provides a standard by which those preferences are evaluated." He notes that "a communitarian state is a perfectionist state, since it involves the public ranking of the value of different ways of life."[62]

Again the specter of coercion raises its head as liberals are often troubled by the communitarian belief that certain ways of life ought to be cultivated, while others should be repressed. But this, too, may be a bit overstated. The current manifestation of the argument centers on the question of self-determination and private choice. Liberals contend that individuals are free to choose for themselves which type of life to lead and that, furthermore, society is advanced when persons are left alone to determine these private choices. Obviously, communitarians insist on just the opposite; that society both has and requires an organizational principle—a collective moral code—that dictates the best kind of cooperative existence. Authority in the communitarian regime comes from the fact that the moral code or "way of life" is agreed upon collectively through a process of cooperation, consensus, and deliberation. Because any political decision carries with it the consent of an informed and active population working closely together, communitarian theory suggests that the government can and should consciously militate against certain private choices and individual ways of life that may not conform to the recognized good.

How does all this translate into real communitarian politics? Using the image of the secure family as his political model, Bell indicates that the communitarian state must enact specific public policies that promote the endorsed community good. "If the agreed-upon end is a society of secure, strongly constitutive families, political measures should be implemented that help realize that end."[63] Those measures presumably include the law, where particular conduct judged detrimental to the good would be statutorily prohibited; procedures, where specific routines and practices, depending on their relation to the subscribed way of life, would either encourage or deter public visibility or access; and entitlements, where certain actions and groups that may be recognized as supportive of the good would be publicly and financially sustained.

Suppose, for example, the conception of the good life regarded by the community as constitutive involved some belief that the "classical" arts were important to the overall development of individual citizens, and that boxing or wrestling were deemed hazardous. In other words, in this particular community it is understood that a life spent pursuing the arts is far more valuable than a life dedicated to the sport of physical confrontation.[64] Under a communitarian system, the government has the specific duty to enforce, by utilizing its vast resources, a life that includes regular exposure to (among many others) the paintings of Rembrandt and Picasso, and the drama of Shakespeare and Williams, but that simultaneously prohibits (or regulates) the participation in, or viewing of, combat sports. Accordingly, the state may sponsor—at the expense of those who perhaps do not care about art but who love boxing—specified theater groups, museums, or art exhibitions. Of course, the law may also prohibit the display of paintings thought, by the community, to be "inconsistent," or it might forbid the production of more daring theatrical events; but the main point is that all governmental decisions are made specifically in the name of the community good.[65] In the end, the liberal understanding of unfettered individual choice is sacrificed, but the communitarian promise to safeguard the collective will remains firmly in place. Personal choice may be somewhat narrowed by a community intent on following a prescribed good, but the overall polity itself, communitarians claim, is greatly strengthened. The benefits of achieving a "constituted" or "embedded" citizenry far outweigh the negatives often associated with a cautious and selective curtailment of certain personal freedoms.

For Barber, as we now know, the good life is spent contributing to the civic vitality of the polity. Toward that end, he has proposed a number of different policy initiatives aimed at cultivating civic-mindedness. Among his many proposals, one is especially interesting in that it highlights the communitarian belief that the state should actively sanction particular ways of life. Barber was instrumental in making Rutgers University, the State University of New Jersey, a model institution for the promotion of civic education.[66] As a prerequisite for graduation, students at Rutgers must now complete a mandatory community service course. In other words, Rutgers undergraduates are required to complete a certain number of credit hours volunteering in the community at large. Some students have chosen to participate in literacy programs in Newark or Jersey City, while others have spent their time helping out in soup kitchens or homeless shelters around New Brunswick. Still others have even selected their service from a list of campus initiatives. But the point is that the service-learning component of the curriculum is mandatory; there is no way to avoid it and still graduate from Rutgers.

It seems public officials in New Jersey have embraced the communitarian notion that the state can and should sponsor particular values (altruism, voluntarism, community service, etc.) while discounting others (self-interestedness, egoism, laziness, etc.). Barber argues that the policy can be justified (1) in the name of greater political awareness; (2) because it will help bridge the gap between rights and responsibilities; and (3) in that it will inevitably lead to a broader understanding of freedom for all of us. We may even agree that these values are the ones the state ought to foster. Nonetheless, the Rutgers initiative is a communitarian policy through and through. It is a measure in which the state takes an active role in the promotion of a particular conception of the good. Financial resources, school budgets, state personnel, and so on, are allocated for this educational plan and not for others. Students who either cannot or will not participate in the program are not given an exemption but are instead precluded altogether from receiving an education at the state's primary public university. They are told that voluntarism is mandatory, and if they don't like it, they can go elsewhere. ✳ *forcing one to volunteer does not have positive appeal*

The idea of state sponsorship is not unique to Barber's vision of the ideal college curriculum. Other organizations have adopted similar policy programs. The Responsive Community Platform, for example, speaks of the need for the state to subsidize working families so that parents can remain at home with their children. It further advocates providing incentives (financial and otherwise) to schools and churches that teach "moral education." It even prefers a particular interpretation of the Second Amendment. The power of the communitarian state to promote one way of life over another thus appears quite impressive. But with state sponsorship, inevitably, comes the label of intolerance. Perhaps uncomfortable with the "perfectionist" or "particularist" classification, the communitarian movement has attempted over the last decade to shed its most controversial component.[67] The movement's more vocal proponents have insisted communitarian polities can be pluralist, that they can be tolerant of many ideologies while also introducing a higher and more meaningful level of citizen attachment to each other and to the polity itself. Communitarians, in fact, are quick to tell us that their vision of a political society is little different than the one we currently inhabit. The only distinction, they would say, is that uninhibited choice is, in some way and in some cases, limited for the advantage of the entire state.

In a final attempt to defend the controversial communitarian policy, Daniel Bell suggests that the liberal understanding of free choice is not always as alluring as it may seem. Consider, he says, the question raised by Peter Singer that asks whether individuals should be offered, in a liberal free-market system, the choice to sell their blood in addition to giving it away voluntarily. Both Singer and Bell answer with a resounding no, and the reason they supply

involves the suggestion that the moral character, public disposition, and overall spirit of cooperation of the community will greatly suffer from such free
enterprise. "Turning blood into a commodity means that if no one gives it, it
can still be bought, which makes altruism unnecessary and so loosens the
bonds that otherwise exist between strangers in a society," says Bell.[68] In the
communitarian political construction, where institutions and policies ensure
that a community-endorsed conception of the good is both identified and
attended to, those bonds, Bell remarks, would be infrequently loosened.

Conceptions of Justice and the Public versus Private Distinction

The vision of a functioning communitarian polity is now almost complete.
In place is the mechanism of political decision making, the authoritative institutions of the community, and the endorsed practice of sponsoring certain
values. All that remains is a few less procedural and more substantive issues
that derive from the earlier discussion, including questions about justice and
the connection between state and society in a communitarian system.

In the construction of a hypothetical communitarian polity, the system of
justice is defined by the group's shared comprehension of the good. Walzer and
Bell at different times stipulate that the system of justice and the distributional
scheme recognized as authoritative in a communitarian state ought to reflect
the shared meanings and understandings of the residents. So that it can effectively constitute the entire citizenry, the communitarian system of justice
should closely (if not exactly) approximate the moral and ethical limitations of
the community's institutions. If the endorsed vision of the good life resembles
some religious doctrine, for example, then the overall structure of justice for
that particular community will somehow depict that teaching. Similarly, if the
community's shared moral understanding prohibits slavery, or places a higher
value on art rather than boxing, the community's system of justice should in
some fashion reflect that collective thinking. In *Spheres of Justice*, Walzer remarks that justice and the implementation of a distributive system involves a
fundamental respect for one's collective moral meanings. Walzer has elsewhere
noted that justice may very well require close attention to the particulars of
both small and large-scale communities.[69] As we proceed through the building
of a communitarian polity, it appears that the final piece of the puzzle—the
theory of justice—must also reflect and celebrate the public's collective will.

Throughout the entire construction of an envisioned communitarian polity, the one constant has been that all components of the design are informed

and animated by the community's shared or collective understandings. Political institutions and associations as well as private or social relationships are all guided by the relatively specific moral and legal parameters set by the conceived communal good. Most, but certainly not all, communitarians propose that the collective will (as realized in the form of the good) is sovereign across all spheres—both public and private. This is so because, unlike liberal theory, communitarianism stresses the need to view the public and private realm as deeply interconnected. In fact, the distinction made between communitarians and liberals on the function and form of political institutions goes to the center of a larger debate between the two about the separation of state and society. For most community-centered pragmatists, humans, as instinctively social creatures, are also naturally political beings. Thus, the liberal insistence on separating state and society is grossly misleading.[70] Communitarianism often subscribes to the thinking that politics is not a hobby or an activity meant to be taken up only once or twice a year, but it is a full-time endeavor, a "way of life" that helps ensure a collective future. Politics under communitarian theory centers almost exclusively on the conception of the good, and because the shared understanding of the good is the authoritative and informative principle for both the communitarian state and communitarian society, it stands to reason that the public and private should be inseparably linked.

An indispensable part of the communitarian reform agenda, therefore, is to reconsider the dominant political mentality so as to notice more readily a deep connection between the collection of individual subjects in the private sphere and the decision-making bodies of the public domain. A communitarian polity attempts to tap into those institutions that most effectively bridge the gap between the social individual and the political state and then use those agencies to help maintain, at both ends of the line, the allegedly constituted nature of the polity. Institutions such as schools, clubs, churches, and synagogues can be instrumental in disseminating (downward to their constituents) the state's deliberated policies, while also broadcasting (upward to the institutions of government) the community's collective mind set.[71] This, of course, is not radically different from the duties of liberal institutions. The principle variation is that communitarians contend that the barriers separating the public sphere from the private should be lowered and that a much fuller, more immediate connection between the sovereign people and their institutions should be encouraged. Hence, because communitarians assert that we should be simultaneously "rulers and ruled," institutions should constantly and actively reflect our cooperative thinking. Consistent with the first principle of communitarian thought—collective action—the unified interpretation of state and society as one within the polity encourages citizens to partake in all aspects of the political process, not just the ones, like voting for a representative, that require only infrequent attention.

The same reasoning motivates communitarians to regard subnational levels of government as critically important, and in some cases far more significant, than the larger national administration. State and local authorities under a communitarian order function in the same way as local nonpolitical institutions like churches and community centers. Because they are in close proximity to their constituents and more in tune with their collective will, subnational institutions are better equipped to voice the thoughts of the embedded constituency while also reflecting their collective vision of a good life. Referring specifically to America's liberal state, while echoing the central message of most conservative communitarians, Bellah remarks that "most of the founders imagined a nation with a modest central administration and a great deal of local control. The growth of a massive centralized state and an even more pervasive legal system must be understood as human responses to human needs, but also as responses that have sometimes shaped us in ways we neither expected nor desired."[72] Instead of the impersonal central governmental scheme, Bellah suggests, "the national government must actively strengthen federalism and local responsibility that are part of the American political tradition. The federal government needs to encourage new institutional arrangements that engage individual citizens and organized groups to become active participants in planning and administration."[73]

Bell imagines that a "fully developed communitarian society" would resemble the current political design found in Switzerland, "very decentralized with a lot of political participation at the local level."[74] Conservative communitarians are not so direct as to isolate Switzerland as the ideal communitarian polity, yet they still share with Bell a firm commitment to a political regime that empowers local associations. The agreed-upon cultural understandings would come from the localities, whereas the central state would be responsible (at most) for organizing in political form those shared traditions.[75] "One consequence of the bonds of commonality that citizens of nations feel for each other will be an attempt by the national community to organize politically so as to meet the historically agreed-upon needs of citizens; and a successful attempt at doing so, i.e., a reasonably fair redistributive scheme, will in turn reinforce those bonds of commonality."[76] In short, Bell is proposing that any envisioned communitarian polity structure itself so that the national government becomes the political institution that protects a system of justice meant to distribute social needs in a way that is consistent with the shared meanings of the constituents, while also promoting those principles that bind one citizen to another. And if that dual relationship can be fostered, a fully functioning communitarian polity just might be realized.

The Liberal-Communitarian Impasse

The image of the communitarian polity is now complete. And yet the wounds inflicted by both liberals and communitarians cannot simply be mended by reference to a hypothetical communitarian blueprint or by identifying any one component of the overall community-based strategy. The debate between the two powerful intellectual forces, that is, cannot be resolved by conventional means. It will take more. Instead of talking to one another, communitarians and liberals have, unfortunately, commenced to talk above one another. Communitarians paint the liberal self as rootless and unconstituted and the liberal polity as disembodied; anticommunitarians argue that community is often parochial and particularistic.[77] Liberals such as Amy Gutmann, Robert Thigpen, and Lyle Downing have all chastised theoretical communitarians for conceptualizing liberal theory in strictly dualistic terms.[78] They are, in other words, opposed to the caricature of liberalism envisioned and subsequently condemned by the communitarian advocates. Yet in much the same way, that is exactly what anticommunitarianism does when it depicts community as coercive. By subtly portraying theoretical communitarianism as hostile to the notion of freedom and autonomy and to the existence of particular individual rights and liberties, liberals and feminists alike have significantly mischaracterized the entire communitarian project as too extreme.[79] For the most part, the arguments of Sandel, Walzer, MacIntyre, and Taylor are not wholly antagonistic to personal independence; they simply see a need to control potentially excessive individuality when it conflicts with the power of the state to conceive of a particular good. Also, Etzioni, Glendon, Barber, and Galston at different times explicitly praise a more moderate approach to individualism and rights as necessary for the continued survival of the American political experiment. Certainly they should not be perceived as adverse to the idea of a private sphere. The impasse in the liberal-communitarian debate comes into sharp focus, therefore, when both sides (because of mistaken interpretations of the fundamentals of each opposing position) begin by asking different questions and pursuing different agendas.

So what can be done to break the impasse? What should be done to get the discussion back on a more productive track? I am not sure anything can truly be accomplished without first considering what is essentially at stake in this debate. And what is at stake is nothing short of political (albeit peaceful) revolution. The earlier theoretical communitarians, in attempting to disarm the liberal paradigm, are at once commenting on the feasibility and the normative appeal of the liberal plan. But in so doing, they are also commenting on the type of ordered political system that should be comprehensively embraced. Liberalism, they maintain, does not work. And even if it did, it is certainly not the best way to organize our many political institutions. Additionally, the later prescriptive branch of the newly formed communitarian movement has also focused on the sometimes excessive individualism that seems to be paralyzing the American body politic. The result of that rebuke is a community-based political scheme that carries with it an altogether new form of ordered politics.

What is most remarkable about the renaissance of American communitarianism, however, is that the deeper, more fundamental questions of constitutional order and political modeling have been largely overlooked.[80] In fact, the profoundly interesting question that motivated the early Anti-Federalists to oppose the ratification of the American Constitution—the pursuit of constitutional excellence—has at best been redefined as an indistinct part of the debate over the merits of a liberal hegemony. Communitarianism is about fundamental change. It is about the pursuit of the political ideal of constitutional excellence. Once again, it is very much about political modeling. The present question at the base of the argument between liberals and communitarians is the one every new regime must ask and every stable regime must continually contend with: What sort of political order do we want? or What kind of people should we be?[81] Why, then, has no critic of the communitarian school challenged them on the level of constitutional theory? Oddly enough, the contemporary disagreement between liberals and communitarians over the primacy of the right and the good is, in practical form, a purely constitutional debate. Moreover, communitarians regularly speak of the value of "constituted selves," yet rarely consider the meaning of "constitution." They often support their particular argument by defending a need for common roots and values, while at the same time neglecting to consider the constitutional form that must accompany their communitarian enterprise.

It seems to me that the theory of constitutionalism—the principle that in some concrete way governmental or public power is both self-consciously created and purposefully limited—presents an opportunity to move beyond the impasse. Indeed, constitutionalist theory offers the most productive means to move the liberal-communitarian debate to a different plane. Is it possible to conceive of a polity that is attentive to the principles of constitutionalism while concurrently being governed by communitarian institutions? Until now, the liberal-communitarian debate has all too often been mired in name-calling and tactical rhetoric. Yet by addressing the possibility of a simultaneously constitutionalist and communitarian polity, we can perhaps reconsider the nature of the entire debate. Reintroducing the primary issue in politics—constitutional organization—and then relating it to the modern communitarian plan will perhaps reestablish the liberal-communitarian debate at its central place in the realm of practical and theoretical politics.

By suggesting a popular alternative to America's current political design, the contemporary community-centered movement is resurrecting the positive legacy of Anti-Federalist thought. What the Anti-Federalists did for the development of this country was nothing short of questioning its first principles and challenging its constitutional order. To be sure, they contributed mightily to the shape of that order by gaining important concessions from the Federalists in the form of a bill of rights and in particulars about the scope of delegated power. But beyond that, they forced America's first generation to contemplate the magnitude of their venture; and as such, they made us reveal what type of political society we as a country wanted. Indeed, Anti-Federalists should be considered an indispensable part of American constitutional development.[82]

Contemporary communitarians, in markedly similar fashion, appear to be carrying on the tradition of the Anti-Federalists by planting the seeds of fundamental constitutional reform. They are beginning to question the merits of liberalism in general and the United States constitutional charter in particular. In the process, they are hoping to achieve, through debate, a fundamentally different institutional design. To borrow a famous phrase from the *Federalist Papers*, American communitarians—from the founding to the present—are currently endeavoring to "establish good government from reflection and choice" rather than "accident and force."[83] We must now seriously consider their choices.

Part II / The Communitarian Constitution

CHAPTER FOUR

The Constitutionalist Challenge to American Communitarianism

The United States is currently witnessing a heated debate between two distinct ideological camps over the constitutionally endorsed merits of liberal individualism, state neutrality, and democratic majoritarianism. Similar to the one that pitted the eighteenth-century Federalists against their Anti-Federalist rivals, the contemporary dispute once again ponders the all-important issues of political modeling and public order. More specifically, with the rise in popularity of communitarian theory over the last few decades, the very foundation of a liberal-democratic constitutional regime is now under attack. Is the notion of a political order that places greater value on individual freedom than on the collective consciousness a concept that is now outdated? Should our constitutional system continue to permit, and even celebrate, an individual's mostly uninhibited freedom of choice, or should it strive to order its institutions so that free choice is somewhat limited but community-based deliberative decisions about the good are permanently fostered? Is the best vision for a political order one that places ultimate authority in the hands of independent individuals, or, instead, in those of collectively deliberating communities? Finally, would our answers to these and other questions differ if we did not face a future made increasingly uncertain as a result of the events of September 11, 2001?

As part of the recent communitarian opposition to the tenets of modern liberal theory, those theorists who most enthusiastically advocate the principles of the community canon cannot avoid commenting on the appeal of a constitutional order that incorporates mostly liberal ideals. Even though the vast majority of communitarians overlook the issue of constitutional ordering, it is a mistake to believe that they do not have an instinctive opinion on the merits of certain constitutional forms.[1] H. N. Hirsch correctly notes that although none of the contemporary communitarian scholars presents a straightforward account of the mechanisms needed to maintain a communitarian polity, we would be remiss if we did not recognize that any general challenge to liberalism includes a specific challenge to those constitutional orders that embrace the liberal creed. Hirsch is suggesting that as an inseparable part of their general resistance to liberal theory, communitarians must also seriously oppose the image of the liberal constitution.[2]

This is so mainly because the overarching liberal-communitarian battle is inherently a political contest centered on the proper ordering of society's institutions and values. To say that a society run by Mill's or Locke's or even Rawls' understanding of liberty is seriously troubling also suggests that any constitution subscribing to those principles of individual freedom and autonomy is probably doomed. Similarly, to claim that identifying the conception of the good is and must be a collective decision rather than a personal one is to insist that any constitutional ordering of procedures, institutions, and values that does not comply with an equally consistent form of communalism is problematic. Yet challenging the properties of liberal constitutions is much different than offering a fully developed communitarian constitutional vision. In fact, constitution making may prove to be a rather arduous task for the communitarian sympathizer, since it is more difficult to conceive of a working constitutional scheme than it is to criticize ones that inform and animate already extant political societies.

Communitarian theory is now at the point at which it needs to look precisely at the first principles of political regimes. Indeed, the communitarian theoretical impulse continues to claim that a complete overhaul of the liberal image—from the self to the polity—is warranted because of the massive decay and detachment that accompanies a society bent on celebrating hyperindividualism. But if the communitarian movement is serious about its plan and seeks to move beyond the realm of theory into the world of real politics, that proposed overhaul must commence with the adoption of an authoritatively functioning communitarian constitution. If not immediately, then soon thereafter, the community-based reform movement must consider the importance of constitutionally grounding the principles of communitarian thought in the words of an organizing text.

The Classical Theory of Constitutionalism

By nature, the constitutionalist is a pessimist. Any conception of constitutionalism and any corresponding push to draft a constitutional text stems initially from a belief in the inherent corruptibility and imperfectability of human nature. The chief concern of the constitutionalist is that if given the chance, most people would likely choose to abuse others while attempting to preserve personal power. The constitutionalist warns that such a view is a realistic one. For example, James Madison, in describing the need for an organizing American doctrine, wrote in *Federalist* 51: "But what is government itself, but the greatest of all reflections on human nature? If men were angels, no government would be necessary. If angels were to govern men, neither external nor internal controls on government would be necessary. In framing a government which is to be administered by men over men, the great difficulty lies in this: you must first enable the government to control the governed, and in the next place oblige it to control itself."[3] The essence of Madison's fear is that without divine intervention, or at least clearly articulated limits or restraints on public power, a government made up of self-interested, narcissistic individuals will routinely degenerate into a tyrannical or oppressive regime. The antidote for this fear, he notes, is a legitimate and authoritative constitution.

When we think about constitutions, we often think first of the American constitutional text. And indeed, many outside the borders of the United States similarly consider the American Constitution to be the paradigmatic example of the modern political charter. Perhaps because of the relative economic and political success of the American regime over the past two hundred years, the world has often tried to emulate the exact organization of political values and institutions mandated by this country's formal constitution. But even in light of this backdrop, it should be noted that the American Constitution, although admittedly different (and rightfully revered) in form, is essentially no different than any other political charter in function. Like all constitutions informing public and private relationships, the U.S. Constitution performs particular and extremely precise duties.

Fundamentally, *constitution* refers specifically to order: "To constitute means to make up, order, or form; thus a nation's constitution should pattern a political system."[4] All constitutions will organize the political community in a very specific way. Indeed, the constitution is a designed model used to structure society around some reflective political strategy and toward some desired goal. In the United States, the Constitution (as manifest most clearly in the Preamble) reflects the Founders'—and subsequently the constituents'—desire for "justice," "tranquility," "liberty," and "general welfare." Accordingly, the institutions of our political society (including those values grounded in the Bill of Rights) are designed, or ordered, in such a way as to perpetuate that broad and general mandate.[5] Similarly, the organizational structure (the constitution, if you will) of a university or college will order the institutions (disciplines) of its academic "polity" in a way that supports that academy's specifically designed interest in educating students. Some universities, like MIT or Caltech, may place a premium on science and technology, whereas others, say Berklee or Juilliard, may more strongly support the arts. The point is that the organization of each of these institutions will reflect in its design the priorities or values of its constitutional structure.

Constitutions achieve the desired sense of order by various means. Obviously order is attained, and the ultimate aim is furthered, by strategically and procedurally organizing the institutions of the polity to reflect a certain agreed-upon pattern. Separate powers or a federal system of government, as in the case of the American design, may fulfill the desired interest of the sovereign to distribute power for the purpose of ensuring stability and justice. Moreover, individual and religious freedoms may signal a strong desire on the part of the founders and ratifiers to foster domestic tranquility by promoting the substantive values of liberty and tolerance. But as much as constitutions order through self-conscious design, it is also fair to say that they also achieve a level of strategic order through what they prohibit the state from accomplishing. As Stephen Holmes has argued: "The basic function of a constitution is to *remove* certain decisions from the democratic process, that is, to tie the community's hands."[6] In the United States, the Preamble's concern for securing liberty is mitigated by placing procedural and judicial restraints on the overarching authority of its institutions. To avoid the clashes that often plague a pluralist nation, a constitution sets up significant limits on the power of the sovereign or, more accurately, on the institutions of government that represent the sovereign.[7] Hence order, in this instance, is realized, not by what the government can do or how society's political institutions are structured, but precisely by what those institutions are proscribed from doing. In the end, the hope is that "rule of law" will replace the "rule of men."

If all constitutions somehow order or organize the political community in a particular way, then why is it that certain constitutions come quickly into disfavor? Why do many polities end up discarding their original constitutions in favor of another, perhaps less reflective design? The answers to these questions lie firmly in the concept of constitutionalism. A working constitution exists in this age only if it is attentive to the theory of constitutionalism. At the risk of overstating the obvious, a constitution will legitimately and feasibly organize the political society only if it accepts and closely observes the main components of constitutionalism, defined as those specified principles that both create and control political power. A country's ordered design (its tangible constitution),[8] if it is to be generally regarded as authoritative and reasonable, must adhere to the sometimes intangible or abstract elements described broadly by the core constitutionalist principles of "restraint of public power" and "distribution" or "validation" of political authority. To further illustrate the point, consider a final and perhaps even more obvious given: a nation's constitutional text will have no meaning if it does not somehow, in accordance with the dictates of constitutionalism, authorize and constrain the many agents of political power and the various institutions that exist within the public sphere.

All that being said, the insurance that constitutionalist maxims will ultimately inform a community's sovereign charter is not as self-evident as it may at first seem. Graham Walker has written, "In a simple sense, every polity, in so far as it is a polity, has a constitution, but not every polity practices constitutionalism."[9] Presently, we can identify many countries that have written constitutions but that do not subscribe to the principles of constitutionalism. Indeed, it is fair to say that the existence of a constitutional text does not always presuppose the existence of a constitutionalist government.

The former Soviet Union provides a clear example of a political society that fell under the watchful eye of a largely irrelevant text. The constitution of the former Soviet Union included a guarantee of individual rights as well as a description of procedures for the exercise of governmental power. In fact, the Soviet constitution contained many provisions that resemble the system of restraints we are so familiar with in the West. Yet the Soviet constitutional text was nothing but a facade. It did not constitute the citizenry, nor did it provide an objectively authoritative means to check governmental power. Procedures, rules, laws, and policies were determined solely by the Communist Party elites, with little or no cognizance of potential constitutional restraints and conflicts.

The Soviet example is not unique to the history of political rule. Even before the reign of monarchs in the fifteenth through eighteenth centuries, individuals and groups who were troubled by the sovereign's all-too-regular pattern of imposing indiscriminate rules and ex post facto laws ventured to minimize the possibility of arbitrary political power by considering the idea of limited government, of dispassionate rather than inconstant rule. They often appealed directly to past rulings, institutional norms, cultural taboos, and natural law in an attempt to bridle the virtually unlimited power of the central government.[10] The aim of these individuals was to somehow harness the dominion of the monarchy through cultural precedents, but the ammunition at their disposal consisted mainly of words (in the form of prior policies and judgments), customs (in the form of institutional norms), and appeals to human reason and natural rights. Bolingbroke captured the essence of this movement— described by most historians as the "classical" theory of constitutionalism— when he wrote: "By constitution we mean, whenever we speak with propriety and exactness, that assemblage of laws, institutions and customs, derived from certain fixed principles of reason, directed to certain fixed objects of public good, that compose the general system, according to which the community hath agreed to be governed."[11]

Like the Soviet leaders of the twentieth century, pre-modern sovereigns and their representatives often felt it necessary to draft a constitutional charter or at least acknowledge constitution-like restraints, only to then ignore the charter's self-imposed limiting provisions. It was often difficult to determine the difference between valid and invalid political action, between justifiable and arbitrary directives, because the legitimacy of any action, whether it was "constitutionally" mandated or not, was solely the prerogative of the medieval rulers.[12] If the central authority demanded that certain policies be implemented, then regardless of the consequences to personal freedom, individual safety, or the "constitution" itself, those political measures were eventually realized. All political power—from legislation, to execution, and, finally, to interpretation— was vested in the form of a single monarchical leader; thus, it followed that any general restraints on the central state were also the sole privilege of that leader.

The enforcement of meaningful constitutional restraints depended mostly on the benevolence and good will of the sovereign. When those virtues were absent, the principle of constitutionalism evaporated.

The belief that subjects of the sovereign could limit state power with only the force of promises and the strength of cultural habits, of course, proved to be a myth. Any significant attempt to disarm the ancient concept of ruling prerogative through the use of institutional norms and prior governmental decisions was, until the eighteenth century, mostly a fruitless enterprise. In referring to this point, Schochet even goes so far as to conclude that constitutionalism was "something of a fiction."[13] Constitutionalism as a practical notion based on the principles of limitation and constraint was ineffective; but just the same, constitutionalism as a political ideal was, at this historical moment, becoming theoretically fashionable. Indeed, it was during this period of monarchical rule that constitutionalism, although largely impotent, began to take on the early appearance of its more developed form.[14]

What emerged from the early effort by the people to limit the expanse of sovereign authority was at least a fledgling and heretofore untested image of restrained or bridled government. To alleviate the tendency in favor of discretionary politics, ancillaries to the sovereign began to demand a fundamental reallocation of political power away from the single titular head and toward a more widespread base. Instead of holding the entire reins of power and subsequently suppressing its many subjects, the monarchy, it was thought, should either give up some of its authority to other political institutions or provide some objectively neutral mechanism—a legitimate and discernible constitution—with which dependents of the throne could directly appeal. In an endeavor to create a source of power beyond (or at least in addition to) the sovereign ruler, calls for constitutionalist government in the premodern period were intended to put an end, once and for all, to the existing pattern of wanton and capricious leadership.

The initial realization of constitutionalism in the premodern era thus centered on a broad and general attempt to limit in some way the expansive scope of state power. Inhabitants of a kingdom sought to curb unconfined power by appealing to communal precedents, while placing certain institutions potentially beyond the reach of the highest state authority. Indeed, citizens of the political realm conceived of constitutionalism as a means to block the power of monarchical prerogative. Yet it was not until the nature of political sovereignty changed that constitutionalism gained some teeth. The modern understanding of constitutionalism subscribes to the same general principles as classical constitutionalism—some degree of "limited rule" and "purposive distribution of power." But, perhaps because of historical events and the shifting of sovereignty from the few to the many, the idea of constitutionalism is now defined by those axioms contemporary constitutional theorists believed to be largely missing from earlier versions.

The Modern Theory of Constitutionalism

The Enlightenment marks an important period in the development of modern constitutionalism. Man's retreat from the dictates of theocracy and dogma into the realm of science and rationalism was, in many ways, as surprising as it was progressive. And yet the shift from absolutist faith not only signaled a belief in the independent power of human reason but also a renewed interest in the capacity of humans to design their own political forms. Embracing new models of political organization was at the forefront of the eighteenth-century rejection of traditional social, religious, and political practices. Gone was the blind adherence to the ways of the ancien régime—where monarchical rule and unlimited authority were the norm—and in its stead arose a radically new philosophical belief based on the principle that humans could manage their own individual and collective destinies. Simultaneously, subjects residing in various parts of the world initiated a series of movements that rejected the often cruel and irrational practices accompanying nonsecular authority. Thus, they threw off, in the words of Rousseau, the chains of their oppression. The birth of modern constitutionalism followed.

No regime was more successful in capturing the spirit of the Enlightenment than the United States. The Founders were passionate followers of the major Enlightenment thinkers: Montesquieu, Voltaire, Locke, Beccaria, Delolme, Grotius, Pufendorf, and many others were widely quoted by both statesmen and laymen alike. What is more, the founding generation mastered the art of constitution making. They constructed a political document that would not only endure major challenges to its longevity like the Civil War, but one that was also entirely novel in its design. Features of the U.S. Constitution reflect the changing attitude of the Enlightenment in that they forsake any religious influences, instead, adopting ones issuing chiefly from the secular world. Political authority, for instance, originates from below—from the people—and not from God; the chief executive is not the anointed leader of the church; and the Preamble does not begin with any reference to religious faith. The U.S. Constitution is in many ways a text that has been scientifically engineered to be distinct. The Founders learned from the mistakes of past political regimes— chiefly, the widespread rejection of meaningful constitutional limits—and vowed not to repeat them.

Hamilton, for one, was acutely aware of history. The "new science of politics," he argues in *Federalist* 9, has received "great improvement" since the decline of petty, unstable republics in the ancient world. He describes the regimes of the past as existing in a "state of perpetual vibration between the extremes of tyranny and anarchy." In contrast, modern regimes—and in particular, the one he defends so passionately in the *Federalist Papers*—were constructed with an eye toward the handful of mechanisms that could ensure strength and constancy. That is to say, the antidote for regime instability could be found in the structure of government itself. Hamilton refers to the components of constitutionalism as means "by which the excellences of republican government may be retained and its imperfections lessened or avoided." He wrote: "The regular distribution of power into distinct departments; the introduction of legislative balances and checks; the institution of courts composed of judges holding their offices during good behavior; the representation of the people in the legislature by deputies of their own election; these are wholly new discoveries, or have made their principal progress towards perfection in modern times." Keeping power out of the hands of one individual or one political body was thus both an untested idea and a normative aspiration. Limiting governmental control through constitutional design, Hamilton concluded, would be essential to the success of the modern polity.[15]

Charles McIlwain, perhaps the foremost authority on the history of constitutionalism, describes the development of constitutionalism, from the ancient or traditional understanding to the modern one, as primarily involving a plea by subjects of the ruling body for greater accountability.[16] He remarks that the classical notion of constitutionalism commenced with the ancients but reached its heyday only in the modern era, when individual and group subjects sought to limit the power of the ruling monarchs by instituting rules and laws that were, theoretically at least, outside the jurisdiction of the highest "earthly" authority.[17]

Constitutional theorists have since taken McIlwain's historical teaching a step further by suggesting that the shift from the classical understanding of constitutionalism to a more robust modern variation corresponds directly with the introduction of the written constitutional text in the late eighteenth century.[18] Probably due to the pressure to control political authority more completely and thoroughly than was done in the past, modern constitution makers have since sought to ground their ideas and principles by integrating the written word within concrete, formal documents. The U.S. Constitution provides the most obvious example. The American founders, seeking to design a powerful but limited national government, chose the instrument of the textual constitution rather than an unwritten body or even a nontextual leviathan to execute the critical task of creating a political regime and, at the same time, controlling its jurisdiction. Presently, most countries around the world have followed the American example and embraced the idea of limited government through textualism.

In response to the lessons learned from a long history of political oppression, a modern constitutionalist polity is one that now recognizes and articulates a *meaningful* constraint on public power, the self-conscious limitation (by various means, including boundaries and active involvement) of governmental authority. The limitation on public authority can come in many forms, from individual rights to separation of powers, but some form of it is absolutely necessary for the modern polity to qualify as constitutionalist. McIlwain observes that "all constitutional government is by definition limited government. . . . [I]n all its successive phases, constitutionalism has one essential quality: it is a legal limitation on government; it is the antithesis of arbitrary rule; its opposite is despotic government, the government of will instead of law."[19] Constitutionalism, to put it another way, blocks unfettered power; it proscribes the rise of tyranny by coordinating and confining the power of institutions and individuals and by keeping all accountable to certain preexisting rules.[20]

If, however, constitutionalists appear to be fixated by the notion of limits, how then is the modern conception of constitutionalism, with its standard approval of the core constitutionalist tenet, infinitely more successful than its classical counterpart in its effort to "control the governed" and subsequently "control itself"? Another way of asking the same question is to inquire how the modern version specifically and fundamentally differs from the traditional notion of constitutionalism: What was added to the earlier understanding of constitutionalism as "limits" to make it a significantly more potent, or meaningful, term?

The modern variation of constitutionalism starts with the classical call for limits but then proceeds to place an important conceptual qualification on the earlier understanding of governmental restraints. In other words, ensuring some form of limits on governmental authority remains the primary motive of any constitutionalist polity, but the means to achieve that end have been carefully, and importantly, redefined. It is no longer sufficient simply to appeal to internal laws, institutions, customs, and habits in an attempt to bind the power of the sovereign ruler. Those mechanisms did not have the force to control the will of the sovereign in previous eras; there is no reason to believe they will be any more successful in controlling governmental organizations now. In the modern era, where institutions and lives are more complex and integrated, it seems even more reckless to rely on the good will of the sovereign or its representatives. In fact, constitutionalists regularly remind us that human nature has not changed, but the need for limited, controlled government has become more acute. The history of oppression that has plagued humankind even as we have "developed" and "progressed" reveals this fact. Thus, the answer to the modern dilemma—and the key element that separates modern constitutionalism from the classical variation—must be reconsidered; it must be redefined. The answer, I suggest, can be found within the principle of objectivity.

To assure impartiality, constitutionalism now requires the *objectification,* and not merely the limitation, of created political power. It requires that the means to control the various sources of political power be apparent to all. Because of the confusion that often accompanies such a loaded word, it may be helpful at the outset to identify what I do *not* mean by the term objectification. I am not using the term in the metaphysical sense. Nor do I mean to suggest that there is some objective or universal truth that animates constitutional documents or that there is a good beyond the good of the specific polity that is somehow revealed by the text. What I mean by "objective" is that the constitution is somehow transparent; it can be understood and is in some concrete way discernible. In defending his particular liberal theory from attacks by critics, John Rawls claimed in his later writings that his notion of "justice as fairness" was not meant to be "a comprehensive moral doctrine." I consider my use of the word objective in the same way: it is not meant to imply that there is some moral truth that must be captured by a constitutional document in order for that constitution to qualify as modern. In fact, I mean just the opposite.

Objective constitutions are simply ones that recognize and articulate an institutionalized set of agreed-upon conventions, just as statutory law recognizes and articulates specific conventional rules.

Let me be more precise. The modern development of constitutionalist theory has adopted as critically essential an important element of objectivity. A text regulated by the modern version of constitutionalism not only limits the otherwise extensive power of the public sphere, but it does so in such a way as to make clear the political boundaries of the public realm—what government can and cannot do. The constitution not only mandates certain procedural and mechanical restrictions on the authority of the government, but more importantly, it limits the possibility of arbitrary, despotic rule by allowing citizens of the polity to consult the constitution directly rather than relying on the sometimes fickle and always vacillating whim of the ruler's private interests. What is a process marked by the political principles of controversy, dialogue, debate, and compromise—the creation, articulation, and approval of a constitutional text—becomes utterly nonpolitical at the moment of ratification and thus takes on a distinct spirit of objectivity. The debatable, in other words, becomes largely undebatable, while the controversial becomes largely incontrovertible. Indeed, the rules of the game become mostly fixed.

That, of course, is not to say that the provisions of the constitutional text are automatically immune from interpretation and debate. Far from it. Politics, after all, is a necessary and important part of the success of any constitutionalist regime.[21] But in most modern constitutionalist polities, what is up for discussion is not the fundamental source of political authority but the specifics of that authority. The principle of objectivity in constitutionalist theory refers to the idea that the polity's constitution is the one object that is acknowledged as authoritative by the overwhelming majority of subjects both in and out of the political arena. The constitution's goal is to direct the political institutions, not to will them out of existence. It is metapolitical in that its existence as the genesis of political power is not subject to review. Indeed, the constitution acts as a touchstone, representing the aspirations of an entire ratifying people, not merely the whims of a shifting majority. It is different, in other words, precisely because it is the fundamental law—the rule of recognition—and the instrument that orders all other instruments.[22]

The trick for most modern constitutionalist regimes is to get elected officials to pay heed to the provisions of the text and thus to create a workable politics within fixed and stable rules. Constitutions are not self-executing entities; they are documents made up of words and ideas. As such, they can be slighted just as easily as they can be celebrated. Indeed, Will Harris has even described the notion that a constitution is able to order an entire political society as "preposterous."[23] To bring to life a political regime out of "thought and theory" is logically an absurdity. It ignores the fact that underlying the enterprise of constitution making and constitutional interpretation is the perpetual struggle for political power, the push to control both the sword and the purse of the nation-state. Politics, in other words, is deeply infused within the constitutional experiment, and to overlook that reality is to embrace only a partial image.

The pull to abide by the principle of the rule of law, however, can be an equally powerful force. One can never guarantee that all political actors will forever adhere to the idea that a constitution is supposed to control political action; indeed, some will always choose to disregard the provisions of the text altogether. But just the same, in this age of global awareness, condemnation will often accompany activity that discredits the belief that power should not be exercised arbitrarily.[24] What animates America's recent condemnation of China's policy regarding civil rights and liberties is not only a strong faith in the value of liberal ideology but also a steadfast commitment to the rule of law. We take seriously the notion that political power can be a very threatening commodity and that it must, as a result, be both respected and shackled. The conviction that the rule of law is somehow better or more virtuous than uncontrolled governance has swept across the globe, and even though many regimes have not yet adopted a similar posture, the believers outnumber the nonbelievers. Moreover, those believers are often willing to isolate and criticize those who refuse to subscribe to their point of view. To the moral relativist, such an argument may not be overly persuasive, but it seems as clear as anything else that if given the choice, most people would prefer not to be oppressed.

In addition, universal ratification helps discourage unrestrained power seekers, since the ratifiers themselves have a vested interest in the success of their endeavor. But even ratification cannot completely restrain officials bent on ignoring the will of the people. Oaths may provide some ammunition against uncontrolled power, and so may longevity.[25] History has revealed that constitutions successful enough to withstand the test of time carry with them a greater authoritative power than do texts that do not. Indeed, it is logical to assume that corrupt officials are more likely to ignore constitutional principles that are less ingrained in the culture of the polity. But constitutionalist regimes now require more. They must, in addition to these and other factors, be infused with a degree of objectivity that prevents public officials from flouting such principles. Oaths, competing institutions, checks and balances, ratification—all are important components, but without a sense of objectivity, a modern constitution will not flourish.

Three important features ensure a constitution's objectivity. First, a polity's organizing charter must subscribe to the principle of *externality*. That is to say, if it is to carry out its function of ordering the institutions of the polity while constituting the citizens of the community, a constitution must exist separately and independently from the political agencies it creates. Implicit in the concept of externality is the idea that the constitution ought to be supreme. There cannot exist, for example, mechanisms (aside from actually amending the text) that can trump the authority of the constitution itself. Simple legislative acts, state laws, executive decrees, judicial decisions, and so forth cannot replace or supplant provisions of the constitutional document. They can supplement or complement the text, providing important insights into the true meaning of the text, but they cannot displace the document. To be authoritative, the constitution must be the highest law.

Secondly, a constitution will achieve a certain degree of objectivity if its rules, procedures, and values are clearly *discernible*. Unlike in the era of classical constitutionalism, fundamental limits on political power, through procedural rules and substantive safeguards, must be recognized and fully understood by the various public and private political actors. Lastly, the constitution, as the voice of the sovereign, must be informed by *self-imposed limits on governmental authority*. Again, the classical understanding of constitutionalism shunned this critical qualification, leaving the burden of imposing governmental restrictions on the shoulders of the mostly powerless masses.[26]

Externality

For the conception of constitutionalism to be objective—and thus consequential—the limits impressed upon the will of the sovereign and its representatives must in the first place exist separately from the political power centers. On this necessary stipulation Thomas Paine wrote: "A constitution is not the act of a government, but of a people constituting a government, a government without a constitution is power without right. A constitution is a thing *antecedent* to a government; and a government is only the creature of a constitution."[27] Paine has pinpointed a critical component of the modern theory of constitutionalism that was absent from the classical definition. Traditionally, constitutionalism referred to those internal institutions and customs that supposedly limited the power of the government, but, had little practical effect on the ruler and his power. One of the main reasons constitutionalism had no bite in the premodern era was that individuals often confused the constitution and the government. To subjects of the state, the institutions of government were not the "creatures" of an antecedently created constitution, existing only insofar as the original charter grants them power, but were rather the "creators"— the original source of political authority. In essence, the constitution and the government, under the classical definition of constitutionalism, were one and the same.

Like Paine, James Madison was also concerned about the conflation of government and text.[28] He spoke in *Federalist* 51 of the need to establish two separate sets of restraints on the institutions of government. His famous passage is worth repeating. "If men were angels," he wrote, "no government would be necessary. If angels were to govern men, neither external nor internal controls on government would be necessary."[29] Madison insisted that certain controls had to reside within the structure of government itself and within the internalized habits of the people. Popular elections, representation, separation of powers, fixed terms, checks and balances, federalism, and so on, although emanating from the constitutional text, were all designed to create a political system where no single branch of the government would dominate. Furthermore, Madison believed he could rely on the consistency and fallibility of human nature. All men, he argued, were governed instinctually by self-interest, and the competition that would ensue between persons in power would ultimately keep all governmental institutions in line. But as much as he insisted on internal mechanisms of control, he also spoke of external controls. He addressed the need for checks outside the government, primarily in the people at large. The political centers of power had to be shackled by a force that rested outside of the political realm. Yet that external force could not be trusted either. "A dependence on the people," Madison wrote, "is, no doubt, the primary control of the government; but experience has taught mankind the necessity of auxiliary precautions."[30]

A modern constitution that is faithful to the principle of objectivity will avert the possibility of confusing the government and the organizational charter by ensuring that the constitution itself is the object that governs public and private relationships. That is to say, the fully developed form of constitutionalism—the modern form—emerges first by recognizing the distinction between fundamental law and the object created by that law. As the creator of procedural rules, institutional structures, and substantive values, the constitution itself cannot be a part of those creations (thereby potentially being influenced by the very institutions it conceived); for to be authoritative, it must exist apart from the form—the government—it is creating. The constitution, in short, cannot simultaneously be the creator and the created.[31]

In trying to bridge the gaps that shackled the more traditional depiction of constitutionalism, McIlwain notes that the modern comprehension of the theory has attached the ideas of objectivity, externality, and detachment to the earlier notion of limits in an attempt to fortify constitutionalism's meaning and give it additional force. McIlwain posits that because constitutionalism "before the late eighteenth century was a set of principles embodied in the institutions of a nation and neither external to these nor in existence prior to them," the probability of introducing consequential limits on state power was minimal.[32] What is required in order to constrain the exhaustive authority of the governors/rulers is more than just a simple appeal to particular customs and institutions. Without modifying the image of constitutionalism to include an element of objectivity, citizens cannot always rely on their leaders to adhere to those restraints that may emanate from prior decisions, institutional norms, and cultural habits. The government, under the less exacting classical definition of constitutionalism, was not created or informed by an objectively separate doctrine, but rather was functionally equivalent to the very constitutional restraints meant to inhibit it.

We can consult the American Constitution for an illustration. With few exceptions, the text creates and then distributes the sources of decision-making power. The states enjoy certain powers, while the national government enjoys others. Similarly, on the national level, the executive, legislative, and judicial branches all function differently, yet simultaneously share a common aim that is described in quite general terms by the Preamble. The point is that by mandating separate branches and thus constitutionally separating the agencies of political power, the Constitution of the United States has wrested the polity away from those, like the president or the justices of the Supreme Court, who occupy significant positions of power. It has, in short, seized the polity from the very political agents it created. In so doing, a stable and dispassionate doctrine—the Constitution—and not the potentially arbitrary caprice of an unconstrained leader (or in this case, majority) is now the "object to be reckoned with."[33] What the drafters of the U.S. Constitution did was to organize the political system with tools like separated powers and checks and balances so as to ensure that no institution or politician can (without extraordinary means) tamper with the main provisions of the text. As such, they have enabled the Constitution to function independently, in an overarching capacity, from the country's political institutions.

In general, then, a constitution is a polity's aspirational strategy, which is to say that it is the instrument in which the polity's values, principles, and structure are publicly articulated.[34] Beyond its practical function of political organization, the constitution's purpose is to supply the polity with the authoritative and foundational source of political power. The constitution manages this by occupying a position above the polity itself: it is, in short, *metapolitical.* In other words, because it organizes and confines all political actors as well as their actions,[35] it must extend beyond the reach of those who currently wield that power. And to do that, it must construct a definitive line between the polity and the politicians. Its authority, therefore, is sustained by its objectivity. The constitution becomes the citizens' primary protection against unfettered rule because it is the polity's one overarching political instrument that exists above the subjectivity of politics.[36] In defending the partition of government and constitution, Theodore Lowi and Benjamin Ginsberg suggest that "to be a true constitutional government, a government must have some kind of framework, which consists of a few principles that cannot be manipulated by people in power merely for their own convenience. This is the essence of constitutionalism—principles that are above the reach of everyday legislatures, executives, bureaucrats and politicians."[37] By placing certain "principles above the reach" of those currently in power, the constitution can not only establish a significant source of stability but also, in response to its primary mission, stave off any real threat of tyranny.

Discernibility

If objectivity is the primary requisite inspiriting the modern conception of constitutionalism, and detachment or externality is the first critical means to achieve the appropriate level of objectivity, then discernibility is the second requirement. For a constitution to be objective, its substantive as well as procedural meaning must be easily discernible to all subjects of the polity. That is to say, the society's population and its rulers alike must be as clear as possible as to the substantive and procedural message of the constitutional charter. Only that way will the text maintain the high standard of legitimacy needed to constitute the polity objectively.

In many instances the constitutional effort to limit the power of the state prior to the modern period was hampered by an unwillingness on the part of the ruler to identify those provisions and mechanisms that did, in fact, act as restraints. For example, a monarchical ruler may have self-consciously subscribed to a particular moral or religious code (especially during the golden age of the "divine right of kings") without revealing the particulars of that belief to his subjects. In keeping them hidden, the subjects of the monarch were prohibited from challenging policy decisions that did not fully comport with the parameters of the leader's moral or theological principles. Hence, keeping the monarch externally accountable to the dictates of that potential source of constitutional-like limits proved to be virtually impossible. Moreover, in certain cultures it was thought that the ruler enjoyed a personal kinship with God, but the nature of that relationship and the corresponding restraints on his power that may have emanated from it were largely unrevealed to the populace. Dependents of the ruling body, despite identifying particular customs and precedents, were routinely kept in the dark as to the interpretation or execution of those customs and precedents. As a consequence, under the guise of classical constitutionalism, individuals had no recourse from the arbitrary caprice of the political leader.

The modern definition of constitutionalism, by contrast, includes a strong concern for "knowability" so as to further buttress the ongoing campaign in favor of justice and fairness. The movement toward greater awareness of fundamental limits on government authority corresponds directly with the push to ground political power in a formal, written text. Prior to the eighteenth century, when most constitutional constraints were based predominantly on natural law teachings, appeals to human reason, or the common law, few polities could boast a universal understanding of the instruments of restraint. Nowadays, although some governments still refuse to observe all constitutional restrictions, the presence of formal texts have rendered the likelihood of widespread ignorance a rarity. Thus, again, the motive behind ensuring determinability is to eliminate, to the greatest extent possible, the capacity for governmental abuse. Moreover, publicly acknowledging the various features of an organizing doctrine helps to ensure that the government will be the object held directly responsible to "general public standards." "The existence of knowable rules," Schochet remarks, "provides an important check on the activities of governing officials. Where their interpretations of constitutional permissibility are questioned, there exists a public standard to which to refer."[38]

At this point it is important to note that a modern constitution requires interpretation, and the principle of discernibility is attuned to this reality. Open-ended constitutional provisions can often lead to quite nasty political controversies involving the text's core meanings—thus, the need for some form of institutional interpretation.[39] Yet interpretation is possible precisely because most modern constitutional provisions and procedures are, broadly speaking, fixed. That is to say, a constitution can be knowable without also being static, particularly when there is significant agreement over time on the meanings of certain constitutional principles. For example, there is general (and in some cases quite substantial) agreement on the meaning of the core provisions of the U.S. Constitution. Even the Due Process Clause of the Fourteenth Amendment, with its general language and open-ended texture, does not include protection of liberties *not* deemed fundamental. And while it is certainly conceivable that an institution (like the judiciary) responsible for the interpretation of the constitutional text can interpret the document in admittedly wild and erratic ways, such interpretations typically call into question the credibility of the interpreting institution more than of the Constitution itself.

In the same vein, arguments that constitutional interpretations are somehow equivalent to the altering of constitutional texts through the amendment process are indeed provocative, but they do little to further this particular argument.[40] To be sure, the judiciary in the United States is regularly approaching the line that separates interpretation from amendment, but it rarely crosses over that imaginary barrier. The journey to that line and the constitutional interpretations that fuel that journey admittedly alter the "meaning" of the text in subtle and important ways. But we must remember that those interpretations do not carry with them the same import as does the constitutional amendment, both because of the extraordinary process that accompanies the passage of most amendments—indeed, the public's clear declaration of consent—and the belief that interpretations are at least partially based on the "good faith" of the interpreter.[41] Discernibility in constitutional meaning, I suggest, can still be achieved even with significant variations in institutional interpretations.

Self-imposed Limits

The final stipulation of modern constitutionalism involves shifting the responsibility for limiting the power of political institutions directly to the sovereign. Consistent with the principles of externality and discernibility, the motivating force behind the self-imposition of limits is to suppress even more fully the possibility of arbitrary and tyrannical rule. It should be recalled by our earlier account of traditional political societies that subjects of the ruling body often recognized the need for real constitutional constraints. In fact, they were the individuals who consistently raised objections to the largely un-checked authority of the state. This is part of what plagued earlier conceptions of constitutionalism, since it was difficult to get rulers to agree to proposed restraints imposed from below.

For this reason, modern constitutionalism insists that the sovereign itself— whether that be in a democratic regime or an aristocratic one—introduce limits, at the moment of founding, on its own political authority. Included in this formulation must be self-conscious limits not only on the sovereign itself (for example, the people), but also on *representations* of the sovereign (namely, majorities and governmental institutions). As Jon Elster has remarked, consti-tutionalism in the present "refers to limits on majority decisions; more specifi-cally, to limits that are in some sense self-imposed."[42] In the United States, the Constitution is the voice of the sovereign people, and by placing important constitutionally endorsed restrictions (in the form of the executive veto, the unelected judiciary, and the protection of minority rights, among other things) on the power of the majority to make decisions, the sovereign has imposed crucial restraints on (practical reflections of) itself. For a constitution to be objective and thus subscribe to the principles of modern constitutional-ism, the limits and restraints on the created power of the state—the arm of the sovereign—must originate from the sovereign itself.

The particulars of these self-imposed limits should be evident at the mo-ment the constitution is ratified or amended. They can take many forms, including the separation of judicial bodies for adjudication or the articulation of certain rules for elections and representation, but central to their legitimacy is the fact that self-imposed limits must be given greater status than mere legality. In the same way that the constitution stands apart—as "supreme" law in relation to ordinary governmental regulations and provisions—the sov-ereign's self-imposed limits must possess greater force than mere legislative enactments. Indeed, this is what separates modern constitutionalism from its classical or traditional predecessor: the fact that the sovereign has abdicated its own power and limited its capacity to control all future activity. Under classical constitutional regimes, the sovereign identified boundaries on his own power, but those constraints were not adequately binding. They could (and were) ignored without fear of consequence. Now, constitutions announce bills of rights, independent counter-majoritarian institutions, difficult amendment procedures, and other mechanisms that specifically and *permanently* obstruct the power of the majority, all in an attempt to structure political conflict more objectively.

Madison's constitutional experiment for the United States is illustrative here. What he and the American founders managed to accomplish was the realization of objective constitutionalism through the limitation of political power. His constitutional politics combined a realistic and vigorous account of democratic life with a controlled and limited government. Indeed, the Madisonian dilemma refers to the paradox of his constitutional vision: how best to maintain majoritarian control without that control degenerating into tyranny. But when the will of the majority clashed with the clauses of the constitutional text, Madison was unwavering in his belief that the nature of constitutionalism was paramount. The sovereign, through its elected representatives, had wide latitude to engage in policy making, but the scope of that berth was not unlimited.[43]

Self-conscious limitations on practical reflections of the sovereign further fortify the specific aims fashioned by the dimensions of externality and discernibility. That is to say, in order for the requirements of objective constitutionalism to function properly, all three characteristics must be present. A modern constitution like that which informs the political society in the United States or Canada depends on the combined effort of all three components. The principles of externality and discernibility both ensure some sense of impartiality, some notion of control over the political arms of the state; while the notion of self-imposed limits further supports that mission by placing certain powers and practices outside the realm of majoritarian control, thereby continuing the effort to harness political authority. Without one element, then, a constitution cannot qualify as objective; without all three, it cannot qualify as a modern constitution at all.

The Constitutionalist Challenge to American Communitarianism

The U.S. Constitution, with its normative principles of liberalism, republicanism, and democracy, provides an example of a text that is attentive to modern constitutionalist guidelines. As fundamental law, it orders the polity objectively by occupying a position outside and above the national political community. Following the lessons provided by Madison, Paine, Hamilton, and McIlwain, the Constitution was established prior to the existence of the federal state, and furthermore, it produced a government rather than the government producing it. It created the procedural boundaries necessary for an efficient, vibrant polity, yet its major tenets are not wholly subject to review from within the system it has created.[44] In addition, the document sets up a structure that is both discernible and self-consciously limited. Individual rights and liberties are isolated and placed beyond the reach of government, while federalism, bicameralism, checks and balances, and the separation of the branches all act together to inhibit the possibility of arbitrary rule and to forestall the concentration of power. As such, the Constitution has embraced neutral principles—among others, liberalism, tolerance, and democratic participation—that are objective as well as manageable.[45] Certain broadly defined values are neither dictated by those in power, nor are they controlled by an ever-changing public whim; they remain simply authoritative.

The same cannot be said for the current conception of American communitarianism. Subtle constitutional problems arise for the contemporary communitarian when considering the principles of externality, discernibility, and self-conscious limitation. True to its definition as a political ideology committed to the celebration of community, communitarianism must rely on those fundamental principles and values that are internally derived. Procedurally, communitarian advocates support the idea of full and active participation in the shaping of the public sphere. Substantively, the key for most communitarians is locating and preserving a binding series of values that will (in the long run) act as a form of adhesive, grounding the citizens to each other and to the polity. As a result of relying on these internally driven principles, however, communitarianism cannot confidently support an objective or modern constitution. In other words, a communitarian constitution, by its very nature, cannot exist external to the governing institutions that represent the sovereign.

In addition to its inability to sustain an external or detached constitutive document, a communitarian constitution cannot be informed by clearly understood limits on political power. Discernibility of the constitution's fundamental meaning, not to mention its rules and guidelines, is problematic precisely because constitutive values are presumably always changing. Indeed, what is the constitutional lesson of Etzioni's observation that the constitutive values of the fifties must be replaced by brand new ones that reflect American thinking today? What happens, we might ask, when the constitutive idea falls out of favor and another, dramatically different value takes its place? In common political language we refer to similar events as revolutions, but in communitarian terms, this type of circumstance is theoretically consistent with the movement's mantra that it will always be piloted by the community. To be sure, a political regime could not call itself communitarian if it did not closely follow the self-proclaimed values of the community, yet those self-proclaimed values—or "constitutive principles"—must also remain flexible.

Finally, the constitutionalist insistence that limits must be self-imposed by the sovereign is troublesome for the communitarian advocate. If certain substantive conceptions of the good are antecedently outlawed by the constitutional text, then the first principle of communitarianism—that the people collectively and through mutual cooperation determine their shared fate—can never be fully realized. Communitarianism celebrates above all else the idea of collective decision making and the community-wide determination (or discovery) of a common good. All obstacles, therefore, that may potentially hinder the realization of that primary mission must be eliminated. And that presumably includes the elimination of all constitutionalist restraints (other than the ones that speak directly to the various democratic procedures).

Before we embark on a discussion of the various constitutional flaws attributed to the communitarian ideal, we should again be reminded of the variety of communitarian strains. There is little doubt that the challenges of modern constitutionalism succeed best against the democratic species of communitarianism, and that other forms of communitarian thought—liberal, conservative, radical, moderate—may be able to satisfy one or more parts of the modern constitutionalist agenda. But all communitarian positions, I will argue, suffer from some constitutional maladies. The democrats and liberals suffer most obviously (but not exclusively) from their desire to place authoritative control of the polity's destiny in the hands of a fickle, often self-interested population. It may be helpful at this point to recall that certain communitarian proponents (Barber most particularly) eschew any allegiance to the representative model. They believe not only that the sovereign populace is capable of deliberating about its most important policy initiatives, but that common action by citizens is a critical means to increased communal awareness. I mention this here so as not to cause any confusion below, when I self-consciously shift my focus between discussions of the sovereign and similar discussions about majorities or representatives—in other words, between the sovereign itself and practical reflections of the sovereign. They are distinct, to be sure, and yet they both must be controlled. If one strain of democratic communitarianism insists on bypassing representative institutions, while another condones those same representative bodies, we must account for both. For some democratically minded communitarians, drawing a distinction between the sovereign people and governmental institutions that may represent the sovereign is a trivial exercise; they are, and should be, one in the same. For others, representation is an important component of efficient governance. For the constitutionalist, however, it does not matter which model is adopted: a modern constitution aims to control both the sovereign and practical reflections of itself.

Conservative communitarians can be a bit more subtle. They try to escape constitutionalist scrutiny by marginalizing the nation-state altogether, suggesting instead, in a decidedly Anti-Federalist posture, that local communities ought to retain primary control of their own constituents' destiny. Yet neither this argument nor its logical converse can truly satisfy the modern constitutionalist. Large-scale republics that rely exclusively on the collective wishes of the entire population and that are not also accompanied by an objectively limiting text, simply mirror the problems of the ancien régime. That is to say, the contemporary community can be just as arbitrary and oppressive as the classical image of the monarch. Small-scale republics, which the conservative communitarians favor, suffer from the same constitutional maladies that Madison so cleverly highlighted in *Federalist* 10. They are "spectacles of turbulence and contention," and have been "as short in their lives as they have been violent in their deaths."[46] Homogeneous local communities that exist without meaningful constitutional restraints, Madison would no doubt argue, do not differ from states (or nations) in their capacity to abuse and to eventually self-destruct.

Communitarianism's Internal Constitution

To get at how the communitarian constitution is primarily internal and thus premodernly constitutionalist, let us assume that the community-based claim that liberals mistakenly refuse to recognize the importance of community bonds is true. After all, I think even most liberals would readily admit that individuals are innately social beings. As a necessary part of that claim, however, communitarians further insist that individuals cannot escape their social environment, that their identities are a product of the various cultural, historical, and moral communities that surround them. If that principal communitarian argument is correct, what, we might ask, is the practical consequence of this knowledge for constituting new political regimes like those found in Eastern Europe or reconstituting existing ones like the United States?

For communitarian theorists, the constitutional ramifications of our social nature is surely to pattern public institutions in such a way as to recognize concrete communal bonds, to translate our social existence into an organizing doctrine. In fact, it would seem implausible for a communitarian to suggest that humans are social creatures and that a community's institutions are "patterned ways of living together,"[47] but that the polity's fundamental law need not also in some way reflect that underlying sociality. Thus in postcommunist Eastern Europe or in the reconstituted United States, the framers of a new communitarian political design should make sure that they secure, in constitutional form, certain community-wide shared understandings and practices.

The problem for communitarian advocates is that this political mentality renders the prospect of an external or detached constitution a virtual impossibility. In fact, a communitarian constitution that exists apart from the communitarian power centers depicts an illogical image; for on the one hand, a modern constitution is charged with the responsibility of creating a functioning government; but on the other, a communitarian polity takes its lead from none other than the community itself (and certainly not from some metapolitical instrument whose provisions may conflict with the wishes of the community). The goal of any modern constitutionalist charter is to be objective, and one of the means of ensuring objectivity is to insist on the clear separation of the fundamental law from the institutions that practice everyday politics. Yet as suggested by Sandel, MacIntyre, Walzer, and Etzioni, communitarian societies must be "constituted" (using their terminology) by the very moral values and substantive principles inherent within the community, and not by any "constitutive" values and principles that exist beyond the boundaries of the particular polity.[48] Furthermore, Barber and other prescriptive communitarians maintain that the polity should be constituted by those decisions that are reached collectively, through the mechanisms of participatory democracy and democratic consensualism. The result of combining the theoretical and prescriptive positions is a general communitarian observation that a political society simply cannot be organized by principles that are imposed from without,[49] that are not part of the "shared understanding" or common roots that exist within the community itself. Instead, constitutive values must reflect the particular moral teachings that are best realized by "keeping [a] nose so close to the ground" that the shared understandings of the community become patently obvious.[50]

What specifically are we referring to when we claim constitutive values in the communitarian movement must be internally derived? A clear example is Walzer's famous argument that a polity's system of justice requires close attention to the particular—and internally unique—workings of the community's collective heritage.[51] Identifying and securing an authoritative system of justice is, of course, one of the most important tasks of a constitutional framer. In the United States, as in most liberal-democratic regimes, the constitutionally endorsed system of justice is a mostly procedural (and substantively neutral) one that rests on a broad notion of equality and fairness and that incorporates, along with an independent judiciary, clearly discernible, metapolitical rules. Limits on the power of the government to determine the scope of justice are therefore authoritative and legitimate precisely because they are not wholly or readily subject to the unstable disposition of a collective citizenry. Those limitations on the power of the creature of the constitution are predetermined by the text and can not be ignored without abandoning the principle of modern constitutionalism altogether. In certain nonliberal societies, the system of justice may not be entirely neutral and may not even include procedural mechanisms, but in adherence to the principles of constitutionalism, it most often exists apart from the day-to-day workings of the functioning polity.

In Walzer's hypothetical communitarian construction, by contrast, the system of justice is neither neutral nor metapolitical. Rather, it is fully dependent upon the common "understanding" of a collective citizenry, whatever that may turn out to be. He writes:

> We cannot say what is due to this person or that one until we know how these people relate to one another through the things they make and distribute. There cannot be a just society until there is a society; and the adjective just doesn't determine, it only modifies, the substantive life of the societies it describes. There are an infinite number of possible lives, shaped by an infinite number of possible cultures, religions, political arrangements, geographical conditions, and so on. A given society is just if its substantive life is lived in a certain way—that is, in a way faithful to the shared understandings of the members.[52]

Each community, in Walzer's construction, will presumably endorse its own particular version of justice; but, similarly, and more importantly from a constitutional perspective, each community's version of justice will reflect a fully internal scheme—"justice," Walzer says, "is relative to social meanings."[53]

All this means that the first principle of modern objective constitutionalism cannot be adequately realized in Walzer's communitarian form.[54] In the first place, communitarianism cannot create a constitution antecedent to the existence of the polity; in fact, communitarian constitution makers must, prior to the adoption of a constitutional design, pinpoint those values and ideas that most effectively root the citizenry to each other and to the state. Daniel Bell has explicitly admitted that "the whole point of communitarian politics is to *structure* society in accordance with people's deepest shared understandings."[55] Yet constitutionalists like Madison and Paine are convinced that if it is to be objectively authoritative, a constitution has to exist both prior to, and externally from, the formation of the government. In opposition to these essential lessons, it is clear that the "internal perspective," and not some externally derived principles that are imposed on the polity, rest at the organizational core of all communitarian politics—from the form of political decision making to the strategy employed to foster collective decisions. Or to put it another way, internal institutions and customs supply the boundaries of governmental conduct in communitarian schemes, yet it is the essence of modern constitutionalism that internal mechanisms should not completely predetermine the difficult project of objectively organizing the polity.

Part of the problem for communitarians, I believe, is the principle that a constitution is founded at a fixed moment in time. At that moment, a regime's founders presumably capture the intangible or tangible spirit of the polity and transform that spirit into the constitutional text. To be sure, a constitution should initially reflect the priorities and the values of a constituting citizenry during the founding period. The U.S. Constitution did in the late eighteenth century, as does the new South African constitution now. The difference between these texts and the one proposed by communitarian advocates is that the U.S. and South African charters can accommodate changes or developments in the citizen's value system. Constitutions that are neutral to competing conceptions of the good—primarily liberal constitutions—have the capacity to adapt to changing social and environmental needs. Indeed, constitutions that value neutrality above all else enjoy a certain amount of flexibility that permits them to remain current. Communitarian constitutions do not share this virtue. They are by nature reflections of the will of the community, and sometimes that will changes. In those instances, either the constitution is supreme and the community loses, or the community prevails and the constitution is rendered meaningless.

Several of Abraham Lincoln's choices while facing the possible implosion of the Union highlight this paradox. He was willing—some might even say eager—to look beyond constitutional directives to find political ammunition for his cause. Certainly John Merryman can attest to the reality that the Constitution was outrightly ignored at various times during the Civil War. And yet Lincoln's unconstitutional suspension of habeas corpus is just one example of his belief that the provisions of the constitutional text should relinquish authority to the will of the community when national security is at stake. He refused to allow the government to "go to pieces" in order to save one law, even if that one law was the Constitution itself.[56] It was illogical to rally behind a belief in unfettered freedom when the very future of that liberty was in doubt, he continued. In the end, we may not disagree with the president's decisions, particularly if we consider the urgent circumstances that made them necessary. But make no mistake: Lincoln's actions were antithetical to the first principle of modern constitutionalism. When he suspended the rules of habeas corpus, the president was influenced by the emotions of the northern alliance and not by the binding commands of the constitutional text; he was driven by internal political choices and not by external constitutional ones. As such, Lincoln's political maneuvers were not sanctioned by the text, but rather they were guided by the passions of the community he governed. A communitarian logically makes those same choices.

Turning away from domestic history, Israel may provide the closest approximation of a communitarian regime and thus it suffers from the same constitutional malady that plagued Lincoln.[57] There is no single textual constitution in Israel that informs the political realm. Rather, the Israeli constitution consists of a series of documents—the 1948 Declaration of Independence, the 1950 Law of Return, the 1952 Covenant Between the State of Israel and the World Zionist Organization, and the Basic Law—that have been granted constitutional status.[58] They do not structure the institutions of the polity in the way more traditional constitutional documents do, nor do they articulate particular rules that may guide individuals in the practice of public life. But what they are successful in doing is announcing a clear vision for Israel, a vision that is entirely based on the teachings of the Jewish faith. That is to say, the precise compact between Jews and their God informs the various documents Israelis believe to be constitutionally sovereign. But at the same time, these documents are importantly particularist and leave no room for manipulating Israel's core values. Absent the violent overthrow of the state, there is no possibility of an anti-Jewish Israel, and thus there is no attempt (or any need) to separate the constitution from those who control power. The unwritten nature of the Israeli constitution and the fact that it ignores the principle of externality renders it unapologetically premodern. I will have more to say on this point in chapter 6.

A modern constitution, it must be remembered, acts as a touchstone, an object that all institutions and policies must satisfy before being included within the public sphere. To qualify as objective, a constitution must create institutions in its image, not the other way around. A communitarian polity relies exclusively on the community; it is inherently and logically a grassroots project. As a consequence, however, the line that separates the constitution (as the instrument that informs all that is public) and the community (the instrument that governs a communitarian polity) becomes blurred.

Thus, in remarkable similarity to the classical notion of constitutionalism, contemporary American communitarianism endeavors to limit the power of the government by referring solely to the cultivating power of internal institutions. Again, Paine argues "that there is a fundamental difference between a people's government and that people's constitution . . . [and] that in any state in which the distinction is not actually observed between the constitution and the government, there is in reality no constitution."[59] As it is presently conceived, communitarian theory suffers from this very disability. Interpretation of the constitutive values of a communitarian polity comes from the grassroots level rather than from an authoritatively extra-governmental source. Indeed, achieving constitutional objectivity is hamstrung by the communitarian aversion to distinguishing the constitution from the polity—the creator from the created. In the end, communitarian constructions cannot "pry the polity away from the holders of power and make the constitution the object to be reckoned with" precisely because the very notion of a communitarian collectivity makes the polity and the sovereign essentially identical.[60]

Problems of Discernibility

Constitutional objectivity is further obscured by the communitarians' insistence on organizing institutions and citizens around the collective will. Essential to the communitarian critique of liberal theory is the idea that individualism carries with it no clear conception of a constituted self. In Sandel's mind, the fact that liberal individuals are at best "unencumbered" suggests that liberal theory can support only a "cooperative" or "voluntary" notion of the community. Communitarianism, on the other hand, posits that individual identities are deeply rooted or encumbered by the various roles they inhabit; and as a result, the image of political society that emerges from this understanding is "constitutive as against merely cooperative."[61] A constitutive community—defined in no other way than a community "dependent upon the idea of a constitution"—is one that recognizes individuals as belonging to many formative groups all shaping their personalities and identities. Moreover, constitutive or formative communities can be as small as a family or a church group, or as large as a nation.[62] What marks them as constitutive, Sandel proposes, is that they "situate us in the world and give our lives their [shared] moral particularity."[63] But what is troubling from a constitutionalist perspective, and what most communitarians like Sandel refuse to consider, is this: What happens to the concept of a constitutive community when its binding values (the things that provide individuals with their identities while keeping all citizens rooted to the idea of a community) substantially change? What, for example, happens when a community's traditional values become outdated, as in the case of the American South at the turn of this century? The answer must be that unless the change is met with widespread acceptance, the individuals who inhabit those "roles" (and who perhaps fight the inevitable change) become largely unbounded, unrooted, and ultimately unconstituted—a disastrous fate for any serious communitarian.

It must be remembered that the constitutionalist views politics in a very particular way. He accepts its inevitability even as he is working to keep it from getting out of control. Again, harnessing the political is possible because of the essential difference between the constitution as a metapolitical force and the nature of ordinary politics. One clearly governs the other under modern constitutionalist rules. It is incumbent upon us to recognize the difference, then, between an event that causes the constitutional principles of a polity to change and one that results in a mere change in the political values of that same polity. In the view of the modern constitutionalist, the latter scenario presents no serious problems, while the former is seen as deeply troubling and, in fact, could inevitably lead to revolution.

Thus, the possibility that internally derived constitutive principles can change has serious ramifications for the determinability or discernibility of the communitarians' constitutional project. The communitarian insistence that the polity be constituted from within suggests that substantive political order—or constitutional order—is dictated by particular communal principles and distributional schemes that are currently dominant, not by objective ones that (1) originally ordered the political society, and (2) permanently limit governmental power. In the communitarian instance, with all aspects of public life (including the general organization of institutions) coming directly from within the borders of an existing community, a change in primary values means a change in the substantive meaning of the allegedly authoritative organizational principles. In other words, due to the communitarian insistence that any society must be regulated by principles distinctive and internal to that one community, changes in a polity's moral form will result in a dramatic change in the polity's constitutional content. Altering the values that are derived from ordinary politics may not have serious consequences for the constitutional stability of the regime, but a corresponding change in the meta-political fabric most assuredly will.

To put the point as simply as possible: a society governed primarily by the wishes of the community cannot afford to identify *permanent* or *recognizable* limits on the will of that community without also erasing the very purpose of its communitarian nature. Communal values will always and inevitably clash with constitutional provisions. It is not difficult to imagine a community that silences a minority in direct defiance of a constitutional provision that protects free expression, or a society willing to introduce ex post facto laws even when the constitutional text explicitly forbids it. Moreover, what should we think of a liberal society, faced with an external terrorist threat, that is anxious to modify or even suspend the constitutional rights of particular ethnic groups simply because they share the same heritage or skin color as the original evildoers? I suspect the answer to this question will depend at least partially on whether one embraces a communitarian vision or a constitutionalist one. A communitarian, by nature, must safeguard the interests of the community; a constitutionalist, the constitution. The problem arises when the two forces collide.

A more concrete example may help. Imagine if the United States abandoned its central tenets of individual freedom, personal liberty, equal justice, and universal democracy. Such a profound and fundamental alteration of constitutional principles would surely result not only in an essential loss of what it means to be a citizen of the United States but also in a general confusion as to the domain of governmental action. This type of change is obviously far different than even dramatic variations in, say, gun control policy or health care reform. Political changes are part of the normal process of governance, but switching from a democratic republic to an aristocracy, or from a predominantly capitalist regime to a socialist one, would have ramifications beyond mere policy. With a change in the constitution's authoritative purpose comes the very real problem that subjects of the polity cannot clearly discern the fundamental meaning (and rules) of the constitutional charter. It follows that when viewing a communitarian constitution, one is basically thrown back to the period in history when constitutionalism and the limits that supposedly went with it was but a meaningless fiction.

The prescriptive communitarian literature can further illustrate this point. Part of what is so nettlesome to communitarians like Etzioni is that the moral code that was in place in the fifties was not "followed by a solid affirmation of new values" in the last quarter century.[64] Of course, identifying new values and cultural trends is something the citizens of the United States almost take for granted. But Americans can afford to be casual about shifting values because the constitutional principles guiding their decisions do not substantially and abruptly change. Thus, the principle of religious and secular freedom found in the First Amendment may certainly contribute to the recognition of new values, but the meaning behind that overarching constitutional provision does not similarly deviate. In contemporary communitarian scholarship, the same cannot be said. There is no externally objective constitutional system that can remain stable while values and cultural habits vacillate. Indeed, it is those internal and purportedly "constitutive" values themselves that form the core of a communitarian polity.

Consider Bruce Frohnen's conservative vision of communal life. He speaks admiringly of the period in colonial history when inhabitants of the Americas were controlled primarily by religious covenants.[65] "Covenants," he writes, "bound a group together under a specific set of corporate rules by binding specified people in a limited geographical area and for specific public purposes, be they religious, political, or economic." The specifics of the religious doctrine found in the covenant dictated to citizens what they could and could not do. Furthermore, the covenant also set substantive limits for the majority: "One outgrowth of American covenantal relations was the conviction that majority rule is inherently limited. The majority rightfully could control only those matters relevant to the community's purposes, as set forth in the covenant. Acts aimed at controlling other matters or undermining these purposes were improper and could rightfully be resisted." "If necessary," Frohnen thus concludes, "dissenting minorities had the right and even the duty to respond to oppression by leaving to form their own government and people."[66]

In one respect Frohnen is correct when he says, "The covenant *is* the basis of American constitutionalism."[67] But in another respect, Frohnen ignores a major component of America's covenantal history—namely, that religious covenants are no longer constitutive in any real sense. They do not order political communities—large or small—with the same uniting force they once possessed. They are no longer the preferred political tool to keep majorities—indeed, all governmental institutions—in check. There is little doubt that religious covenants at one point ordered all types of communities. But now political constitutions have succeeded religious covenants as the means to forestall the authority of the community. Both Donald Lutz and Bruce Frohnen agree that colonial covenants have given way to "later constitutional forms."[68] Such a transition, of course, raises a series of questions: What happened to the constitutive power of the covenant? Why was it eventually supplanted by political constitutions, and why have they not resurfaced in force? The answers, I suggest, shed additional light on the problems associated with communitarian constitutionalism.

Covenants came into disfavor for any number of reasons, but surely one of the reasons they were discredited is that they stopped reflecting the core values of their most devout adherents. Communities, quite simply, stopped seeing covenants as constitutive.[69] Frohnen himself suggests a possible explanation for their ultimate demise. He argues that covenants were based on the principle that God stood as the primary witness to the pact, that the relationship between God and his subjects was based on a belief that if one violated the agreement one would have to pay the consequences in the afterlife, and that fear of a disapproving God went a long way toward controlling the citizens of a covenantal community. Yet once God is removed as the primary witness—a scenario that occurred time and time again during the Enlightenment—any religious covenant will inevitably carry less meaning. The core values of a community have changed when a previously devout group ceases to live its collective life according to the proposition that God is watching and instead embraces a mostly secular existence. Frohnen celebrates the fact that "later documents called on the people rather than God as witness to the pact," suggesting that later constitutions borrowed important constitutive lessons from earlier covenants. But their *demise* is what is critical: when a covenant's principles become out of sync with the wishes of the community, the constitutionalist insists that the community's values must yield. In admiring the early American covenant and suggesting that it should be the model for contemporary texts, Frohnen—the communitarian—seems to be advocating just the opposite. He is suggesting that covenants—early constitutions, in his mind— can and should be discarded *before* the will of the community is either examined or thrown out.

Doubtless some will argue that replacing religious (and thus largely intolerant) covenants with more liberal (and presumably tolerant) constitutions was a good thing. I would agree—but only from a moral or political perspective, not from a constitutionalist perspective. As much as we may celebrate the transition to a greater standard of tolerance that historically accompanied the abandonment of early religious compacts, we must also remember that the opposite is equally true: fascist and authoritarian regimes (particularly in the twentieth century) regularly abandoned liberal constitutional texts when they no longer served the oppressive purposes of tyrannical leaders. The point is not that covenants, or *any* constitutional texts for that matter, reflect a more or less politically correct mentality, but rather that the exercise of adhering first and foremost to the will of the community and not to the dictates of the constitutional text when they conflict with that will, violates the first principle of modern constitutionalism.

Thomas Jefferson understood this component of modern constitutionalism with unique clarity. In a letter to Samuel Kercheval dated July 12, 1816, he writes of his concern that "the progress of the human mind" would eventually render incompatible the desires of the majority and the specifics of any constitutional document. "As [the mind] becomes more developed, more enlightened, as new discoveries are made, new truths disclosed, and manners and opinions change with the change of circumstances, institutions must advance also, and keep pace with the times." Otherwise, he thought, a civilized society will remain captive to its old habits, including the tendency to abuse and oppress; leaders will resort to violence to maintain control, and reason will be lost.[70]

According to Jefferson, the constitution is the most important institution that is directly threatened by changing societal norms. As such, it is imperative that it continually reflect the priorities of a developing population. And yet it is equally critical that a constitution remain authoritative through time. Jefferson's solution to the problem of a progressing society in conflict with a constitutional text that is written and ratified at a fixed moment in time is to convene periodic constitutional conventions, not to simply ignore existing constitutional provisions. The aim of these gatherings is to alter the specifics of the text to better reflect society's shifting priorities. "Each generation is as independent of the one preceding as that was of all which had gone before," he writes. "It has then, like them, a right to choose for itself the form of government it believes most promotive of its own happiness."[71] Jefferson's ideal constitution is one that "provides for its own revision at stated periods." By his estimation, a new convention should thus be called every "nineteen to twenty years," the result of which might be an altogether different constitutional design.

Jefferson's strategy of a constitutional revision every generation or so is certainly provocative and may even sound enticing to many communitarians. What is critical about his proposal, however, is that it includes an unwavering commitment to the principle that constitutions delimit power. Rather than sacrificing the text in favor of a developing collective will—arguably a much simpler way to fulfill Jefferson's desire to recognize new generational values— he insists that the constitution remain paramount and that, for the period between conventions at least, no public want can transgress the specifics of the document. From convention to convention, the constitution performs all of its intended duties: it constrains the will of the majority while empowering the institutions of government to carry out policy initiatives. At the moment the old constitution is replaced by the new one, the cycle begins anew; the text is once again elevated to its position outside and above the vacillating world of real politics. As such, it does not bow to the political pressures of a unified community. It regulates governmental institutions for a distinct period of time, until the moment when the next constitutional convention is convened.

As part of this general discussion, let us conclude by exploring Walzer's *Interpretation and Social Criticism*, a book in which the author certainly gravitates toward a more constitutionalist stance. Walzer draws an analogy between liberal constitutions and sacred texts, suggesting that each provides an example of an authoritatively limiting document. Religious sources, in other words, restrict clergymen in much the same way that constitutions constrain the political power of statesmen. Walzer insists that both are effectively precluded from abusing their positions of authority by the specifics of the particular document. But unlike liberal constitutions, sacred texts like covenants cannot easily accommodate change. In fact, it may be fair to say that all particularist constructions will have difficulty sustaining modern constitutionalist principles because they do not permit the possibility of meaningful reform.

Take Israel (again) for an example. Israel's constitutional government is founded on the idea of Jewish statehood; its existence rests precisely on the authority and legitimacy of (to use Walzer's analogy) a series of sacred texts. These documents may in fact satisfy the principle of externality (although I have my doubts here too), but they are in no way objective. If a community's wishes somehow conflict with the provisions of the sacred texts, the texts could be (and are) ignored.[72] The authoritative weight of Israel's "constitutional" documents is thus regularly placed in question; when the documents cannot be understood in light of policies aimed at maintaining Jewish statehood (rare as that may be), they are simply put aside. For example, some Jews residing in Israel call for the renunciation of religious statehood—a claim that certainly defies the central premise of Israel's "constitutional" texts. And yet these groups are often silenced in contradiction of the spirit of freedom and liberty *also* found in the "constitutional" documents. That is to say, the opportunity to question the first principles of the regime—a practice that is at least allowed even if not encouraged by the texts themselves—is often suppressed in practice. In the end, we may not disagree with Israel's judgment, but if we are serious about the principles of modern constitutionalism, we are justified in exposing them.

The communitarian political design may at first appear to be subject to knowable rules. A communitarian regime like the one proposed by most prescriptive theorists may seem to articulate meaningful constraints—through the entrenchment of individual rights and liberties—on the decision-making power of government organizations.[73] As they are in liberal constitutionalist polities, those restraints on political power can be viewed as limits on the central communitarian sovereign. Nevertheless, those limits are specifically and solely dependent on current political viewpoints. Etzioni in fact calls for the "careful adjustment" of rights from time to time.[74] In referring to the Eighth Amendment provision against "cruel and unusual punishment," he notes that in certain instances (such as the need for increased public safety) the allowable limit of punishment may be significantly modified; and furthermore, the body responsible for "adjusting" or modifying those constitutional safeguards is not an independent judiciary but rather (and consistent with the overall idea of communitarianism) the collective citizenry.[75] If that is the case, what is to stop Etzioni from suggesting that in other instances, various other constitutional provisions may be modified, some even being modified right out of existence?

The main thrust in all of this is that modern communitarianism is left with a political posture that resembles those that preceded the rise of modern constitutionalism. The classical notion of constitutionalism stressed concrete limits on public authority, but more often than not, those limits were constantly in flux. If the sovereign opposed a particular limit on his authority, he simply changed the rules. In current communitarian lore, those constitutional values and principles that limit the power of the government and that supposedly give citizens common roots or a "shared substantive life" can similarly fluctuate. As a result, consistent interpretation of a communitarian order becomes impossibly difficult, and citizens are left literally unprotected by the constitution's malleable principles. A certain degree of stability is thus sacrificed, for constitutional revolution occurs every time the values and "shared understandings" of the community change.

In the end, then, contemporary communitarianism cannot adequately comfort the modern constitutionalist. Modern constitutionalism requires objectivity, yet communitarian theory is designed, not around principles that exist independently of the polity and thus that objectively inform the institutions and citizens of the political society, but rather on those internal mechanisms and moral values that supposedly "bind" an entire citizenry. Constitutionalism has attempted, in its modern version, to shelter persons more thoroughly and objectively from the hazardous effects of erratic or indiscriminate government. But because communitarianism depends on the collective and substantive consciousness of the community's inhabitants and not on authoritatively external, discernible maxims, the result of a communitarian political experiment is a constitution that exists only in premodern form.

CHAPTER FIVE

Communitarian Democracy

In Tension with Constitutional Theory?

Perhaps the most concrete and important provision of constitutionalist thought, the self-conscious restraint of political power, takes us directly into the heart of communitarian politics. What is at stake in fully contrasting constitutionalism and communitarianism is the very essence or power of collective decision making, unitary democracy, and the generation of consensus. In fact, what is principally at stake every time the constitutionalist banner is raised is quite simply the capacity of the sovereign (or representations of that sovereign) to determine freely and completely its own political path. Indeed, by now it should be clear that modern constitutionalism comes at a very real price: the uninhibited freedom of the community's citizens to determine for themselves the exact direction in which they want their overall polity to go.[1] Under the strict guidelines set by modern constitutionalism, certain aspirations or visions of communal existence will be forbidden solely because a piece of paper and an organizational design mandate it, while the collective will of a modern people will very often be silenced precisely because of the words and phrases of an ancient pact.

Each time a new constitutional framework is designed, the engineers of that republic face a serious paradox: they must endeavor to grant political power to the people while simultaneously recognizing the need to seize or recapture (through congruent institutional means) a good amount of that newly bequeathed authority. In understanding that the best form of politics is one that places normal decision-making jurisdiction somehow in the hands of the democratic citizenry, those framers must be ready to confer authority upon the collective whole. But in so doing, they must also be leery of the abuses that may stem from an intemperate, unfettered citizenry, particularly in its majoritarian form. Accordingly, the architects of a newly formed polity must specify legitimate and powerfully self-imposed constraints on the government's authority. They must concede that the will of the people (often through their representatives in government) is ultimately sovereign; but that will, at the same time, is not totally uninhibited.

In the late eighteenth century, the drafters and ratifiers of the American constitutional text were not only cognizant of this paradox but were also successful in finding a workable solution to its main problem. The question in twenty-first-century America is whether the current conception of communitarian politics can ensure the same self-conscious or self-imposed limits on the power of the people in their self-governing capacity. One is right to wonder whether the advocates of a communitarian polity are able to constrain themselves with enough force to allay the fears of most modern constitutionalists. Indeed, should they have to? Why should the people be forced to relinquish some of the authority originally granted to them? If all decisions are conceived collectively, why should we be forced to erect obstacles that will combat the agreements made by me and my neighbors? Finally, and perhaps most urgently, how does the constitutionalists' call for self-restraint play into the continued drive by prescriptive communitarians to reframe the American political system in the image of a more bounded community?

A response to these questions must acknowledge a small but important communitarian victory. The preliminary construction of a communitarian regime at the end of Part I revealed that the form of political decision making most often embraced by communitarian thinkers was participatory democracy, or what I dubbed "communitarian republicanism." What is the idea of participatory democracy in the communitarian canon if it is not specifically an attempt to reach political decisions by employing all citizens of a distinct community in a predominantly conversant manner? The very notion of a political community presupposes a collective unit resolving shared problems through participation, deliberation, and cooperation. For communitarians, collective action is not only a means to achieve necessary political measures, but it is also an attitude that goes a long way toward constituting or bounding a citizenry. Barber, for example, understands the activity of engaging in politics, not as a tedious obligation, but as a "way of life."

Correspondingly, he and others note that the decision-rule favored by most communitarian supporters is not majoritarianism, with its tendency to foster privatism and individual interests, but rather "democratic consensualism," where private interests can be fundamentally transformed into shared or communal desires. According to Barber, "The ideal ground of strong democracy is *creative consensus*—an agreement that arises out of common talk, common decision, and common work but that is premised on citizen's active and perennial participation in the transformation of conflict through the creation of common consciousness and political judgment."[2] Combined with the plea by Barber and others that the decision-rule best complementing full and active participation is consensualism, the complete extent of the communitarian political form thus comes to light. In the end, full and active participation, coupled with a call for negotiation and compromise, will give the citizens of the communitarian polity a solid handle on which shared values or conceptions of the good the state ought to endorse.

This qualification of consensualism in community-centered politics should be viewed as a potentially substantial procedural limit on the otherwise exhaustive power of the collective citizenry and their representatives. Presumably, some mechanism for compromise—the endeavor to transform personal interests in order to reach a degree of solidarity—would likely be implemented by the communitarian design. In fact, it is safe to assume that Barber's notion of consensus would be found somewhere within the procedural provisions of a hypothetical communitarian constitution. As such, the people in a communitarian regime are in a sense constrained from what they can will into existence because they are forced to consider all aspects of a political debate. Hypothetically, a communitarian society wrestling with the heated issue of abortion would presumably have to consider, and subsequently incorporate in the deliberation over policy, both the pro-choice and the pro-life positions. Any public initiative on abortion (if all goes well) would thus reflect the compromise or consensus reached by the warring factions. To that extent (and if all goes extremely well), both the pro-choice and the pro-life movements will be (somewhat) satisfied with the universally endorsed settlement.[3]

Instead of running roughshod over the minority view and not granting particular groups a voice in the political process, the communitarian demand for a degree of consensus allows all members of the polity to contribute to the political bottom line. Unlike contemporary utilitarianism, where politics is based on pluralism and victory is dependent on aggregating interests, communitarian systems mandate that all ideas—no matter how polarized—be awarded some stake in the political outcome. Ideally, there would be no conception of a majority and minority in the communitarian world, only a feeling that all citizens will contribute equally to the resolution of conflicts, as well as consensually agree upon the final results. No single group enjoys complete control, but no single group is ignored. In that respect, a clear limit on the authority of the sovereign is self-imposed.

However, that is as far as the communitarians feel it is necessary to go on the subject of self-restraint, and for the constitutionalist, that is not far enough. Once consensus has been reached and a decision has been rendered, the feeling is that there are no losers, only winners. Within the communitarian universe, the belief exists that at the end of the political process all should be satisfied with the community-sponsored compromise. But a deeper question remains: Does a condition of consensualism fully establish a valid self-imposed check on the will of the collective citizenry? Is it any more successful against simple governmental institutions that might represent the community? How can the collective population, even if it is told to cooperate and compromise, truly bind itself in such a way as to certify or guarantee a sufficiently limited scope? Indeed, can a political regime that places primary stock in the value of collectivism and democracy locate a legitimate counterbalancing force to offset the authority of the popular sovereign and prevent the rise of arbitrary, tyrannical, or capricious rule?[4]

Perhaps the immediate answer to these and other related questions can be found in the bedrock of communitarian theory: because we all contribute to the resolution of shared problems, we trust that we will also agree, in solidarity, to the notion of self-limitation. Much like American judges who are appointed rather than elected and hence largely unaccountable to the public, an entire communitarian populace will surely subscribe to an internal doctrine of self-restraint.[5] In fact, communitarians might even contend that self-restraint is not necessarily inhibiting, but rather it is in itself a form of power.[6] They could claim that owing in part to the insistence on active and universal participation, self-restraint should not be viewed as disabling, but instead, as potentially empowering, and thus a likely outcome of collective action as well as an indispensable precondition.

Like James Madison and Alexander Hamilton, modern constitutionalists are not nearly as trusting and deferential. The framers of the American Constitution were so concerned—obsessed, even—about the possible rise of tyranny, that despite the establishment of an objectively detached and interpretable constitutional text, they thought it necessary to further curtail the scope of power by introducing, among other things, complicated political procedures, checks and balances, and separated institutions. Speaking primarily as a constitutionalist and not specifically as an American founder, Madison once wrote that "power" must be "surrendered by the people."[7] In his mind, the way to bind the authority of the government was to proscribe the concentration of power through the constitutional implementation of such experiments as overlapping governmental functions and separate institutional branches. In order for the government to "control the governed, and in the next place oblige it to control itself," Madison understood that "auxiliary precautions" might be necessary. He wrote in *Federalist* 47: "The accumulation of all powers, legislative, executive, and judiciary, in the same hands, whether of one, a few, or many, and whether hereditary, self-appointed, or elective, may justly be pronounced the very definition of tyranny."[8]

Thus, within the constitutionalist framework of American politics at least, there is a democratic component and a nondemocratic component; there is a means for the people to voice their opinion, but, at the same time, there is an equally potent check on the influence and scope of that voice. There exists, in short, the capacity for the majority to get its own way, but that capacity is in no way absolute.[9] The important constitutionalist point provided by the American example is not that there must be separated branches, checks and balances, or complex governmental structures (these are merely the tools used to check the imminent governmental power), but rather that every constitutionalist polity requires mechanisms that legitimately and forcefully enjoin the power of the democratic citizenry. Walter Murphy, James Fleming, and Sotirios Barber capture the essence of this critical qualification when they contend that "the constitutionalist insists on institutional limitations beyond those of open political processes to curb government."[10] And although fixating on the principle of individual rights, Madison's sentiment is also informative: "In our Governments the real power lies in the majority of the Community, and the invasion of private rights is *chiefly* to be apprehended, not from acts of Government contrary to the sense of its constituents, but from acts in which Government is the mere instrument of the major number of its constituents."[11]

Although conceptually dissimilar because the communitarian notion of "collectivity" is admittedly not equivalent to our contemporary definition of "majoritarianism," current communitarian theory still cannot adequately assuage the modern constitutionalist of his uneasiness. What the constitutionalist is deeply concerned about is exactly what communitarianism, as a political ideology, stands for: the idea that (1) all institutions of public power will eventually become subordinate to a collective body determining its own political fate; and (2) the democratic process, if properly designed around consensus building and compromise, can and should render all other institutional checks and restraints mostly unnecessary. To be sure, democratic rule—whether it results in a mere majoritarian victory or a unanimous collectivity—is an important procedural value in most constitutionalist regimes (including the United States). But it is not the only (or even the dominant) political value, as it has become in contemporary communitarian theory. In both liberal and nonliberal constitutionalist polities, there exist distinct measures—the unelected judiciary, the unelected and antidemocratic process of appointment in many nonliberal, particularist communities—that directly combat the authority of the collective citizenry, again, for the purpose of preventing arbitrary and unfettered rule. In communitarian polities, however, any measure that successfully combats the will of the community must be seen as largely unfaithful to the very definition of that ideology, to the centerpiece of communitarian thought, which, again, Sullivan describes as "the common pursuit of the public good."[12]

Let us try to tackle this complicated and subtle idea from a slightly different angle. Glendon, Barber, Etzioni, and even the "Responsive Communitarian Platform" all contend that the future of politics must celebrate full and energetic participation, governmental accountability, and responsible political actors. Legitimate policies, they argue, come directly from a collective citizenry seeking consensus and acting in unity. Majoritarianism, privatism, and individualism are out; while consensualism, public interests, and communalism are in.[13] The ultimate aim of any communitarian regime is to travel the envisioned path determined collectively by all of the community's citizens, for it is that particular conception of the good life that binds us together and makes us a community.

It is an appealing aim, one that many regimes would strive to duplicate. But if that is, in fact, the goal, it seems implausible to suggest that the communitarian would risk sponsoring constitutional restraints that may at once be required to minimize the possibility of unfettered rule, but that may also prevent some collective visions of the good from being realized. For the communitarian who is truly governed principally by the will of the community, it is illogical to accept the fact that a constitution "remove[s] subjects from the public sphere" while those "subjects" may be the very ones that could most effectively provide the community with its common roots.[14] Admitting that a single shared vision endorsed by the community can be constitutionally prohibited would in essence plunge a dagger directly into the very heart of the modern communitarian belief. Communitarianism rests so completely on the idea that a polity is ordered around a collective and specified shared conception of the good that it would be virtually impossible for the communitarian to self-impose concrete limits on the community's authority to follow a particular vision. Indeed, to do so would essentially be the same as renouncing one's own identity and risking the possibility of becoming unbounded or unconstituted.

True to his basic communitarian instincts, Barber proposes concrete constitutional changes aimed at fostering a greater sense of civic engagement.[15] Many of the suggestions are profoundly interesting and may, if implemented, create the environment Barber so desperately craves. A cornerstone of his approach is the idea of a "National Initiative and Referendum Process," a scheme whereby national referenda are used to galvanize the public as well as to identify the polity's general will. In proposing initiatives and referenda, Barber is trying to alter both the perception that the American system of government is not conducive to active popular engagement and the reality that Americans are largely uninterested in the political process. He suggests that allowing the general population to have more direct control over political policies—rather than simply voting for representatives—will alter the widely shared belief that a single voice really does not amount to much. His ultimate goal, it should be recalled, is for an engaged and civic-minded populace to take control of its collective destiny.

Yet when examined more closely, this strategy encounters certain constitutional problems. It is easy to criticize the process of referenda from a number of different perspectives. In fact, Barber himself identifies some of the structural difficulties associated with such a plan. "The resistance to a national referendum process," he writes, "derives in part from Madisonian fears of popular rule. These manifest themselves in the modern world as an anxiety about elite manipulation of public opinion, the power of image and money to influence the popular vote, the private interest character of the balloting process, and the plebiscitary dangers of direct legislation."[16] On the surface, these criticisms are based on some constitutional measure. Nonetheless, what is missing from Barber's list is a concession that the process of national referenda can result in direct conflict with the constitutional document. That is to say, national votes on substantive matters are no less immune from constitutional conflict than are other types of legislative processes. In reference to this concern, Barber later acknowledges the importance of constitutional checks and admits that to discard America's system of separated powers, checks and balances, federalism, and a separated judiciary would be unwise.[17] But he is silent on whether the results of a national referendum will not trump certain substantive provisions of the constitutional text. Likewise, it is not clear from Barber's argument how the independent judiciary will carry on as an institution whose primary responsibility is to put a brake on constitutional violations. Indeed, he has little to say about the judiciary. Barber speaks of the need for (among other things) a "second reading" and a congressional veto to counter the negative effects of a national population run amok. But why should we believe that representatives of the people would be any more altruistic or restrained than the people itself? A second referendum separated by six months of debate and deliberation may be a good idea, but a congressional veto, where the politicians depend for their very jobs on the same populace voting in the referendum, would amount to a superficial check at best.

Consider some issues that are currently ripe for national referenda but that would also face serious constitutional challenges. The recent disconnect between the First Amendment's protection of free speech and the population's call for some mechanism to prohibit the burning of the American flag is one. Privately, many people agreed with the Supreme Court when it ruled in *Texas v Johnson*, 491 U.S. 397 (1989), that the constitutional guarantee of free expression safeguards the actions of those who choose to protest by destroying the flag. Yet because of the intense passion for the flag as a symbol of American freedom and power, few members of Congress were willing to publicly defend the Constitution. They might have recognized the tension, but most were unwilling to risk political suicide by embracing the "unpatriotic" side of the argument. The recent decision by the Ninth Circuit Court of Appeals that the Pledge of Allegiance violates the First Amendment's Establishment Clause is another example.[18] National polls indicate that an overwhelming majority of Americans view the Pledge of Allegiance as sacred and that public school children ought to be forced to recite the entire pledge, including the statement ("one nation under God") that offends the Constitution. In this era of terrorist threats and domestic anxiety, we can also imagine national referenda that seek to curtail the civil liberties of particular ethnic or religious groups. Tragically, I suspect that these would pass rather easily and that a "second reading" six months later or a "congressional veto" aimed at checking the will of the public would be mostly ineffectual in preventing serious constitutional encroachments.

The constitutional dilemma that emerges from Barber's initiatives can be seen more clearly if we focus on his plan to implement a "Civic Education Postal Act."[19] Here, Barber would like to subsidize the dissemination of information by providing free or low-cost postal rates for "newspapers, magazines, journals of opinion, and certain kinds of books." Information, he sensibly argues, is critical for the maturation of the individual and the development of the collective citizenry. The problem arises when he proposes that only "legitimate" publishers would benefit from the subsidy. Although he does not elaborate on what constitutes a legitimate publication, I think it fair to say that publications that either do not conform to the community's conception of the good or that directly endanger the democratic process will likely not qualify for support. But who will decide? And how will the decision be affected by a constitutional provision that protects, say, freedom of speech? The communitarian instinct is always to promote a particular way of life while implicitly (or even explicitly) denouncing all others: a life spent engaged in political pursuits, communitarians like Barber regularly assert, is somehow good; while a life spent ignoring the political ramifications of particular policies is somehow bad. That is to say, Barber is a true communitarian insofar as he defends a particular version of the good life. The only way to realize his societal image, however, is to remove certain constitutional restraints from the equation. More specifically, the challenge to Barber's plan, if implemented, will come directly from the First Amendment. Proponents of the scheme will then be forced to make a very difficult choice: Should they follow through on their communitarian impulse and ignore the troubling constitutional provision(s)? Or should they embrace constitutionalism and, reluctantly, concede the proposal? Either way, one powerful principle loses.

Revisiting a previously discussed hypothetical example may also prove useful in highlighting the communitarian difficulty with constitutional limits. Walzer's self-proclaimed purpose in writing *Spheres of Justice* is "to describe a society where no social good serves or can serve as a means of domination."[20] He is not interested in constructing such a society, nor is he concerned with "sketching a utopian regime." Instead, what he is mainly interested in is identifying which political mechanisms our particular society requires in order to foster a sense of meaningful (or complex) equality. His response is to identify a system of distributive justice that is "radically particularist" but that is roughly based on the idea that goods cannot be distributed and used outside specified spheres. Walzer insists that our contemporary system of justice is not, as Rawls might once have proclaimed, based on universal principles and hypothetical contracts, but it is rather grounded on our shared particular tradition and centered on the idea that justice requires the fair distribution of goods within separate and autonomous spheres. For example, Walzer recognizes that there is a separate and detached sphere devoted to medical care and that within that sphere there is a tradition of distribution grounded solely on need.[21] Justice, therefore, mandates that the distribution of medical care should be based on necessity and nothing else. The problem for Walzer occurs when individuals bring other goods—say, money or influence—into the sphere and try to use those goods to obtain health care. That, he says, becomes a problem precisely because it violates the community's original "shared understanding" that medical care should be provided based solely upon need.

Now imagine that, despite the mandate that suggests health care should be distributed around need, the democratic people, perhaps in a moment of unreflection, determine that medical care will now be distributed according to wealth and not according to necessity.[22] The result of the hypothetical change, of course, is a serious conflict between the original conception of medical care as being based on need, and the changing will of a democratic community. If we conclude, as I think it is right to, that under communitarian guidelines the original shared understanding is somehow constitutionally authoritative (or at least has constitutional import), then the clash becomes increasingly serious. The fundamental question now becomes which substantive form of distributive justice—the one articulated by a constitutionally authoritative tradition, or the one advocated by a whimsical but unified people—should dominate. Which conception of justice should rule?

For the constitutionalist, the answer is simple. In cases where the democratic people have sponsored a policy that directly opposes a corresponding provision in the constitutional text, the constitution must prevail.[23] Accordingly, the original shared tradition (if in fact it had constitutional import) triumphs over the will of the present citizenry. In communitarian theory, however, the answer is not quite so clear. If, on the one hand, the communitarian defends the original constitutionally endorsed tradition, then he will obviously be ignoring the will of the current community. That, as we have noted previously, appears to be anathema to the very definition of communitarian politics. But on the other hand, if the communitarian chooses to side with the collective citizenry, he will essentially be admitting that either: (a) there is no authoritative constitution through which one can appeal, or (b) the constitution is mostly, if not totally, impotent.

Lest we think the reluctance to articulate clear limits on the sovereign is the fault of only liberal-minded communitarians, consider also what some conservative communitarians willingly defend. There is no doubt that conservative communitarians—from Frohnen to Shain—long for us to recapture the spirit of localized political control and republican virtue that characterized early American history. Most of their writings imply that America can be great once again if we adopt some form of the decentralized structure and moral fortitude of an earlier era. Specifically, conservative communitarians often assert that small local communities in the eighteenth and nineteenth centuries successfully ordered and constrained the citizenry by defining the moral parameters of individual and group action. Communities like the family and the church were organized around a clear hierarchical structure, with the father or the priest occupying the highest positions of authority. More often than not, instructions (moral and otherwise) from these authority figures were followed unconditionally. It was thought that one should not question the teachings of those who had the experience and wisdom to know the difference between right and wrong. "For most colonial Americans, serving God and leading a fulfilled human life depended on membership in a hierarchically structured household and a locally controlled congregation and community," writes Shain. "In turn, each community was to be guided by appropriate transcendent morality that, in effect, defined it as a community."[24] In other words, the hierarchical nature of certain institutions, combined with their mission as purveyors of morality, enabled those institutions to regulate individual behavior and maintain public order. The implication from certain conservative communitarians is that modern institutions retain a similar capacity for regulation.

According to Shain, the success of these early communities (and the hope of modern ones) derives principally from their ability to use informal mecha-nisms—humiliation, public shaming, communal disapproval—to maintain a relatively ordered and stable existence. If one did not follow the lead of the community in an earlier time, one was likely to find oneself ostracized from it altogether. Of course, formal law was (and still remains) a necessary compo-nent of all generations of American history, but it was much less decisive in the period surrounding the nation's birth. Tocqueville, for example, wrote that it was not necessary to "coerce those who did not think like themselves: public disapprobation was enough; a sense of their loneliness and impotence [would] overtake them and drive them to despair."[25] Customs, traditions, and the fear of reprisals from one's peers kept citizens of the community in line.

In at least one respect, the conservative communitarians are right to cham-pion informal means of social control: no free society has ever existed on the strength of formal sanctions alone. But the constitutionalist does not share the conservative communitarian's confidence that informal mechanisms will eventually restrain individuals. Indeed, the constitutionalist simply does not have the faith that the pressure to conform will be as successful in controlling the sovereign as Shain is suggesting. At the foundation of modern constitu-tionalism is the expectation that humans will abuse each other. Sad as it may seem, the constitutionalist project relies on the knowledge that individual behavior is often marked by the worst aspects of human nature; again, the principal characteristic of the constitutionalist is pessimism. Customs, tradi-tions, and informal means of social control are all necessary in limiting the power of individuals and leaders alike;[26] but alone they are not enough, and they certainly cannot replace formal law (including constitutions) as the pri-mary means of bridling power. The possibility of limiting the sovereign, a true constitutionalist insists, is at best ambiguous without the help of formal in-struments—instruments that the communitarian for many reasons might have trouble accepting.

A parallel challenge can be leveled at MacIntyre's image of community. In his provocative essay "Is Patriotism a Virtue?" MacIntyre explicitly states that a true community is one that accepts certain questions as beyond rational dis-cussion. MacIntyre makes the claim that any legitimate community will recog-nize that certain subjects cannot be questioned because rationality dictates that any individual with a true commitment to the community would not even think about doing so. Patriotism, for MacIntyre, is one of those subjects. He notes that patriotism is a "loyalty that is in some respects unconditional, so in just those respects rational criticism [of patriotism] is ruled out." Unlike the liberal conception of patriotism, where individuals are encouraged to constantly reflect on its meaning and on their personal commitment to the polity itself, MacIntyre's communitarian understanding assumes that certain subjects are "immune from being put in question and perhaps rejected." He continues: "The morality of patriotism is one which precisely because it is framed in terms of the membership of some particular social community with some particular social, political and economic structure, must exempt at least some fundamental structures of that community's life from criticism." MacIntyre's general claim, in short, is that our comprehension of a political community, and subsequently our own allegiance to a homeland, is illogical if its components are tenuous.[27]

The main point that I am trying to convey is that MacIntyre's assertion that certain questions be "ruled out"—removed, in other words, from the public sphere—may be compatible with the modern constitutionalist principle that self-imposed limits are necessary. MacIntyre seems to be suggesting that rationality can serve (roughly) the same purpose as constitutions in restraining the community's desires—and he might be right. But surely MacIntyre would also admit that the existence and recognition of rationality requires an understanding of *irrationality*. That is to say, rational thought presupposes the existence of *irrational* thought. And it is precisely the possibility that irrationality can seep into and eventually infect the political universe that is most troubling to the constitutionalist. For example, the democrat in Aristotle's *Politics* who believes that dividing the possessions of the wealthy among the poor is somehow just because the sovereign (the poor masses) decreed it, is acting irrationally. He is influenced by his anger (politics) and not by reason when he asserts that because the sovereign has endorsed the policy, it must be so.[28] He is not thinking rationally, and thus he needs something beyond mere rationality to harness the consequences of his thoughts. And this is where a constitution comes in. The constitutional enterprise acts as a critical safeguard against the kind of irrationality Aristotle so aptly describes. Precisely because humans are so unreliable and their thoughts and actions often so irrational, the constitutional enterprise requires security beyond mere reason.

But perhaps I am being unfair. Perhaps there is more to the argument that informal mechanisms can restrain the communitarian populace than I am willing to concede. Perhaps the very nature of conservative communitarianism suggests that we ought not view a communitarian polity through a decidedly liberal or modern lens, but rather through a more republican one. We might ask: Is it possible to imagine a community's deep *moral* commitments as performing the same limiting function as do constitutional forms? These commitments presumably guide individual action, and yet they are extra-constitutional. Turning the tables a bit, communitarians may point to Rawls' construction of decisions by persons behind a veil of ignorance as such a device. Rawls imagines a scenario in which persons will make collective decisions about justice without any knowledge of their individual strengths and weaknesses, the consequence of which is a conception of justice that presumably binds, in a quasi-constitutional way, the participants to their collective decision. His construction is extra-constitutional, but it still has the necessary force to shackle and restrain the polity's principal decision makers.

Conservative communitarians are probably correct to assume that deep moral commitments can have a restraining effect on all sorts of actors. But for the constitutionalist, faith in the power of communal commitments alone is not enough. Rawls himself is perfectly aware that his scenario is wholly imaginary, that in the real world of politics individuals are not necessarily limited by their deep commitments. More is required to ensure that the conception of justice that emerges from the original position is followed once the veil of ignorance is lifted. Once again, a constitutionalist is forever guided by a pessimistic belief that human nature inevitably leads to the abuse of power. Hence the need for law.

In *The Last of the Fathers*, historian Drew McCoy wrote that Madison "believed in a permanent public good and immutable standards of justice."[29] However, taking his cue from David Hume, Madison was not so foolish as to admit to a belief that immutable standards would ever trump man's private interests. "Such was the frailty and perverseness of human nature," he and Hume both thought, "that it proved impossible to keep men faithfully and unerringly in the paths of justice. Sometimes a man found his interests to be promoted more by fraud and rapine, than hurt by the breach which his injustice makes in the social union; just as often, he could be seduced from his great and important, but distant interests, by the allurement of present, though often very frivolous temptations. And this calamitous inversion of the proper hierarchy between the immediate and the remote—between temporary, selfish advantage and the real and permanent interests of the community

—was especially likely in popular regimes."[30] Madison's answer to the reality that collectives or majorities or representatives often mirrored individuals in their abusive nature was to construct constitutional documents that promoted, among other things, power-sharing principles. The question communitarians must answer is this: How can the community's deep commitments be formed and channeled to protect the public good, including the good of minority populations, and still remain circumscribed by the limitations of the constitutional text?

To further illustrate the larger discussion about constitutional limits, let us return to the founding of the American nation and explore two related theoretical and historical points, one involving Hamilton's vision of a constitutional polity and the other relating to the Anti-Federalist demand for a tangible list of constitutional rights. First, consider not what Hamilton says, but rather *how* Hamilton argues for an autonomous judiciary in *Federalist 78*. After broadly arguing in favor of a strong separation of powers and an independent judiciary, Hamilton remarks that "where the will of the legislature, declared in its statutes, stands in opposition to that of the people, declared in the Constitution, the judges ought to be governed by the latter rather than the former."[31] Many contend that this statement gives implicit support to the idea of judicial review, and that may in fact be true. But for our purpose, the important notion addressed by Hamilton is that there are two democratic peoples, and that "the former" (as represented in the legislature) are not the primary institution in a constitutionalist regime. Instead, the constitution, as the voice of an unrestrained ratifying populace as sovereign, is supreme. In other words, there is a distinction between the "people as political decision makers" and the "people as founders." "The people as political decision makers" are constrained from what they can do precisely because of what the "people as founders" originally mandated. What is more, "the people as political decision makers" in all legitimately constitutionalist regimes have accepted the fact that with regard to certain "subjects," their hands are essentially and importantly tied. They understand and recognize that because of what the "people as founders" agreed upon, the scope of their overall authority is narrowed. The only act of unrestrained or unfettered sovereignty was the original act of ratifying the constitutional text.[32] All subsequent actions are in effect limited since the people (acting as the sovereign *or* through their representatives) enjoy only qualified power after implementing a complex governmental network that works to offset the force of popular government and stave off the possibility of arbitrary rule.[33]

Communitarians, by contrast, have made no analogous pledge to accept the agreement of themselves as sovereign founders and to constrain the authority of themselves as a governing collective. In fact, communitarians have largely confused or ignored the distinction made by most constitutionalists between the two separate democratic peoples, implicitly insisting that the two are equivalent.[34] To be sure, there can be no clearly authoritative founding people in modern American communitarian theory; for to identify a distinct communitarian founder would be to take decision-making authority out of the hands of the particular community. To suggest that their hands may be tied by a commitment to some predetermined agreement or charter is to admit that the current collectivity is not worthy of making the most important political decisions themselves. Accordingly, and because modern communitarian theorists implicitly refuse to subscribe to such a notion, Hamilton's distinction between the "people as political decision makers" and the "people as founders" becomes conflicted; democrats and founders in the communitarian canon become one in the same.

Turning now to the second theoretical/historical point, I contend that the Anti-Federalist press for a bill of rights to constrain the federal government *advances* rather than undermines the claim that communitarians are unable to sustain the principles of modern constitutionalism. Indeed, it may seem a bit curious to argue that a direct call for constitutional limits actually furthers the opposite position, but it seems all too clear that the Anti-Federalist clamor for constitutional restraints was of a different sort and was directed at a different constituency than that expressed by proponents of ratification. And this subtle difference is critical from a modern constitutionalist perspective. By insisting on a bill of rights, Anti-Federalists hoped to give *communities and states* freedom to cultivate their own conceptions of the good. They wanted to clear the way for states to be distinct and to remain largely insular and homogeneous. The Anti-Federalist referred to as Agrippa insisted that "the idea of an uncompounded republic, on an average, one thousand miles in length, and eight hundred in breadth, containing six millions of white inhabitants all reduced to the same standard of morals, or habits, and of laws, is in itself an absurdity, and contrary to the whole experience of mankind."[35] He, like so many Anti-Federalists of his generation, believed that local communities and states were more easily managed precisely because their inhabitants shared common roots. "It is impossible," he wrote, "for one code of laws to suit [both] Georgia and Massachusetts."[36]

Of course, this is completely in keeping with the modern communitarian agenda. Modern communitarians, and particularly modern *conservative* communitarians, are far less interested in cultivating shared bonds at the national level. They would much prefer to allow states and localities to promote particular values independent of federal interference. Yet it is precisely the constitutionalist who responds that states and localities—like nations—are not immune from a capacity to tyrannize. Human nature does not somehow change simply because the scale of the polity is smaller: if given the chance, local and state political figures, and the local communities themselves, will still abuse power. The Federalist constitutional structure is designed to limit this abuse; the ideal Anti-Federalist constitution, in contrast, would have done just the opposite. It would have permitted the states to ignore the rights of the minority, and to do so in the name of greater homogeneity and efficiency.

To put the point another way, the push by Anti-Federalists to include a bill of rights limiting the authority of the federal government was aimed at maximizing the autonomy of the local communities. The Anti-Federalist movement to adopt a bill of rights was in many respects a political maneuver in response to the emerging reality that the Articles of Confederation—their preferred constitution—was being replaced. If they could not have a constitution that created an impotent federal government, a constitution whose powers could be trumped by simple state legislation, they at least wanted assurances that the new federal government would not interfere in the affairs of their individual states and communities. In that respect, Anti-Federalists were genuinely interested in constitutional limitation—but only insofar as the national government is prohibited from imposing a single conception of the good on individual states. We need only recall the earlier passage by Agrippa condemning the consolidation of moral standards under one central government as proof of the Anti-Federalists' more peculiar definition of constitutionalism. For the true constitutionalist, restraint that does not reach all the way down to the smallest communities is never sufficient, because localities have the capacity to oppress just as easily as nations do. Consider Madison's position opposing small-scale republics in *Federalist* 10, or his identical concerns in "Vices of the Political System of the United States," which, because of their relation to our entire discussion of human nature and constitutional limits, ought to be quoted at length:

> In republican government the majority however composed, ultimately give the law. Whenever therefore an apparent interest or common passion unites a majority what is to restrain them from unjust violations of the rights and interests of the minority, or of individuals? Three motives only: 1) a prudent regard to their own good as involved in the general and permanent good of the Community. This consideration although of decisive weight in itself, is found by experience to be too often unheeded. It is too often forgotten, by nations as well as by individuals that honesty is the best policy. 2) Respect for character. However strong this motive may be in individuals, it is considered as very insufficient to restrain them from injustice. In a multitude its efficacy is diminished in proportion to the number which is to share the praise or the blame. . . . 3) Will religion the only remaining motive be a sufficient restraint? It is not pretended to be such on men individually considered. Will its effect be greater on them considered in an aggregate view? Quite the reverse. . . . Place three individuals in a situation wherein the interest of each depends on the voice of the others, and give to two of them an interest opposed to the rights of the third? Will the latter be secure? . . . Will two thousand in a like situation be less likely to encroach on the rights of one thousand? The contrary is witnessed by the notorious factions and oppressions which take place in corporate towns limited as the opportunities are, and in little republics when uncontrolled by apprehensions of external danger.[37]

Moreover, the Anti-Federalist reliance on state constitutions as mechanisms to constrain unfettered political power was hardly more comforting. The Anti-Federalist purpose in opposing ratification in the first place sprang from a belief that small-scale republics, with mostly homogeneous populations, were more easily governed. State constitutions, therefore, were not concerned with the relationship between the majority and the minority; indeed, they often reflected the beliefs (religious and otherwise) of the state's dominant group. But again, these constitutions did not truly limit the power of those insular populations or, more accurately, the representatives of the dominant group. Certainly the Massachusetts state constitution did not constrain the singular religious beliefs of its largely Protestant population. In fact, the Massachusetts Constitution of 1780 unabashedly embraces a singular religious faith within the document itself. Article III clearly places Christian religious beliefs ahead of all other competing ideologies for scarce state resources. It is important to quote it again:

> To promote their happiness, and to secure the good order and preservation of their government, the people of this commonwealth have a right to invest their legislature with the power to authorize and require, and the legislature shall, from time to time, authorize and require, the several towns, parishes, precincts, and other bodies politic, or religious societies, to make suitable provision, at their own expense, for the institution of the public worship of God, and for the support and maintenance of public Protestant teachers of piety, religion, and morality, in all cases where such provision shall not be made voluntarily.

What the federal constitution did (and does) differently is adopt a largely neutral stance on the good. In doing so, the liberal U.S. Constitution objectively, which is to say explicitly, blocks the ability of representatives of the sovereign to abuse power. The same cannot be said for those state constitutions that the Anti-Federalists preferred.

In short, then, a modern constitutionalist willingly surrenders the idea of attaining certain communal aspirations in favor of objective control and stable rule.[38] Hence, in the same way that sovereign Americans are enjoined (because tolerance and neutrality are fundamentally constitutional values in the United States) from implementing (through political measures) a strictly white supremacist or Neo-Nazi platform, communitarians must admit that to qualify as constitutionalist, some of their shared visions (even if one of them is not tolerance) may never come to fruition. And that poses a serious problem, for any restraint on democratic authority in the communitarian universe is tantamount to a limit on the ability of the people to determine for themselves their shared future, and needless to say, that runs counter to the first principle of communitarian theory.

At issue here is the communitarian propensity to place collective decision making—or democracy—at the forefront and foundation of all political life. To the pure communitarian democrat, the idea that the current people can be bound by an external contract, particularly in such areas as determining the community's collective future, is anathema. It is clear from the communitarian literature that community-based theorists recognize the importance of establishing certain alternative institutions. Galston, for example, argues that in

many situations judicial review is an absolute necessity to thwart the sometimes oppressive tendencies of majority faction.[39] Nevertheless, as a necessary
part of the current conception of communitarian polities, these institutions
play a predominantly subordinate and supplementary role to the collective
citizenry, whereas in constitutionalist regimes they occupy an equal and counterbalancing position.[40] The basic idea of communitarianism and the internal-
ist nature of the ideology suggest that any check on the will of the true collective is antithetical to the community's central purpose. Whether right or
wrong, deference in communitarian regimes is always given to the imminent
sovereign (or its representatives) and its ability to mandate a conception of the
good life; after all, it is that good life that ultimately forms and binds us
together. But simultaneously, that attitude ignores one of the fundamental
features of modern constitutionalist thought.

The Tension between Constitutionalism and Democracy

This discussion highlights one of the more controversial aspects of constitutional theory: the fact that publicly approved policies can be flatly prohibited, not by force or by reason, but by a written document. One of the
questions that has plagued most constitutional observers since the Enlightenment centers on why the present community of individuals should be constrained or limited by the actions and covenants of past individuals or groups.
In other words, at issue here is why, specifically, "should a constitutional
framework, ratified [in prior generations], have such enormous power over
our lives today?"[41] Admittedly an advocate of strong constitutionalism, Laurence Tribe is even perplexed. He has wondered "why a nation that rests
legality on the consent of the governed would choose to constitute its political life in terms of commitments to an original agreement?"[42] Why should
a political regime that places sovereign authority in the hands of the people
not similarly trust those people to make appropriate and warranted political
judgments?

At the base of this inquiry lies the fundamental tension between constitutionalism and democracy. On the one hand, democracy celebrates the notion of
collectively (and freely) willing a shared future, but on the other hand, in order
to avoid the possibility of arbitrary, capricious, and tyrannical rule, constitutionalism works specifically to hinder the full realization of that aspiration.
Murphy, Fleming, and Barber have considered this tension at length.[43] To them,

constitutionalism, like democratic theory, celebrates the notion of human dignity and the "moral worth of the individual"; but unlike democrats, constitutionalists "tend to be more pessimistic" about the precise distribution and practice of political authority. "Constitutionalism is constantly concerned with the human penchant to act selfishly and abuse power," and as such, it is willing to "reject the primacy of process."[44] Similarly, Francis Sejersted has studied the perceived incompatibility of constitutionalism and democracy and has concluded that the friction produced by the two political principles stems from the need, in modern regimes, to provide an outlet for positive liberty while still maintaining a high level of stability.[45] Democracy connotes something positive—the granting of freedom to determine a collective will. In contradistinction, constitutionalism connotes an equally negative force—the circumscription of state power. Together, the two appear to be mostly incongruous.

Thus, to place primacy on democratic rule is, from a constitutionalist perspective, deeply problematic. The trouble occurs when stability is sacrificed in favor of positive liberty.[46] A polity grounded principally on the democratic process can possibly deteriorate into a tyrannical or totalitarian system, where rule by popular sovereignty often leads to the suppression of alternative views. As a result, modern constitutionalism, while it approves of democratic procedures, is careful to articulate institutional checks on the power of the democratic representatives. In essence, constitutionalism provides a powerful antidote for the occasional abuses that might plague a system based ostensibly on democracy and popular government. In the end, therefore, democracy must be acknowledged as simply one important feature of a vast constitutional framework. "Modern constitutionalism does not reject the democratic processes, it treats them as a means—and though necessary, still an insufficient means—to achieve what it considers the ultimate civic purpose of protecting individual liberty."[47]

The deeper sentiment expressed by Murphy, Fleming, and Barber that democracy is but an instrument to fulfill constitutional ends is largely correct. That is, they accurately depict the more profound notion that democracy (regardless of any connection it might share with liberalism, I would add) must be seen as part of a process that undergirds or supports the theory of constitutionalism.[48] In the world of contemporary politics, where legitimacy and stability are forever coveted, democracy can be an important means to achieve those two critical goals, but it is also and fundamentally just that—a means. John Hart Ely, who more than perhaps any other constitutional theo-

rist praises the virtues of democracy, would even admit that democratic conduct must be viewed as an mechanism or component of a polity's larger
constitutional design. His theory of judicial review suggests that "rule in accord with the consent of a majority of those governed is the core of the
American governmental system." But "just as obviously," he continues, "that
cannot be the whole story, since a majority with untrammeled power to set
governmental policy is in a position to deal itself benefits at the expense of the
remaining minority." As such, Ely correctly observes that the Constitution
"contains several sorts of devices" meant "to combat" potential majoritarian
tyranny.[49]

The constitutionalist's preference for constitutionalism over democracy is
self-evident. Majorities—even those that approach unanimity—have throughout history abused individuals and groups, all purportedly in the name of the
"community." In the United States alone (and in spite of this country's largely
objective constitution), minority groups have long been oppressed. But the
ideals of constitutionalism have also been powerful ammunition for these
same groups. One need only look to the NAACP's attempt to use the judiciary
to further policies of desegregation to realize that if the ideals of justice and
fairness are ones to be pursued and celebrated, then constitutionalism, and not
the principle of collective decision making, provides the best vehicle to achieve
the desired ends.

Because of the value communitarians place on the images of democracy,
consensus, discussion, and deliberation—values that most American communitarian practitioners would admit are primary—the tension between constitutionalism and democracy becomes all the more acute. Communitarians are
essentially and thoroughly democrats; while constitutionalists, although not
antidemocrats, are not exclusively or even principally democratic. Utilitarian
theorists who subscribe to constitutionalist rules willingly accept the fact that
in pluralist societies, democracy and public participation can only get one so
far, and that in the end, constitutionalism must step in and restore limited and
purposeful order.

Daniel Bell, on the other hand, contends that the political process, the practice of democracy, and the principle of cooperation can, alone, achieve similar
results. To this point, Bell argues that nation-states should attempt to incorporate the attitude prevalent in small-scale "psychological" communities—that
politics is best when participation is based on face-to-face interaction—within
their overall decision-making scheme. Although difficult to implement, the

type of cooperative attitude that is typical in small-scale communities will go a long way toward eliminating the atmosphere of divisiveness that so often plagues pluralist societies, the climate that in constitutionalist regimes is alleviated by restraints on power. "Widespread, civic-minded participation," Bell says, may be an unachievable aspiration, but that is not to say we should stop aspiring to reach that goal. "Put positively, even if our deepest aspirations are unrealizable in their fully developed form, we should still strive to realize those aspirations;"[50] for it is those aspirations that will ultimately save us.

The communitarian impulse, therefore, rests most profoundly on the notion that the community as a whole, and in solidarity, should work together to resolve shared controversies. One of the major goals of any communitarian thinker is to eliminate (or at least downplay) the rampant dependence on private interests that accompanies a hyperindividualistic liberal society. The privatization of wants and needs, Glendon remarks, "is less about human dignity and freedom than about insistent, unending desires."[51] In his own words, Bellah even hopes that "at every level, new forms of citizen involvement should transform the very conception of interests."[52] From Etzioni to MacIntyre to Sandel, communitarians universally maintain that the way to attenuate private interests is first to recognize and resurrect the idea that private desires can be reframed in terms of public or communal interests, and second, to organize political society around that credo. Institutions of the private and public sphere are thus placed within the communitarian design specifically to help isolate, identify, and embrace the community's shared understanding or collective consciousness, and not primarily to prevent the abuses that often result from collective action. They act as facilitators more than as restraints.

Such a stance can be deeply troubling for the modern constitutionalist. It is, after all, those competing interests and the various political institutions where the competition is played out that help ensure limited government. If the "constitutionalist insists on institutional limitations beyond those of open political processes to curb government," then the communitarian, who relies solely on the procedural call for consensus and compromise, cannot be a true constitutionalist. That is to say, because the communitarian doctrine rests principally on the process of consensus building and compromise, constitutionalism, which requires something more than mere democratic processes, cannot fully be realized in communitarian form.[53] And in terms of constitutional restraints, a communitarian has to rely on the notion of consensus. To admit that the community and its innate capacity to recognize and celebrate shared constitutive values is in any way hindered by a force that exists from without is to subscribe to an altogether different image of communitarianism, one that is not reflected in the contemporary American movement.

Until now I have been primarily interested in challenging the communitarian position from a constitutionalist perspective. I have argued that community-centered ideology cannot sustain the principles of modern—that is, objective—constitutionalism. But perhaps the standards I have set are too high. Perhaps I am subjecting communitarianism to a measure that no other ideology, including liberalism, can satisfy. Perhaps, in short, I have inadvertently exposed communitarian thought to a constitutional double standard. Before closing this chapter, I will turn my attention briefly to the possibility that liberalism can successfully replicate the modern constitutionalist project. I need not go into great detail because throughout this work I have embraced two related positions: that the U.S. Constitution provides the best example of a modern constitution, and that the U.S. text is primarily liberal. But a more direct discussion of the relationship between liberalism and constitutionalism certainly seems warranted.

To begin, let us consider sections 136 and 137 of John Locke's *Second Treatise of Government*, where he defends a decidedly modern constitutionalist position. Earlier in the work, Locke writes that "the great end of man's entering into society" is the "enjoyment of their properties in peace and safety," and the key to that enjoyment is the establishment of the legislative power.[54] He continues by praising the legislative power, claiming that it is not only "supreme" but also "sacred and unalterable." And yet it is not unlimited. He writes: The authority of the legislative branch "is not, nor can possibly be, absolutely arbitrary over the lives and fortunes of the people." Nor can it "assume to itself a power to rule by extemporary, arbitrary decrees, but is bound to dispense justice and to decide the rights of the subject by promulgated, standing laws, and known authorized judges." The legislature, in other words, cannot be left to follow its own will, for as Locke notes, no man should be a judge in his own case and no governmental body should be left unregulated to restrain its own self-interest. In fact, Locke contends that man enters civil society in order to find the stability that comes from knowing that clearly discernible rules have replaced the laws that existed in the state of nature. The existence of a social compact that identifies certain prearranged and agreed-upon sets of rules, he says, is precisely why the individual is willing to leave the uncertainty of state of nature and enter civil society.

In section 137, Locke is even more explicit in his disdain for arbitrary and impulsive power. He insists that "whatever form the commonwealth is under, the ruling power ought to govern by declared and received laws and not by extemporary dictates and undetermined resolutions." Furthermore, he is convinced that individuals will be far worse off in a situation where the established civil government rules by capriciousness than they might have been had they simply refused to unite and remained captives of the state of nature. Indeed, in the same way that individuals need laws to restrain their arbitrary actions, governments require some force to bridle their urge to rule by self-interested preferences. "For all the power government has," Locke claims, "it ought to be exercised by established, promulgated laws; that both the people may know their duty and be safe and secure within the limits of the law; and the rulers, too, kept within their bounds and not to be tempted by the power they have in their hands to employ it to such purposes and by such measures as they would not have known, and own not willingly." The greatest irony for Locke is that mankind can escape the brutality and insecurity of the state of nature only to be confronted with an equally uncertain future as citizens of the civil society.

Locke, arguably the leading liberal voice of the modern age, is here defending the need for objective constitutionalism. Not only does he endorse the idea that the legislative power requires limits, but he also backs the notion that laws, including the fundamental law, should be knowable, discernible, and transparent, and that the rules directing the power of government ought not to be confused with the government itself: neither men nor governments, he repeats, should be judges in their own cases. Not coincidentally, the emerging influence of Locke's more individualistic theory signaled the decline in some regimes of the classical idea of republicanism. Indeed, the Enlightenment marks a paradigm shift in which the old notions of human virtue and holistic communalism gave way to the self-interested narcissism of the modern liberal self. The lessons of sections 136 and 137 of the *Second Treatise* appear to be consistent with that paradigm shift: Locke's liberal self is a pessimistic self; his liberal institutions of government are thus not to be trusted without accompanying restraints.

Enlarging on Locke's initial thought, the founders of the American constitutional regime understood that the individual's sense of security, so rooted in modern liberal theory, depends on the very presence of an external, discernible, and self-consciously limiting constitutional document. But there is more to the need for constitutional restraints than just maintaining security. Once the legacy of classical republicanism was replaced by modern liberalism somewhere around the time of the American founding, the objectives of the federal government changed dramatically. Whereas a republican vision of political society seeks to foster virtue not only for the betterment of private individuals but also for the development of the community's welfare, the liberal vision seeks roughly the opposite: to celebrate above all else the diversity of individual conceptions of the good and to suppress the notion of society as some sort of organic, autonomous entity whose good can be identified independent of its individual members. In the end, an enduring faith in the principle of self-restraint that accompanied the republican tradition, and that figures like Thomas Jefferson heralded, was replaced by the pessimism or realism that characterized the more liberal leaning thoughts of, say, Alexander Hamilton. No longer did the people of the United States share a belief that humans could be trusted to control themselves. Instead, they argued for assurances. Indeed, the contrast between the republican ideals of the past and the liberal values of the future was all too real at the time and manifested itself in constitutional form.

Primarily liberal constitutions like that which organizes the American polity are designed to be mostly neutral to competing conceptions of the good. It would be antithetical to suppose that a society bent on celebrating the diversity of individual goods could also permit the state, through constitutional means, to promote one good over all others. Liberal ideology therefore necessitates that constitutional measures be taken to ensure that the power of the state not be used to sponsor particular conceptions of the good. Some of those measures come in the form of rights guarantees; others appear in the form of institutional restraints. For better or worse, a modern liberal polity—a polity whose primary objective is the cultivation of individual interests rather than collective ones— requires meaningful constitutionalism to bridle the inevitable tendency of majorities, or communities, or representatives, or whomever to prefer their conceptions of the good over others. An external, discernible constitutional text that identifies limits on the will of the sovereign is the preferred choice among liberals to achieve that lofty ambition. It may not be the perfect antidote to tyranny, but it is the one liberals employ most frequently.

The Enabling Function of a Constitution

Hitherto we have been concerned chiefly with constitutionalism's call for limited or restrained power. In the last chapter we examined the principles required to satisfy the notion of objective constitutionalism, and the inquiry revealed that a polity attentive to the tenets of modern constitutionalism will likely need to ratify a separate or detached constitution that incorporates self-conscious limits with clearly discernible rules and values. In this chapter we have continued that primary inquiry by relating the idea of constitutional restraint to the contemporary communitarian penchant for democracy and absolute self-rule. But the exploration of constitutional limits and the corresponding introduction of democratic theory brings another critical component of modern constitutional theory to the fore. Indeed, constitutionalism cannot just be about limits on the power of the sovereign but must also include the patterned distribution or *enabling* of power. As Stephen Holmes has indicated: "In general, constitutional rules are enabling, not disabling; and it is therefore unsatisfactory to identify constitutionalism exclusively with limitations on power."[55] A constitution not only limits or confines the authority of the political leadership, but also, as a further way of legitimizing authority and making rule possible, grants power and distributes jurisdiction to various public institutions.

Modern constitutionalism suggests that the distribution of some political authority to public agencies is, in fact, a good idea, with the constitutional text acting as the primary enabling doctrine. In order for the institutions of a polity to possess the necessary energy to make elected officials as well as the public take notice, the fundamental law must have the capacity to infuse those institutions with power. The process begins when part of the community's original and complete freedom is given up, by the ratification process, to the constitution itself. Yet it is equally clear to the modern constitutionalist that once political power has been delegated, the constitution should then attempt to redistribute that transferred political authority, but this time to other institutions or agents.[56] The entire ratification process follows three separate stages. Prior to ratification, the sovereign enjoys all the power. We know this to be true because the sovereign can just as easily choose to reject the proposed constitution, thereby retaining all of its original authority. But if we assume that the sovereign does decide to ratify, then the second step in the ratification process involves the symbolic surrender of both pure freedom and unlimited power by the sovereign. In the critical third step, the constitution then delegates authority to various institutions, thereby enabling and empowering them on behalf of the sovereign to work within the rules set by the constitutional text. Obviously, the major concern for the modern constitutionalist is assuring the acquiescence of power so as to safeguard "a sense of fair play." But the third stage, the one that is in effect distributive, is of critical importance as well.

This idea that a constitution distributes power can, of course, be seen as an extension of the limitation principle of modern constitutionalism, but the key to completely understanding what is meant by constitutional delegation is to view the process, as Holmes does, from a positive rather than a negative perspective:

> One of the main pillars of constitutionalism, the separation of powers, is routinely described in purely negative terms, as a machine for preventing encroachment. Authority is divided to avoid excessive concentrations of power. One branch of government can "check" another, inhibiting despotism and disclosing corruption. But here, too, the negative connotations of constitutional binding obscure the positive purposes of institutional design.
>
> As a corrective to the conventional view, it is useful to conceive the separation of powers as a form of the division of labor, permitting a more efficient distribution and organization of governmental functions.[57]

Specifically, a constitution distributes power over a wide range of political institutions to make rule possible, to make it legitimate. The enabling function of a constitution is needed so that the actions by representatives of the sovereign (majorities, other institutions of government, even unified collectives) are considered valid and authoritative; for without this theoretical maxim, the practice of politics is once again rendered arbitrary.[58] Delegation and distribution of authority, therefore, are meant precisely to ensure that all institutions of government enjoy the necessary power and legitimacy to prevent the rise of tyranny, while at the same time, efficiently and effectively practicing the art of politics.[59]

The theoretical argument can be seen more thoroughly by again considering the distinct roles played by the different "peoples" in a constitutionalist regime. In constructing a constitutional system, the people as founders enable or empower the people as political decision makers. They construct institutions that act as agents for the citizens in the practice of everyday governance, and they do so in order to give legitimacy and validity to: (1) the institutions they create, and (2) the policies that emanate from those very institutions. In essence, they create a division between the constitution and politics so that the latter, with its tendency toward arbitrariness and caprice, can stand for something and be considered meaningful. Without a legitimate distribution of power from an external and authoritative source, the argument goes, majorities and other purely political institutions in constitutionalist regimes are largely groundless, their policies mostly vacuous. Absent a specific source to infuse a degree of legitimacy into the various institutions of government, the actual policy initiatives of any political regime will doubtless be seen as arbitrary. The constitution, in the end, provides that essential source of legitimacy.

Corresponding to Publius' argument in *Federalist* 78, the enabling component of modern constitutionalism must be viewed as a series of interconnected deliberative events.[60] The first (and original) deliberative event, referred to as constitution making, involves the sovereign in the act of creation.[61] At the point of founding, the people as constitution makers create a political order by designing institutions and giving them the necessary power and authority to practice politics in a legitimate and effective manner. In fact, what is granted, and thus what specifically legitimizes or validates politics, is precisely the ability to exercise political discretion in the name of the sovereign. At the moment of founding, the sovereign (as founder) is essentially granting authority to the people (as political decision makers) to act in its place, to represent it in the process of political deliberation and policy making. But ironically, the very act of creation signals the end of the founder's role. Indeed, the constitution is the singular act of a sovereign people unified in the common purpose of creating a polity. But once that act is concluded, the people as constitution makers "retire into the clouds, apparently aware of the irony [not only] that too much constitution-making speech crowds out the possibilities of politics,"[62] but also that they have an essential, but most certainly limited, task.

The second deliberative event is ongoing: the common act of political governance. Often tedious and unremarkable, the process of policy making, judicial interpretation, execution of legislation, and so forth are all considered part of this second, ongoing, purely political event. But what is most critical to note is that, in accordance with the enabling principle of modern constitutionalism, the purely political is distinct from, and dependent upon, the original founding. The procedures and outcomes (legislation, executive orders, judicial decisions, etc.) of this second event are considered valid only as long as they comport with the initial mandate. A political institution represents the sovereign only if it fully accepts the sovereign's founding authority. The problem arises when politics and constitutionalism are absorbed into one another, when the political (the second event) and the constitutional (the initial event) become one in the same. At that point, where there is no clear demarcation between politics and constitutions (as when there is no clear separation between the people as founders and the people as political decision makers), the direct distribution of power is not possible, and the practice of everyday governance becomes a largely illegitimate endeavor.

The American political system rests most profoundly on the positive form of this fundamental constitutional theory. In contrast, however, the constitutional delegation of political power has serious repercussions for the current design of communitarian politics. By now the communitarian affinity for democracy, public participation, and the way of life each engenders is well documented. Barber, of course, is perfectly clear about his devotion to the attributes of democratic participation, provided they support some form of "strong democracy." Again, his feeling is that in order to reshape the collective existence of America's citizens, we must rely on the transformative power of active and democratic public involvement. Similarly, the Responsive Communitarian Platform stresses the need to "make government more representative, more participatory, and more responsive to all members of the community." The means to accomplish such a task is first to revamp a corrupt political system bent on protecting private interests, and second, to encourage group participation in the reformulation of a new "moral voice."

Among the theoretical communitarians, perhaps the most aggressive sponsor of a vibrant self-governing polity is Michael Walzer. In fact, Galston even remarks that "of all Walzer's general commitments, the most pervasive is to democracy."[63] Walzer's *Spheres of Justice* reveals a commitment to democracy that goes far beyond the simple endorsement of a "one man, one vote" scheme, or a protection of private interests through electoral procedures. Like Barber, Etzioni, Glendon, and most other communitarians, Walzer insists that the greater the participation in the political sphere, the deeper the constitutive attachments that bind citizens to each other. "The more intense forms of participation," he writes, "actually reduce the distance between leaders and followers."[64] Yet in his relentless support for the idea of self-government, Walzer has overlooked the all-important redistributive element of constitutionalism: he has ignored the important distinction between the political and the constitutional. To this point, *Spheres of Justice* offers a curious statement. "Democracy is a way of allocating power and legitimating its use," Walzer begins, "or better," he concludes, "it is *the political way* of allocating power. Every extrinsic reason is ruled out."[65] Consistent with the general communitarian ideology, Walzer suggests here that democracy and self-government are the principal instruments with which a community should organize itself and that constitutionalism (or any other "extrinsic reason") is not. Democracy will not only help determine the scope of shared interests, but it will also determine which office and which political agent should legitimately possess public authority. If that is the case, however—if democracy is, in fact, "the political way of allocating power" in a specific community—then the constitution, whose job it is to objectively oversee the proper distribution of all political authority, again becomes a largely trivial object. If legitimacy and authority is based solely on a popularity contest—who can get the most votes or who best represents the will of the majority—the possibility that some will be left behind and others will be abused rises exponentially.

In most communitarian systems, institutions, both physical and cultural, have the capacity like no other force to transform individuals. Yet when placed alongside the fundamental tenets of modern constitutionalism, those same institutions are forever rendered subordinate. Instead of counterbalancing the sometimes unreflective or fickle mood of a citizenry, political agencies and cultural traditions are relegated to secondary status, deferring always and entirely to the will of the democratic populace. From a constitutionalist perspective this fact is profoundly troubling, for democracy and constitutionalism remain, theoretically at least, at odds with one another. On the one hand, democracy celebrates the capacity of the people to realize a shared future together, but on the other, constitutionalism ensures that certain visions are never fully achieved. Constitutionalism can support many democratic principles, but it will never fall prostrate before those practices. The constitutional design can never abandon its primary organizational and distributive position, thereby allowing a self-governing community to validate its own internal practices. Unfortunately, modern communitarian theory has confused or ignored that fundamental maxim.

Because communitarians confound the two peoples in a constitutionalist system, they combine the primary and secondary "events" and absorb the political directly into the constitutional. As such, the constitutional empowerment of political agencies or institutions becomes an unachievable goal in the communitarian construction. The organizational system is essentially redesigned every time the community acts in a purely political way because there is no clear distinction made between constitutional order and political practice. Accordingly, the institutions of the political regime or the constitution itself are rendered virtually meaningless in this type of system. There is no legitimate, valid, or effective power in the communitarian universe because there has been no definitive distribution or transfer of that power from the people as founders to the people as political decision makers. Effective legitimacy or validity, for the very policies that emerge from communitarian deliberations, is therefore absent.

This, again, goes directly to the base of modern constitutionalist theory. Contemporary communitarian theory appears to be somewhat ill-defined as constitutionalism, in its modern form, apparently extends a bit beyond the communitarian reach. The core principles of American communitarianism, that is, seem either to ignore or to outwardly conflict with the major tenets of modern constitutionalism, rendering the theory itself pragmatically suspect. Constitutional objectivity cannot always be ensured as long as the communitarian position continues to defend internally derived political values and procedures. Moreover, the identification of self-conscious constitutional restraints within a communitarian polity remains a dubious proposition. In the end, communitarian theory fails to measure up as a serious alternative to liberal constitutionalism; and it does so because of want of self-reflection.

CHAPTER SIX

Mixed Constitutionalism and the Communitarian Hope

The theoretical notion of communitarianism, I have argued thus far, appears to be mostly incompatible with the basic constitutionalist ideal. To put the point slightly differently, it should now be clear that the communitarian challenge to liberal dominance is circumscribed by the inability on the part of major communitarian supporters to envision a community-centered regime that is also attentive to the main components of modern constitutionalism. In the first place, the politics of community cannot adequately sustain an objectively detached and discernible charter; and secondly, the current conception of communitarianism has a difficult time admitting to self-imposed limits or restraints on the jurisdiction of democratic self-government. In the end, what remains a significant and important challenge to liberal theory appears to lack the necessary practical ingredients to make it a viably modern constitutional project.

To this point, I have been mainly concerned with the imaginary construction of a communitarian polity. Using the broadest possible theoretical terms so as to adequately cover a largely undefined and expansive ideological position, I have asked how the principles of contemporary communitarianism and modern constitutionalism mesh. In this chapter I intend to explore the current universe of real constitutionalist polities by singling out two regimes whose organizing charters—"constitutions" in the broadest sense of the term—do not exactly resemble the principally liberal ones so familiar to us. Alternative examples of constitutional texts do, in fact, exist; and in order to complete the study of communitarianism and constitutionalism, we need to explore how these constitutional forms manage to organize and empower their particular political societies. By identifying and investigating two of these alternative models, the hope is that we will more clearly see why predominantly communitarian regimes cannot support modern constitutionalist maxims.

My purpose in exploring alternative constitutional designs is again to highlight, this time in a slightly different manner, the incompatibility of communitarian thought and modern constitutional theory. In the pages that follow, I do not want to suggest that nonliberal or semi-liberal constitutions are defective in any way; indeed, as in the case of Israel, they are often the best matches for the type of political regime desired. Nonetheless, I do want to suggest that these constitutions are not wholly *modern*. For better or worse, the particular constitution that informs the Israeli polity embraces none of the principles of modern constitutionalism. It is neither objective nor impartial. As a series of governing documents, it does not exist outside or apart from the institutions it empowers; nor does it identify meaningful and discernible limits on the power of the sovereign. That, of course, is not to say that the constitution of Israel is not a constitution at all, only that it is not a *modern* constitution.

Similarly, the semi-liberal constitution of the German Republic also does not fully qualify as a modern document. In contrast to the Israeli governing charter, the German Basic Law *does* reside externally, and *is* in some sense discernible. Its liberal pillar permits it to rest on certain modern constitutionalist foundations. But the relationship between the extremes of individualism and community found in the text is at best an uneasy one, and that has very real consequences for the document's capacity to identify self-conscious restraints. Recent history has demonstrated, for example, that the limits supposedly imposed on representatives of the sovereign by a list of individual rights can be tempered or modified by the general will of the community. Tangible constraints on government, that is, can be subordinated by particular policies if the consequences of those policies prove beneficial to the community at large. In those instances, rare as they may be, it is difficult to characterize the German constitution as a document that can effectively obstruct the wishes of the majority. Once again, we are thrust back into a scenario where we must decide between the desires of the community and the convictions of the modern constitutionalist.

Alternative Constitutional Designs

Surely, no one will be too surprised to learn that primarily liberal constitutions—constitutions that do not articulate a specific conception of the good—have been overwhelmingly favored by most newly formed states in the post-Enlightenment era.[1] The success of polities like the United States has resulted in both the transplantation and the replication of many constitutional clauses found in the American document. But these predominantly liberalist texts around the world are not the only constitutions that have emerged over the past two centuries. A variety of nonliberal and semi-liberal constitutions have also been introduced that go a long way toward challenging the dominant position of the liberal-constitutionalist paradigm. Certain polities have, for one reason or another, chosen to compose constitutional organs that celebrate the value of community. These states have preferred to endorse fundamental laws that identify and promote a particularist or specific conception of the good, oftentimes in direct opposition to the interests and concerns of the nation's unconstituted minority.

Still other constitutional foundings have adopted a less-dramatic model. Indeed, those regimes have refused to abandon liberal ideology altogether and instead have attempted to integrate liberal principles with communitarian ones in the same constitutional charter. I would define these constitutions as semi-liberal in that they tend to include some of the most basic liberal ideas (including state neutrality) while also recognizing a critical nonliberal component that often successfully tempers the hyperindividualistic tendencies of predominantly liberal regimes. Characteristic of semi-liberal constitutions is the reality that liberal principles can be juxtaposed with constitutional clauses that isolate the community's (and not the individual's) interests as paramount. Graham Walker refers to these designs as "mixed constitutions," and he reminds us that Publius recognized the U.S. text as, in some ways, an experiment in mixed constitutionalism.[2] Following the lead presented by Aristotle and Montesquieu, the American framers envisioned a political order organized around separate governmental agencies and powerful institutional checks as well as both liberal and republican virtues.

Yet the American illustration is far from the most vivid. The republican heritage of the United States cannot be refuted, but neither can it be denied that other constitutional documents and other political regimes better capture the essence of the semi-liberal constitution.[3] It can be said with confidence that our Bill of Rights and the subsequent liberal provisions of the Fourteenth Amendment do not fully share the same republican or community-based influence that characterizes the original text. When the First Amendment commands that Congress shall "make no law abridging freedom of speech," it does not also include a disclaimer permitting the institutions of government to all but ignore that central lesson when the community's well-being is threatened. Time and again the judiciary has reminded us that the purpose of the First Amendment free speech provision is to protect those messages that we, as a majority, despise. Additionally, the Just Compensation Clause of the Fifth Amendment specifically, and by its very nature, prevents the government from adjusting the amount of compensation in the name of the community, even when the taking would significantly benefit the whole. Consider the recent contribution of the Supreme Court to this debate. Some of the most controversial (and arguably most important) judicial opinions over the last fifty years [*Human Rights Again*] have suppressed the welfare of the community in favor of the rights of the individual: *R.A.V. v City of St. Paul*, 505 U.S. 377 (1992); *Collin v Smith*, 578 F. 2d 1197 (7th Cir., 1978); *Texas v Johnson*, 491 U.S. 397 (1989); *Miranda v Arizona*, 384 U.S. 436 (1966); *Gideon v Wainwright*, 372 U.S. 335 (1963); the Pentagon Papers Case, 403 U.S. 713 (1971); *Lee v Weisman*, 505 U.S. 577 (1992); *Brandenburg v Ohio*, 395 U.S. 444 (1969), and many others, all involved disputes where the community's well-being was pitted directly against the rights of the individual. And in each case, the Court consistently interpreted the provisions of the Bill of Rights as protecting the interests of the individual over the welfare of the community. In each case, the Court weighed the very real threat to the community against the admittedly more narrow interests of the individual and resolved that the protection of personal liberty outweighed the possibility of serious communal harm.[4]

In contrast to the U.S. example, Israel and Germany represent two very different constitutional models whose main rights-based provisions share one striking feature in common: they tend to go well beyond the more traditional methods of promoting the freedom of the individual by including an equally powerful—and importantly offsetting—community-based component. Indeed, both countries are governed by "constitutions" whose main axioms severely regulate the freedom of the individual to act in opposition to the common good. Israel's unwritten constitution places the ideals of liberalism and the corresponding liberal propensity to remain neutral regarding questions of the good far down the list of priorities. In that regard, it can be included among the nonliberal examples. The German Basic Law, by contrast, includes a variety of constitutional clauses that should be defined as, at best, semi-liberal. Particular provisions of the German constitution combine importantly liberal declarations with undeniably communitarian ones. Indeed, the German Basic Law is a far more striking example of the mixed constitutional model than that found in the American illustration.

Non-Liberal Constitutionalism: The Israeli Model

The incompatibility of communitarian principles and modern constitutionalist teachings does not necessarily preclude the existence of a certain type of communitarian constitutionalist regime. Indeed, what may be possible is a regime that is principally communitarian in form but whose governing charter more closely mirrors the *classical* version of constitutionalism, and not the more narrowly defined *modern* one.

Israel represents just such a regime. Gary Jacobsohn is entirely correct when he defines the Israeli constitution as primarily communitarian in nature.[5] The "communal model" in Israel, he says, "represents the idea of an extended community in which collective needs and visions often take precedence over individual ones."[6] The Jewish tradition of group solidarity (in theoretical opposition to liberal individualism), Jacobsohn says, effectively counters the "Western model of the state with its emphasis on impersonal and universal application of legal norms."[7] Individual rights are granted, but collective Jewish unity is primary; liberal tenets are present, but community or nonliberal principles are dominant. What makes the Israeli constitution communitarian, therefore, is the fact that it orders a regime that is committed most profoundly to a particularist or singularly substantive agenda, an agenda that by its very nature must suppress the liberal inclinations of its unconstituted and semi-constituted citizenry. Hence, what makes the Israeli constitution premodern is the fact that the unwritten text makes no attempt to remain objective; indeed, the logic of a particularistic state precludes that very possibility.

In fact, religious states in general appear to be the most obvious exemplars of the nonliberal constitutionalist model. Israel is a nation that is constitutionally committed to a (broadly defined) single way of life, a way of life that fully supports the traditions and culture of Judaism. All politics in Israel is governed in some sense by the teachings of the Torah, while Jewish symbols and values are in every sense of the word constitutive. As a result, Jews in Israel enjoy entitlements not similarly available to non-Jews. Non-Jews, it should be noted, do enjoy certain benefits, and these primarily take the form of specific rights and freedoms; but just the same, these individuals are barred from meaningfully contributing to Israel's common good. Israel, Walker suggests, is a nation that "is constitutionally dedicated to being a Jewish state. Jewish values, symbols and the Hebrew language are officially paramount, and Jews (returning from Diaspora) have entitlements in the Jewish state available to them by accident of birth and not available to Christians, Muslims, Buddhists, Gaians, or Wiccans."[8] In the end, Jews and non-Jews alike are protected by civil rights, but those rights become attenuated just as soon as they interfere with the nation's nonsecular mission.

Joav Peled also examines this feature of Israeli constitutionalism.[9] In attempting to place Arab residents within the realm of Israeli political participation, Peled argues that there are two forms of citizenship in Israel. Jews enjoy "republican" citizenship or "citizenship as practice," whereas Arabs must be satisfied with "liberal" or nonparticipatory citizenship. The distinction between the two formulations resides in the specific capacity to attend to the common good. Republican citizenship is a form of citizenship that encourages —but more importantly allows—members of the community to participate in the shaping of the collective good. Accordingly, all Jews are permitted to fashion for the state a definitively Jewish existence. Liberal citizenship, that which Arab-Israelis are left with, has no corresponding responsibility to define the nation's shared collective future. Citizenship for Israel's non-Jewish population is experienced, not as "practice," but rather as "status." There is, to put the same idea differently, no license to contribute to the determination of the nation's conception of the good, yet there is an understanding that the private convictions and personal independence of non-Jews will be tolerated by the state through legally sanctioned liberal freedoms so long as those personal beliefs do not conflict with the regime's central priority.

The unique nature of Israeli citizenship sheds light on the peculiarities of the Israeli constitution. As a contemporary polity, Israel is one of the few nations not presently constituted by a formal, written text. Indeed, the story of Israel's ongoing dialogue regarding the necessity of a constitutional document has been well documented.[10] During the period of independence, secularist leaders defended the need for a formal constitution, contending that Israel's future stability depended on the existence of a document that ordered the political institutions and identified both the rights and responsibilities of Jews returning from Diaspora. Not surprisingly, their arguments were met with strong opposition by Orthodox Jewish leaders who insisted "the only real constitution for a Jewish state is the Torah and the Jewish Law (*halakhah*) that flows from it."[11] The result was a sort of compromise between the two factions. A promise was made (and subsequently documented in the Declaration of Independence) to draft a formal constitutional text by October 1, 1948, that would attempt to reflect the political and religious beliefs of as many of Israel's Jewish groups as possible. The problem for modern secularists is that the promise was never formally realized.[12]

Instead, Israel's constitutional framework is made up of three important symbolic documents that have been granted constitutional status—the 1948 Declaration of Independence, the 1950 Law of Return, and the 1952 Covenant Between the State of Israel and the World Zionist Organization—and nine organizing pieces of legislation that act in a quasi-constitutional way (known collectively as the Basic Law). The three symbolic documents represent the vision espoused early in the history of the modern Jewish state—a vision of Israel as a haven for the universe of Jews from around the world—and identify certain rights and freedoms shared by all citizens of the state. The Basic Law, in contrast, acts more as an architectural blueprint describing the structures and powers of the various institutions of government. Together, these documents provide the foundation of Israel's constitutional polity.

What is interesting is that saturating all of these constitutional texts are specific references to the primary responsibility of all Jews to uphold their religious tradition and help defend the Jewish homeland. The Israeli Declaration of Independence, for example, speaks of Theodore Herzl's vision of the Jewish state, which "proclaim[s] the right of the Jewish people to national revival in their own country." The Declaration also insists that the "right of the Jewish people to be a nation, like all other nations, in its own sovereign state" is "self-evident." And even more explicit is section 5 of the Covenant Between the State of Israel and the World Zionist Organization, which reads in full:

> The mission of gathering in the exiles, which is the central task of the State of Israel and the Zionist Movement in our days, requires constant efforts by the Jewish people in the Diaspora; the State of Israel, therefore, expects the coopera-

tion of all Jews, as individuals and groups, in building up the state and assisting the immigration to it of the masses of the people, and regards the unity of all sections of Jewry as necessary for this purpose.

Adam Garfinkle has described the widespread support for the preservation of Jewish statehood as part of the "informal side" of Israel's constitutional debate.[13] He reminds us that there is broad social consensus on the belief that "a) Israel is a Jewish state; b) the preservation of national security is the preeminent function of government; c) the army therefore has to remain outside politics; and d) Israel must function as a society defined by communitarian principles if not literal socialist ideology."[14]

What legally empowers the Jewish people of Israel to maintain their particularistic political foundation, and thus what enables the regime to function as a communitarian polity, is precisely the unwritten character of the Israeli constitution. The major texts of the Israeli constitution have been recognized (by the judiciary and other institutions) as enjoying constitutional status. But, logically, they must also be seen as both affirmations of, and importantly subordinate to, the mission of Jewish statehood. When the Declaration of Independence pledges to "uphold the full social and political equality of all its citizens, without distinction of race, creed or sex," or when it "guarantee[s] full freedom of conscience, worship, education and culture" to all religions, it must do so with the knowledge that such a promise has to be qualified when the right of the individual—both Jewish and non-Jewish—impedes the specific priorities of the Jewish state. In other words, the Israeli Declaration of Independence (as well as the other constitutional documents) is at once an important symbol of the Jewish state and a source of liberal protection for all Israeli citizens. And therein lies the contradiction: on the one hand, the exact purpose of the Declaration of Independence is to create a particularistic regime based on a specific religious teaching; but on the other hand, that very document talks of equality and freedom, ideas that conjure up the image of state neutrality. Indeed, Israel is anything but neutral to different ways of life. In the ongoing debate between the right and the good, Israel has come down strongly on the side of the good.

Inconsistencies such as these are only possible in the contemporary era where a regime subscribes to the *classical* constitutionalist model. The unwritten Israeli constitution is not in any way objective, and that is likely the way it ought to be. Israel cannot afford to be governed by a modern constitution because such a particularistic state cannot be controlled by a document that may, by its very design, impose restraints on the collective decision-making body. One can certainly debate whether or not the unwritten Israeli constitution exists externally from the government in an oversight capacity[15] and whether or not the Israeli constitution is truly discernible, but there should be little debate over the question of self-imposed limitations. It must be recalled that what separates modern constitutionalism from its classical or traditional predecessor is the ability of the sovereign to abdicate its own power in certain critical areas and thus limit its own capacity to control all future activity. Israel, as a paradigmatic example of a contemporary communitarian nation, is logically unable to accept this modern constitutionalist premise and still maintain its pledge to defend a principally Judaic foundation. One can easily envision a situation where the two forces may clash. It is not hard to imagine an occasion in which the government has to take action to suppress anti-Jewish activity, and yet if a modern constitutionalist document proscribed that specific political action by establishing preexisting constraints on the power of the state, the very idea of an exclusively Jewish polity would be severely compromised.

A pinch of Israel's history regarding electoral politics provides an apposite and vivid illustration of the nature of this constitutional conflict. The story begins in 1965 when a group of Arab nationalists sought entry into the Israeli Parliament through the conventional method of popular election.[16] Under Israeli law, any political party that seeks election must first submit a candidate list to the Central Election Commission for approval. The Commission will then evaluate the list and declare whether the party can take part in the legislative elections. In this instance, the Commission denied the petition of al-Ard because the political party "denied the [territorial] integrity of the state of Israel and its very existence."[17] The platform of al-Ard, in other words, questioned the legitimacy of the Israeli state, insisting that the Jewish occupation of Palestine constituted an illegal and unjust appropriation of sacred Arab land. The Commission's response was that such a message brought into question the very foundation of the Israeli political experiment and that any political party espousing such beliefs should not be given permission to participate as a member of the state's most important decision-making body. Not surprisingly, al-Ard appealed the Commission's ruling to the Israeli Supreme Court.

The Israeli Supreme Court has long struggled with the conflicting tenets of the Declaration of Independence and its corresponding constitutional documents. The al-Ard case is certainly no exception to this rule.[18] In a 2-1 decision, the Supreme Court upheld the findings of the Central Election Commission, claiming that the party's very existence threatened the principle of Jewish self-determination. During the trial, there were two competing interpretations of the Commission's authority.[19] The first insisted that the Commission's power to reject petitions extended only to determinations about procedure. Specifically, the argument went, the Commission could only bar political parties from appearing on the ballot if they failed to get the appropriate signatures for the petition or if they did not submit the required number of candidate names. The Commission's oversight responsibilities, in other words, did not include passing judgment on the substance of any group's particular platform. The competing interpretation, however, suggested that the Commission's authority was broad enough to encompass decisions about the compatibility of individual party platforms to the central mission of the Jewish state. There was a belief that the Commission's power, in other words, included a substantive component and that it had every right to disqualify a political party if it believed the party might threaten, even slightly, the legitimacy of the country. The majority of the Court ultimately adopted this position. In a decidedly dramatic opinion, President Agranat's ruling in fact argued that the Commission must be allowed to make determinations about the impact al-Ard and similar parties might likely have on the continued existence of a Jewish homeland.

Some time later the Court was once again asked to review the decision on the part of the Central Election Commission to bar two separate political parties from participating in the 1984 general election.[20] This time, however, both parties were primarily Jewish agencies. The Progressive List for Peace (PLP) was a joint Jewish-Arab party dedicated to defending the principle of equality. The PLP's platform called for the elimination of all inequalities that resulted from the particularist nature of the state. All laws that favored Jews or that discounted non-Jews from contributing to the collective good were viewed by the PLP as discriminatory. If Israel was to become a modern state that takes seriously the idea of democracy, PLP officials argued, all differences in terms of political power must be eradicated.

In response to this posture, the Commission disqualified the PLP because the party "believes in principles that endanger the integrity and existence of the state of Israel, and the preservation of its distinctness as a Jewish state in accordance with the foundations of the state as expressed in the Declaration of Independence and the Law of Return."[21] Concepts such as political integrity, self-determination, and distinctness were used over and over again by the

Commission to describe the unique character of the Israeli state. Israel is a nation-state that makes no apologies for its particularistic tradition, and any political party that does not subscribe to that belief cannot, by law, participate in the political process.

Similarly, Kach (the second party) was disqualified by the Central Election Commission, but for different reasons. Kach supported an ultraconservative position on Israel's ethnic dilemma, which included the policy of exiling all Arabs from Israeli land. The Commission found that, like with the PLP, this platform also threatened the tenets of the Jewish state in that Kach would deny certain fundamental rights to a segment of the population. In the same way the PLP imperiled the state because its position was too liberal, Kach placed the state in jeopardy because its was not liberal enough.

Each decision was appealed, and the Supreme Court infused more controversy into the situation by reinstating both political parties. Indeed, the Court argued that Kach could not be barred from participating because its platform was not directed at the abolition of the Jewish state as that state is currently constructed. The implication of the Court's ruling, of course, was that any party that advanced the notion of a purely Jewish state (as opposed to a pluralist one) was not incompatible with the original premise of the Declaration of Independence. Extremist parties were acceptable, the Court intimated, so long as their extremism was of a particular kind.

In contrast, the Supreme Court reinstated the PLP because, in the eyes of the justices, there was not sufficient evidence to suggest that the party sought a fundamental reconfiguration of the state. The Court admitted that the Commission was within its authority to disqualify the PLP, but only if it could demonstrate beyond mere speculation that the party's goals were to negate the first principle of Jewish self-determination. And this the Commission had not done. The Court's ruling in the case obviously differed significantly from its earlier ruling on the fate of Kach. The PLP decision was not based primarily on substantive determinations, but rather on the belief that there was a lack of evidence that demonstrated incompatibility with the state's original mission. In essence, questions of process reinstated PLP, whereas questions of substance were central to the Court's decision regarding Kach.

These opinions—and the fact that both Kach and the PLP were successful in winning seats in the legislature in 1984—ultimately prompted the Knesset to take decisive action. In July 1985, the Knesset amended the Basic Law to include a statute that clarifies the role of the Central Election Commission and gives added support to its tendency to ban political parties that contest the central logic of the Jewish nation. The law reads:

> A list of candidates shall not participate in elections to the Knesset if its goals, explicitly or implicitly, or its actions include one of the following:
> (1) Negation of the existence of the State of Israel as the state of the Jewish people;
> (2) Negation of the democratic character of the State; or
> (3) Incitement of racism.

The words used by Israeli legislators in drafting this legislation were carefully chosen. Proposals, in fact, were made to abandon the wording at the end of section 1 and replace it with a more neutral declaration, a declaration that would instead read, "the state of Israel" or "the state of the Jewish people and its Arab citizens." Both proposals, however, were rejected in favor of the original wording and its communitarian or particularist message.

The legislation is an important confirmation of Israel's first priority. A fundamental right—the right to represent a constituency and participate meaningfully in the political process—has been subordinated by the Basic Law in the name of maintaining Jewish dominance over its own collective future. The primary lesson that resonates from the passage of the 1985 statute is that no agency should be permitted to threaten the enduring legacy of a principally Jewish state, not even predominantly Jewish groups whose agenda calls for increased attention to the values of equality and liberalism. The Knesset viewed the PLP as one of a handful of political parties whose threats to institute a radically different notion of equality might undermine the principle of Jewish self-determination. Instead of celebrating those values, as states that are neutral to the conception of the good might, the main power centers in Israel sought to suppress them by prohibiting their most capable advocates from entering the political arena. Israel's particularist, and thus communitarian, identity transcends even the most passionate cries for liberty.

The preceding account is an admittedly simplistic view of the Israeli constitutional polity. I certainly do not want to suggest that there are no concessions made for non-Jews in Israel or that the rights granted Arab citizens are simply token. Instead, what seems clear is that the notion of liberalism in Israel is not defined by traditionally Lockean principles but is, again, characterized most accurately by the central tenets of Judaism. The critically important right to freely exercise one's religion, or the right to due process that all citizens—

Jewish and non-Jewish—enjoy are very real and should not be questioned. But that reality is tempered ever so slightly by the fact that these protections are distributed with an awareness of the primacy of a Jewish way of life. Pervasive throughout all Israeli policies, in other words, is the principle that Israel is now, and forever will be, governed by an importantly particularist conception of the good. The broader point I am trying to convey is that a defense of this position is not possible without a constitution that eschews the main principles of objectivity.

As a communitarian regime, therefore, the Israeli example is instructive. From the perspective of all inhabitants, the constitutional posture of Israel is protective of individual liberty. On the surface, it is at least a moderately tolerant society in that all residents, regardless of their religious faith, are granted particular freedoms to move about, to associate, and to speak freely. Yet it is still exclusively a Jewish state. Judaism is not only the dominant religion, but it also informs and fortifies all that is political; society in Israel is piloted by the teachings of the Torah. For that reason, Gary Jacobsohn and Charles Liebman have each described Israel in terms of communitarian statehood.

This is not to say that Israel has successfully balanced liberal and nonliberal principles. In fact, it is quite evident that the religious particularism and the communitarian disposition in Israel has been a source of great tension among non-Jews. Jacobsohn aptly captures the essence of the tension when he writes that the problem for the framers of the Israeli state was to "erect a constitutional roof over these walls while also integrating features of the modern liberal democratic style into their architectural planning."[22] As is often the case with nonsecular nation-states, the deep passions of the religious residents almost always overshadow the attempt to locate political moderation through the synthesis of competing ideologies or practices.[23] The group that enjoys constitutional primacy will often (consciously or unconsciously) disregard the interests of other groups in an attempt to maintain control; while at the same time, the minority factions tend not to be fully satisfied with their freedoms. They aspire to participate in the determination of the common good rather than to simply stand on the sidelines and admire their rights and liberties. As is only natural, these groups covet a political voice with which to contribute to the settlement of a collective future. Unfortunately for them, they are often proscribed from realizing that wish. Paraphrasing Peled, there is a limit beyond which the exercise of citizenship rights will not be able to proceed. This limit is located at the transition point between struggling to have liberal rights respected in the conduct of official policy and attempting to challenge the prevailing notion of the common good.[24]

Mixed Constitutionalism: The German Model

The German Constitution is importantly distinct from both the Israeli and American models. Specifically, the German Basic Law represents the paradigmatic example of a contemporary mixed constitution. Mixed or semi-liberal constitutional schemes can be realized through some combination of two distinct approaches, defined separately as "institutionalist" and "ideological." At its core, the institutionalist approach suggests that polities can be successful if they create counterbalancing institutions that forestall the concentration of political power. It will not come as a great surprise that many Western constitutions, including those that inform the American and Canadian polities, have embraced the idea of stability through institutional mixing.

The writings of Aristotle and Montesquieu most accurately highlight the institutionalist approach to mixed constitutionalism. In Books III and IV of *The Politics,* Aristotle is primarily concerned with ensuring two interrelated principles—stability and justice—and to him, moderation is the key to maintaining a stable and just existence, both personally and politically. Extremes, he says, can be disastrous for any political regime. Just like an individual who "finds it hard to follow reason" because he is "over-handsome," "over-strong," "over-wealthy or at the opposite end over-poor," a state can have difficulty functioning if its political structure is also unbalanced. Too much democracy (or rule by the poor masses) can be just as ruinous, he notes, as too little. "Tyranny is a form of government which may grow out of the headiest type of democracy, or out of oligarchy [rule by the rich few]." Accordingly, the remedy, Aristotle argues, is to introduce a "constitution of the middle order."[25]

The second approach to moderate constitutionalism involves ideological mixing. Like its institutionalist partner, the aim of the ideological approach to mixed constitutionalism remains stability through moderation. But this time the tools for stability are not the institutions per se, but the values and commitments of the constitutional regime. What I mean to suggest is that this "new" mixed constitutionalism must try to incorporate both liberal and illiberal tenets; it must recognize an individualistic component within the constitution as well as a communal or social one. In the end, the basic idea of mixed constitutionalism—namely, political moderation—remains the same, but now the means needed to achieve that high aspiration include an ideological component.

The situation immediately following the demise of communism in Eastern Europe gave rise to the present discussion of ideologically centered mixed constitutionalism. For so many who were (and in some cases still are) witness to the somewhat clumsy or awkward birth of new constitutional orders in the former communist bloc, the intense interest in describing a "new" mixed constitution was to propose for the fledgling post-communist countries of Eastern Europe a restored constitutional organization that juxtaposed unfamiliar political strategies with more familiar historical values.[26] In other words, many architects of new constitutional orders in the former Second World are attempting to embody certain Western principles in their reorganized regimes without losing sight of the area's cultural or socialist heritage. The question, of course, becomes whether or not it is possible to blend individualistic ideas with traditionally communal maxims. Can Poland, for example, embrace a political regime that combines religious teachings with the principles of social responsibility, tolerance, and limited individualism? Similarly, can Russia install roughly the same formula in light of its primarily socialist background? Can the Czech or Slovak republics break from their past?

For the mixed constitutionalist, the answer is a guarded yes. A liberal constitutional regime places the individual and his priorities at the forefront of any political decision, and as such, is basically impartial when it comes to promoting a particular conception of the good. That is to say, the citizen—and not necessarily the community—is primary within a constitutional polity informed by liberal tenets, and as a result, each individual is rewarded with the freedom and capacity to direct his own life independent of significant governmental interference. From a constitutionalist perspective, according to Walker, "liberalism has two basic features. First, it makes the *rights of individuals* constitutionally paramount, and in its fullest and most self-consistent development liberalism understands those rights in terms of autonomy-entitlements and choice prerogatives. Second, in the service of individual autonomy, liberalism aims to make state authority neutral among competing visions of goodness and justice in the society it organizes."[27] Thus, what become constitutionally sanctioned are the principles of individual freedom and governmental neutrality. All individuals share freedom and autonomy equally in a principally liberal regime, while the state is proscribed from embracing one particular way of life.

It is not as easy to isolate the defining conditions of nonliberal ideologies. Stephen Holmes, perhaps the foremost contemporary authority on "anti-liberalism," even dances carefully around the topic, stating that the "uniformity" of nonliberal theory consists only "in a handful of basic assumptions plus, above all else, a common enemy."[28] Rejection of liberal individualism, however, can be a powerfully uniting force. At the very least we can certainly surmise that in renouncing radical individualism, all nonliberal ideologies must celebrate some conception of community or group solidarity. Whether it is the white supremacist stance of midcentury continental fascism or the more inclusive modern American communitarian doctrine, antagonism to liberal principles carries with it a base assumption of collectivity. Indeed, Holmes would be the first to admit that most antiliberal doctrines, including those that are tolerant or intolerant, particularist or semi-universalist, place primacy on the notion of unity or commonality. Moreover, the normative position of most antiliberal advocates suggests also that individualistic attitudes and egoism have contributed dramatically to the moral decay and deterioration of twenty-first-century existence.[29]

Modern Germany provides the most tangible example of a constitutional regime that adjoins competing liberal and nonliberal provisions. It is, in fact, the most obvious example of a constitutional polity that is attentive to ideological rather than simply institutional mixing. Aside from the stipulation in the German Basic Law that the government is structured around the principles of republicanism and federalism,[30] the charter also clearly protects both individual rights and communitarian interests. The first section of the German Basic Law is devoted to the enumeration of private rights and liberties. Article 1, in fact, initiates the listing of freedoms by declaring, "The dignity of man shall be inviolable. To respect and protect it shall be the duty of all state authority." It continues by professing, "The German people therefore acknowledge inviolable and inalienable human rights as the basis of every community, of peace and of justice in the world." The German constitutional charter then proceeds to describe in detail the extent of its citizens' personal and political liberties. Freedom of religion is protected in the text by Article 4, whereas freedom of speech is safeguarded by Article 5. Similarly, a personal right to assembly, education, privacy, and property is secured by various provisions of the German Basic Law. In the end, one of the major conditions of liberalism—that the rights of individuals are made "constitutionally paramount"—is met within the German Basic Law by the unambiguous articulation of individual freedoms.

Communitarian principles, however, are equally manifest in the text. In some cases, in fact, communitarian ideals are present directly alongside liberal assurances. Article 2, for instance, reads, "Everyone shall have the right to the free development of his personality insofar as he does not violate the rights of others or offend against the constitutional order or the moral code." At one end of the clause is a definitively liberal protection—the "right to the free development of personality" can easily be rephrased to reveal a constitutionally protected right to free choice—yet at the other end lies the curious statement about offending the "constitutional order" or the "moral code." For Germans, this is merely a reflection of a strong belief in the concept of community, in a fervent appreciation of *Der Staat*.[31] Adherence to the "moral code" is equivalent to a strong fidelity to the mores of the community. One may develop his personality freely, the German constitution states, as long as that development does not impinge on the rights of others or the corresponding interests of the community at large.

From the beginning, West German courts have sustained this particular interpretation. The *Bundesgerichtshof* (the Federal High Court of Justice) has indicated repeatedly that "the limits of the right of personality are imposed by the fact that the individual must integrate himself into society and respect the rights and interests of others."[32] Similarly, the West German Constitutional Court (the nation's highest court) noted in a 1970 decision that "the concept of man in the Basic Law is not that of an isolated, sovereign individual; rather, the Basic Law resolves the conflict between the individual and the community by relating and binding the citizen to the community, but without detracting from his individuality."[33] These judicial bodies are in essence arguing that one's conception of rights in Germany must be informed by an equally powerful obligation to the community—one's freedoms can and should be tempered by the needs of the political regime.

Mary Ann Glendon remarks that the attitude of the German judiciary differs dramatically from that expressed by corresponding courts in the United States. She insists that the American judicial establishment—including the parties to a case, the judges presiding, and the lawyers advocating on behalf of their clients—speaks in a language of rights that suggests absolutism. We should recall Glendon's powerful words on this topic: "For in its simple American form, the language of rights is the language of no compromise. The winner takes all and the loser has to get out of town. The conversation is over."[34] Few in America, she says, acknowledge the social component that pervades all relationships, from our most intimate to our most distant. Even fewer embrace the German notion that rights should be regulated or tempered by the interests or wishes of others. In fact, Glendon argues, America's infatuation with rights (and its corresponding rejection of the responsibilities that she says must accompany those rights) has contributed to the "disorder" that currently plagues the body politic. And she insists that our primarily liberal constitution is at least partially to blame. America's constitutional document does not explicitly articulate a governmental or individual obligation to the polity. In contrast to most European constitutions, the American text favors an image (derived mainly from Locke and Blackstone) of the rugged individualist who feels little or no responsibility to the communities that surround him. The result, she concludes, is a culture and set of institutions (including the law) that simply does not respect the organic nature of the community.

Turning back to the German Basic Law, we see that from a mixed constitutional standpoint, Article 14 is just as intriguing as Article 2. The first provision of Article 14 guarantees an individual right to property. Yet in almost the same instance that the right is granted, it is circumscribed by a strongly communitarian assertion that ownership of property is not a wholly individualistic privilege. Section 2 of Article 14 reads, "Rights impose duties. [The use of property] should also serve the public weal." On this issue notes from the German Constitutional Convention reveal the true intent of the framers. "Ownership entails a social obligation," the framers argued. "Its use shall find its limits in the living necessities of all citizens and in the public order essential to society."[35]

Again, Glendon is instructive. She contends that the German understanding of property rights derives from a distinct tradition nowhere visible within the United States. In contrast to primarily Lockean notions of property that undergird the American psyche, many European nations have adopted Rousseau's belief—borrowed ostensibly from Aristotle and the Bible—that "property rights are always subordinate to the overriding claims of the community; that an owner is a kind of trustee or steward for the public good; and that human beings have a natural right to what they need for their subsistence."[36] Individuals are obliged, as part of this distinctively European interpretation, to perceive ownership of property, not as a personal entitlement, but rather as part of a larger social phenomenon. That is to say, property is simply not private. Indeed, Glendon remarks that it would be exceedingly difficult, in fact, to locate a serious contemporary European who would defend the position that government should *never* interfere with the individual property rights of the citizen. It would seem absurd to argue that government should remain neutral when intervention would enrich the common good.

Further revealing are the different attitudes Americans and Germans have toward their respective Just Compensation Clauses. In the United States, the Just Compensation Clause of the Fifth Amendment is seen as merely an extension of the provision guaranteeing the right to property.[37] When property is seized, the feeling is that the individual has an unqualified right to be compensated for the total value of the taking, regardless of the potential public benefit. In contrast, the equivalent clause of the German Basic Law is seen not as an *extension* of the property right, but as a *regulation* of that liberty. Compensation is disbursed in Germany solely based on the seized property's contribution to the public good. If the contribution to the public weal is minimal, the individual is fully compensated, but if the contribution is significant, and the individual himself (along with his neighbors) will benefit from the appropriation, compensability is seriously attenuated. Thus, unlike in the United States, where the Fifth Amendment suggests that the right to property is virtually inviolable, ownership of property in Germany is tempered by an intensely public or communitarian component.

The social bent also invades the dominion of the German family. Article 6 of the German constitution sets out the privileged position of "marriage and family," stating that the two shall "enjoy the special protection of the state." A "natural" right of the parents to nurture and care for their children is professed by Section 2 of the Article. Correspondingly, however, Section 2 also places responsibility for overseeing the parent-child relationship on the "national community."[38] Indeed, for Germans raising a child is not a singular endeavor; it is a community-wide project that includes all members of the national polity.[39] All Germans recognize some constitutional responsibility to protect the welfare of their own offspring as well as those of others. And although judicial interpretation of the clause has at times been controversial, the major lesson of Article 6 centers on the indiscrete juxtaposition of communal and liberal principles.

The communitarian imprint in Germany comes from the country's tradition of *Sozialstaat*, roughly translated as the "social state." *Sozialstaat* refers to the mentality among Germans that the welfare and collective existence of the citizenry is paramount. Responsibilities toward the physical and economic health of fellow Germans accompany, and in some cases even supplant, any rights that may be enumerated in the text. Furthermore, that posture has been specifically grounded in the body of the constitutional charter from the time of the original founding. The community-centered disposition is one aspect of a tripartite German tradition based on the principles of liberalism, socialism, and Christianity. The combination of traditions at the German founding saw to it that no single belief would dominate. "At the risk of oversimplification," Kommers notes, "the liberal tradition was responsible for the classical freedoms listed in several articles of the Bill of Rights (Articles 1–18); the socialist tradition contributed certain social welfare clauses, including provisions concerning the duties of property and the socialization of economic resources; and the Christian tradition added provisions dealing with social morality, religious education, and the institutional prerogatives of the established churches and rights associated with marriage and family."[40] The liberal tradition is obviously present in many constitutional provisions, but the socialist and Christian heritage have also found a post in German constitutional lore. The result, many would say, is moderation.

One last issue needs to be addressed. In direct contrast to the pure liberal pledge to maintain value-neutrality, the German Basic Law proudly sets forth a number of priorities. Unlike the United States and other important liberal regimes, where the constitutions protect substantive values only incidentally through procedural mechanisms, the German Basic Law is unambiguous about its endorsement of certain substantive values. Interpretation of the document by the German Constitutional Court often includes recognition of a sliding scale, with some substantive values placed higher on the scale. As Kommers observes, "The Constitutional Court . . . rejects the notion of a value-neutral state. Instead . . . it speaks of a constitutional polity deeply committed to an 'objective order of values.' "[41]

The hierarchical ordering of values begins with human dignity, since the principle of human dignity informs all that is public and private. Somewhere near the top, Kommers says, are the basic "principles of government (e.g., popular sovereignty, separation of powers, legality of administration, a multiparty system, and the legitimacy of political opposition)," and on this same level lies the rights of the individual. Also on this plateau rests the value of collective or social existence. Germans understand that accompanying the rights and liberties of the community come many responsibilities and duties. In fact, for most Germans it is incomprehensible to think of rights without also considering their corresponding duties to the state. Private ownership of property is valued, but is not absolute. The parental task of raising children is similarly prized, but it, too, is not left unregulated. Indeed, citizenship in Germany carries with it the understanding that liberalism is but one of three equally important and critically reinforcing traditions. Along with liberty stands a tradition of morality based on Christian teachings and, perhaps more importantly, a social tradition that teaches the benefits of collective action and shared responsibilities. Without any single set of values, Germany is a dramatically different polity; without all three, Germany is not a recognizable polity at all.

Thus, despite the fact that Glendon and Kommers define the balance of liberal and communitarian values within the German Basic Law as "fruitful," the community-based impulse appears to be paramount. This is so because the conception of the good most clearly resonating throughout unified Germany resembles some vague notion of communitarianism. After World War II, when the German Basic Law entered into force, the founders embraced the notion that community-based themes should supplement liberal values. Both were thought to be critical to the survival of the West German state, and thus both were necessary ingredients in a distinctive and holistic charter. As a result, the current German constitution reflects a strong preference for ideological mixing.

The problem is that the strategy of blending ideologies, as appealing as it may seem, is risky from a modern constitutionalist perspective. The constitution's mandate to guide the agencies of government becomes less effectual as governmental institutions—including the judiciary, the executive, and the legislature—are permitted to choose between competing ideological values, each of which can claim equal constitutional import. Sometimes a polity's public institutions, in other words, may favor a liberal disposition, and sometimes they may favor a communitarian one. It is even conceivable that a single institution might favor a liberal disposition at one time and then change its mind and adopt a communitarian one at a later date, or vice versa. But one thing is certain: the decisions of these institutions will be at least partially based on extra-textual factors like the history and tradition of the polity or the personal predilections of the decision maker. Not that governmental institutions under primarily liberal constitutions do things differently, but I think it is fair to conclude that the substantive outcome of judicial decisions and legislative initiatives under mixed regimes is made far more complicated by virtue of the integration of different ideological viewpoints.

The Communitarian Hope

Despite the risk, prescriptive American communitarians would most likely approach the reconstruction of America's constitutional system with something like the German text in mind. Mary Ann Glendon, in particular, admires the German model. To resolve the imbalance between the principles of liberty and community, she and the "Responsive Communitarian Platform" implicitly point to the induction of a mixed political order much like that which currently informs the German constitutional structure. Modern communitarians are quick to admit that their skirmish with America's hyperindividualistic spirit and penchant for privatism suggests a need for an equally potent "social" tradition. That is, when contemporary prescriptive communitarians visualize their ideal political state, they imagine something akin to the German *Sozialstaat*, where both the public and private spheres have a strong social component. Consider what is said in the third paragraph of the "Responsive Communitarian Platform": "A Communitarian perspective recognizes that the preservation of individual liberty depends on the active maintenance of the institutions of civil society where citizens learn respect for others as well as self-respect, where we acquire a lively sense of our personal and civic responsibilities." Or this statement in the fourth paragraph: "A Communitarian perspective recognizes that communities and polities, too, have obligations— including the duty to be responsive to their members and to foster participation and deliberation in social and political life." Or even the fifth: "A Communitarian perspective . . . mandates attention to what is often ignored in contemporary policy debates: the social side of human nature, the responsibilities that must be borne by citizens, individually and collectively, in a regime of rights; the fragile ecology of families and their supporting communities, the ripple effects and long-term consequences of present decisions."

Even more unmistakable is the position taken by the editorial board of *The Responsive Community*, a quarterly publication devoted entirely to the communitarian movement. In the opening statement of their first volume, Amitai Etzioni, James Fishkin, Mary Ann Glendon, and William Galston diagram the strategy to be employed by advocates of the journal. Immediately, and throughout the entire statement, they contend that their communitarian plan seeks to "balance" the "rights of individuals" with "responsibilities to the community."[42] "It is empirically wrong and morally dangerous," they insist, "to view individuals as monads or rights-bearers existing in isolation, or to view the commons as merely an aggregation of individuals."[43] Instead, individuals should be viewed as part of a larger network of citizens, all responsible for the community's collective existence.[44]

More specifically, those who sign on to the prescriptive communitarian code want to make the exchange of personal rights and liberties less one-sided. There is, they say, as much of an interest in protecting the "social-moral climate" of an educational institution as there is in protecting an isolated individual "against wanton expulsion." Similarly, there is an equal desire to provide the community with the necessary "constitutional tools" to "prevent drug dealers from dominating street, parks, indeed, whole neighborhoods," as there is to provide that drug dealer with his constitutionally protected civil rights. The point is that personal rights need not stand alone; they can still function effectively even when accompanied by communal responsibilities. In fact, say many advocates of community, the independence of rights in America may prove in the end to be seriously harmful. In the view of many recent prescriptive communitarians, an enormous social cost is currently being paid for the unregulated distribution of individual rights and liberties.[45]

In Germany, the same attitude is pervasive. The right to property is not absolute, and neither is the right to free speech. Each of these freedoms is moderated or balanced by the community's interest in maintaining a peaceful and collective coexistence. Private usage of property and the freedom to speak one's mind are permitted—up to a point. And the threshold of that limit rests at the point where the community's welfare stands to be threatened. Once the community and its collective will are endangered, rights and liberties are automatically regulated. They are obviously not regulated out of existence, but they are restricted just the same. Priority, in most cases, lies with the community, not with the individual. Hence, responsibility to the German state is authorized and mandated specifically by the constitutional text more than simply through the implementation of law. Accompanying the many rights and liberties in Germany is an equally critical assertion that duties to the state are both necessary and required.

The communitarian movement in America applauds this German stance. When Etzioni talks of a "four-point agenda on rights and responsibilities," his main objective is to reestablish a feeling of "concern for others." If Americans are ever to let go of their introverted, egoistic disposition, they must "correct the current imbalance between [individual] rights and [communal] responsibilities." New rights must be discouraged, while old rights must be regulated. And where "legal rights have been interpreted in ways that hobble public safety and health," he remarks, those rights must be "reinterpreted."[46]

Property, Glendon further argues, can no longer be viewed as inviolate but must instead be considered part of a larger collective dynamic, with the right of ownership being modified by an important communal interest. Glendon's argument highlights what in Germany the mixed constitution successfully avoids, and what in America the predominantly liberal text cannot: that when brought to the extreme, an individual's freedoms, unless mitigated by a communal component, will no doubt clash with the rights of others. "There is a strong discrepancy," she points out, "between our tendency to state rights in a stark unlimited fashion and the commonsense restrictions that have to be placed on one person's rights when they collide with those of another person."[47]

In further comparing the prescriptive communitarian agenda to the German Basic Law, consider also the remark made in the editorial piece that reads: "We [Communitarians] shall pay special attention to the future of marriage and child-raising families; the moral upbringing of the young in schools; the moral condition of their elders in private and public life; and the vigor of political parties and the intermediary bodies that stand between the state and the individual."[48] Any "restoration of America's moral foundation," the "Responsive Communitarian Platform" states, will begin with the family and will also include the schools. Much like in Germany, where Article 6 of the Basic Law identifies a "natural" right to parenthood but also recognizes a community-wide responsibility in the rearing of children, the American communitarian movement acknowledges parents as the primary source of nurturing, yet also insists that we, as a community, can do our part to ease the burden of childcare. Thus the Platform calls for a "change in orientation" by parents and workplaces. Parents must place priority on the development (both moral and physical) of their children, while, simultaneously, workplaces need to offer more flexible options for working parents. Singularly, the parents are charged with the responsibility to morally educate their children, but collectively, the Platform seems to be suggesting, the community can help.

In light of the remarkable similarities between the position of the American communitarian movement and the language of the German Basic Law, it may be more accurate to characterize the communitarians' *constitutionalist* argument, not as communitarian per se, but as semi-liberal. Modern American communitarians (particularly the prescriptive breed) seem to want to bond liberal propositions with community-centered maxims in much the same way that the German Basic Law has done. Rights must be tempered by responsibilities, they argue, while community must be viewed alongside the individual as coequal partners in America's quest for "a more perfect union." But such a proposition may signal the undoing of any contemporary American movement that thinks of itself as purely communitarian. Indeed, Israel's constitutional project cannot be said to include a similar plan, and as a result, few are likely to confuse Israel's purely communitarian constitution with the mixed ideological one that lies at the foundation of the German state. In fact, Israel is not at all interested in balancing the rights and responsibilities of individuals because such a balance would undoubtedly disrupt, or at least cloud, the effort to maintain Jewish self-determination. The individual is not paramount in Israel, nor is the state neutral to competing conceptions of the good. There is little doubt, therefore, that Israel represents a communitarian state. What is doubtful is that modern American communitarians would rush to adopt a similar constitutional model.

Furthermore, the existence of a communitarian pillar in Germany's constitutional structure depends almost entirely on a tradition that places communal values *ahead* of liberal ones. For over two hundred years now, the reverse has been the experience of the United States. When the republican tradition of the American Revolution gave way to a modern liberal ethos sometime during the early part of American independence, we began a journey down a different path. Since then, it seems we have only amplified rather than diminished our affinity for individualism. In the end, the argument in favor of a mixed constitutional design is perhaps best captured by one of the principals of the communitarian movement, Mary Ann Glendon. In an essay entitled "Rights and Responsibilities Viewed from Afar: The Case of Welfare Rights," Glendon hints that the U.S. Constitution, with its virtual silence on the idea of welfare rights, may now be outdated.[49] She argues that the U.S. text, in contrast to the fundamental laws of Canada, France, and Germany, predated (by almost 150 years) the birth of the welfare state. As such, the document, through its silence, implicitly and lamentably rejects the notion of collective responsibility.

Using comparative techniques, Glendon posits that the U.S. textual design is strikingly different than the model used by European constitutionalists. In the United States, government is seen as oppressive or imperial. In continental

Europe, by contrast, that same government is rarely viewed as belligerent; instead, it is purposefully charged with an affirmative duty to protect and foster the well-being of its citizens. Thus, instead of a mostly negative posture, the governments of Europe enjoy a positive role in the development of their constituents. A minimal level of health and welfare is awarded constitutional status in these European regimes. Accordingly, Glendon insists, "The leading European conservative parties espouse openly and in principle what American conservatives have only accepted grudgingly and *sub silentio*: a mixed economy and a moderately interventionist state."[50]

To her obvious disappointment, Glendon's comparisons also highlight the serious problems associated with trying to adopt a European constitutional model.[51] America is, after all, different from its European neighbors. Americans share a distinct cultural and historical past, and despite the fact that its tradition includes a republican component, there are things that make the history of American political development unique. Since 1791 the U.S. government has mostly discouraged the emergence of a national religion, a central component and a necessary ingredient of Germany's "social" heritage. Furthermore, American states are not granted the same independence to implement policy as their German counterparts; they are not always permitted to interpret federal regulations in accordance with their separate customs, habits, and traditions. The result, of course, is only a minimal or limited state community. But even more important than these institutional differences, America's traditions as well as its constitutional mandate have been dominated by the idea of regime neutrality. Individuals, not communities, are given the authority to determine the appropriate conception of the good in the United States. It is a society, in other words, that relies on the principle of individualism, warts and all. Many European countries are currently determining which constitutional ideas and aspirations ought to prevail, and some are not even to that point yet. American citizens, in contrast, have (for better or worse) largely resolved that debate. From a constitutional perspective, Americans have made a commitment to liberalism; and for the time being at least, the constituents will have to live with that selection. Even adopting the more accurate label for American communitarians, therefore, cannot save the movement from the overwhelming impediments to constitutional change.

CHAPTER SEVEN

Conclusion

The Enduring Constitutional Debate

Communitarianism as a political ambition is here to stay. Ever since Rawls almost single-handedly resurrected the subject of political philosophy, the communitarian movement has been at the forefront of the normative debate over liberal values. Central to its mission has been an almost continuous investigation of liberal theory's major propositions. Theoretically, the advocates of community have questioned whether liberalism sufficiently addresses the true nature of the self. Does it adequately capture the essence of personhood? they ask. Because it "neglects" the social character of human existence, can it ever properly organize a vibrant and alluring political society? Furthermore, how can we believe that the abstract contractual setting envisioned by liberals will ever develop into a fully functioning system of justice? Rawls' original position, communitarians say, suffers from internal inconsistencies, while the veil of ignorance simply belies reason. A more realistic vision of political life, they protest, would rightfully recognize an important social or communal element. Continuing the assault on liberal theory, communitarians assert that personal identity is not always determined by individual choice, but rather it is most often attached directly to a specific communal or collective good. In the end, individuals are but part of a larger set of relationships that constitute an entity referred to by most political observers as the "community."

For most communitarian theorists, Rawls' treatise was indeed a call to arms. Stephen Mulhall and Adam Swift have remarked that Rawls' defense of neo-Kantian liberalism "established the terrain" on which all "subsequent political-theoretical battles were to be fought." The work of Rawls, they say, "simply defines the [theoretical] agenda and continues to do so."[1] Furthermore, Gutmann notes that the philosopher's work has "altered the premises and principles of contemporary liberal theory" and that all communitarianism should be seen, in some way, as a reaction to the widespread impact of *A Theory of Justice*.[2]

As I have noted above, the communitarian response to Rawls' liberal stance was, to put it mildly, impassioned. In *Liberalism and the Limits of Justice*, Sandel attempted to depict liberalism as an inherently flawed notion, teeming with mistaken assumptions about the self and even more troubling propositions about the polity. Similarly, in the bulk of Taylor's and MacIntyre's work, Rawls' position is equally chastised. In Taylor's view the "emotivist" liberalism that originated with the revolutionary agents of the Enlightenment and that has witnessed a resurgence under Rawlsianism misunderstands the deep and real relationship between the principles of personal identity and collective good. One cannot know who one is, Taylor insists, without also having some conception of one's place in a community of others.[3] MacIntyre professes that same theme, claiming that to know myself is to know what "social roles" I inhabit.[4] Walzer continues the challenge to liberal political theory by raising serious normative and methodological questions about the station of unconstituted citizens, the promise of neglected communities, and the legitimacy of any "universal" pattern of justice.[5]

The communitarian opposition to modern liberalism does not just end with the major political theorists. The prescriptive communitarian attack on neutral values, inflated rights, and pure hyperindividualism is an equally aggressive second-generation assault on the contemporary liberal opus. Amitai Etzioni and Mary Ann Glendon each lament the loss of responsibility and devotion to country that seems to plague America's youth. They attribute such a loss to the rising importance of (and reliance on) rights and liberties in this country, and they suggest, as a possible way to restore an acceptable balance between "duty" and "freedom," a sharp reevaluation of our individual and societal priorities. Benjamin Barber, William Galston, and Robert Bellah similarly bemoan the country's ongoing predicament, yet they look primarily to institutions as a means to cure America's many ailments.[6] Change American habits, culture, and attitudes, the argument from these prescriptive thinkers seems to be, and one can eventually change the country's basic political framework. Hyperindividualism is but a symptom of a deeper malady—insistence on uncontested liberalism—that can be alleviated only with the devaluation of liberal principles. If not completely rescinding liberal primacy, at least the adjustment of our most essential public institutions should usher in a greater appreciation of communal values and shared interests.

Now that three decades have passed since the publication of Rawls' profound and sweeping theory, we can accurately assess the present status of the liberal-communitarian debate. In addition to the extent to which Rawls' work continues to define the parameters of liberal and political theory, credit should be given to the communitarians who have successfully managed to clarify Rawls' original ideas.[7] But aside from their purely philosophical import, how compelling are these antiliberal arguments? Are we persuaded enough by the communitarian impulse to admit that a society reinforced by liberal supports needs some retailoring? And even if we are, are we convinced that communitarianism represents the best alternative to a liberal-democratic system? Is a political regime ordered by the principles of communitarianism one that we should enthusiastically embrace? In some very tangible way, we are, by asking these sorts of questions, subjecting the arguments of the communitarian spokespersons to the same probing scrutiny that liberals have long endured. That is to say, what spawned the modern American communitarian movement was a profound aversion to the liberal paradigm and a fervent belief that change would bring about a more ordered, peaceful society. Thus, the foundational inquiry for all contemporary communitarians revolved around the inspection of liberal norms and practices. And the questions that arose from that fundamental inquiry were essentially: Is the liberal political design the best we can ever hope to achieve? and Should not a different model organize our political existence? Presently, the tide has turned somewhat as academics and politicians carefully scrutinize the main attributes of the communitarian proposal. Much like what communitarians did to liberals after the release of *A Theory of Justice*, political observers and practitioners are now beginning to consider more closely the principal characteristics of the recent communitarian endeavor.

For quite some time, many prominent political and sociological scientists have been deeply skeptical about the feasibility of the communitarian project. Aside from the most common pragmatic complaints,[8] feminists have opposed the advent of communitarian ideals for no other reason than that they tend to appeal chiefly to patriarchal models; while liberals and libertarians have countered the community-centered strategy by pointing to the unfavorable characteristics of "intolerance" and "exclusion."[9] In this era of "political correctness" and "multiculturalism," the feeling among some liberals is that communitarianism—more so than any other ideology—represents a style of political organization that tends to foster one specific conception of the good at the direct expense of all others. It endorses a single aspiration while at the same time discouraging, and in some cases even forbidding, subordinate visions of the good life. This study has revealed that communitarianism, at least as a practical political design, still has some work to do. In their single-minded drive to reorder liberal (and American) politics around the concept of the community, communitarian theorists and political practitioners alike have almost surely overlooked, if not the qualities of the self and the society, the profound constitutional consequences of their work. I have, in this book, tried to highlight that simple fact.

However, that is not to say that the communitarians are not continually forging ahead with their project. In fact, I think it is fair to say that many Americans secretly (or in some cases even outwardly) applaud the modern communitarians for what they aspire to create. Surveys suggest that most Americans long for some recovery of responsible representation and collective rule.[10] Americans seem instinctively to ask: What could be more appealing than a society based on the notion of complete solidarity? If we can imagine a world (much like the ancient city-state) where politics is a "way of life" rather than simply a means to an end, where participation in the construction of a public life is universal, where civic virtue is cultivated, and where consensus and compromise are regular occurrences, then, it is said, we can imagine a "better" political regime. Moreover, if we can imagine a political order that both identifies and fosters a collective will and a common general purpose, then we can imagine an even richer, more fulfilling political existence. Indeed, the idea that politics can be organized around community-wide decision making, shared values, and mutual respect is certainly one that most of us, if given the chance, would eagerly endorse. What could be better? What else could we as a nation want?

In the United States, political aspirants from Jesse Jackson to Pat Buchanan, from Al Gore to George W. Bush, have wondered about the same thing. Like most politicians (and perhaps as testament to my own perpetual optimism), representatives from both political parties are presumably involved in politics for one reason only: improving the overall position of America's citizens. And like most other modern political actors, these representatives, in trying to realize that singular goal, have begun to consider seriously the merits of a predominantly communitarian platform. Can we, they have asked, reform the electoral system in America to solicit greater communication between the representatives and their communities?[11] Furthermore, can we address what is wrong with American society and place responsibility for fixing it in the hands of the states and localities instead of always relying on the agencies of Washington to locate an appropriate antidote? It would seem from the conduct and the platforms of many contemporary political parties and actors that the ideas articulated by communitarian advocates represent if not the best, at least the most compelling, alternative for meaningful political change. Democrats, over the past decade, have begun to shy away from the hyperindividualistic stance often associated with the more radical members of the left-wing party;[12] while Republicans have, in that same period, more assertively proposed a comprehensive restructuring of political decision-making centers. In contrast to the omnipotence of the federal government, say many nationally recognized conservatives, local institutions and agencies are better equipped with the knowledge and tools necessary to combat internal problems—problems that may, in fact, be unique to just one community. Accordingly, they, and not the bureaucrats in Washington, ought to be given sovereign authority to handle their own local conflicts.[13]

Former presidents have also seized upon the general population's curiosity with respect to communitarianism. While in office, President Clinton and Vice President Gore took communitarian reform a step further not only by employing a more participatory approach to representation (through the advent of "town hall meetings"), but also by implementing—in the form of the national service program called "AmeriCorps"—a more active, community-based mentality.[14] The impetus behind AmeriCorps is the desire to attract committed young men and women to devote their time to the improvement of American communities—from beautifying the environment, to working with the handicapped, to tutoring the learning disabled. Modeled on the Peace Corps, the national civil service group attempts to do for all Americans what the international program attempts to do for the citizens of many Third World nations.

And while the incentives are still based on broadly individualistic interests (travel, money for college, and a small stipend), the motivation behind the induction of the local corps is a purely communitarian one.[15] The expectation from the Clinton administration was that the program would instill in the hearts of young Americans the value and virtues of altruistic behavior. It would develop in those teenagers who participate a communitarian sense of responsibility, shared values, and accomplishment, along with the more "liberal" feelings of individual freedom and personal independence.[16]

It has also become all too clear that many local communities, fed up with the bureaucracy and disorganization of federal government oversight, are taking responsibility for their own activities. Former mayors like Rudolph Giuliani of New York and current mayors like Tom Menino of Boston are seemingly on a crusade to return policy-making authority to their own communities. Throughout his tenure, Giuliani, for example, continued to fight hard for local control of law enforcement and drug prevention, insisting that no two cities are alike and that each, to be successful, must deal individually and independently with the rising problems of crime and drug abuse. Menino, not surprisingly, is equally supportive of this more localized approach to political administration. Similarly, the movement away from a nationally endorsed educational curriculum continues to gain momentum. School systems in Norfolk, Virginia, and Memphis, Tennessee, have abandoned traditional state and nationally sponsored teaching methods in favor of ones that encourage alternative approaches to education.[17] In Norfolk, as in Memphis, the idea is that the community knows best how to educate its children, and thus the community itself will be responsible for the determination of an appropriate (yet still comprehensive) school curriculum.[18]

Add to this accelerating embrace of communitarian principles the actions of the current president and vice president. There are numerous accounts of President Bush's strong affinity for communitarian ideals.[19] His faith-based initiatives, combined with his comprehensive plan to foster "Communities of Character," have revealed a decidedly communitarian edge to his administration's domestic strategy. Moreover, communitarian strategies have now seeped into his foreign policy agenda. In the wake of the September 11, 2001, tragedy, the Bush administration has squeezed civil liberties by holding indefinitely, without formal charges, hundreds of suspects, while threatening many others with military trials. He has considered the possibility of suspending habeas corpus for terrorist suspects and has toyed with the idea of abandoning traditional law enforcement restrictions aimed at regulating official covert surveillance. His mandate for these various actions derives from an overwhelmingly sympathetic public—even one year after the tragic events of September 11, 2001, a Gallup poll survey indicated that a strong majority still supported these initiatives.

Of course, Bush's plan is strikingly familiar. President Lincoln used these very same tactics during the Civil War. The suspension of habeas corpus was introduced by the president as a mechanism to forestall threats to our national security, and it was bolstered by widespread popular support from the North. Individuals like John Merryman were told that their constitutional rights were not as important as safeguarding the existence of the Union; they were inconsequential when compared to the overall wishes of the Northern community. Acting as a federal court judge, Roger Taney's relatively narrow interpretation of presidential power was thus challenged. Lincoln scolded him for interfering in the effort to save the country. And because the Union forces were fiercely aligned with the president, the chief justice was eventually forced to relent.

President Bush has now adopted a similar posture. In this period of global uncertainty, he speaks of the need to place the safety of all Americans ahead of the rights of a few. His recent rhetoric downplays the constitutional constraints on governmental officials while simultaneously highlighting the increased threat to national security. Indeed, the famous questions Lincoln posed when justifying his suspension of habeas corpus—"Are all the laws, *but one*, to go unexecuted, and the government itself to go to pieces, lest that one be violated? Even in such a case, would not the official oath be broken, if the government should be overthrown, when it was believed that disregarding the single law, would tend to preserve it?"[20]—could just as easily be attributed to President Bush.

The current president regularly remarks that the activities of the terrorists are symbolic of what is wrong with the contemporary world; that these wrongdoers preyed on American freedoms and values in order to realize and ultimately carry out their specific brand of evil. Time and again since that fateful day in September 2001, Bush has identified renewed faith in religion, the family, neighborhoods, schools, civic organizations, clubs, and other institutions as the panacea for our troubles. The president has reshaped his political image: he now exhibits the principal characteristics of a communitarian.

Is all this to suggest that communitarianism, as a political ideology, is gaining ground? The most realistic answer is perhaps. As part of the acceptance of various communitarian ideas by a number of vocal political leaders, maybe we should now admit that certain antiliberal stances are, indeed, picking up speed. But similarly, communitarians are quick to point out that we should also proceed cautiously, for to remark that America is undergoing a community-based revolution would almost certainly be premature. Simply because components of the communitarian platform are seeping into the programs and platforms of prominent political actors, we, as a country, are not headed down the road toward communitarianism. Certainly, American liberalism is in no real jeopardy of losing its favored position, if in fact it is under any real threat at all.

An increased presence does mean, however, that the merits of communitarianism must be given continued serious consideration. At the very least, the communitarian impulse has contributed mightily to the overall health of America's constitutional aspiration. The Preamble to the constitutional text unambiguously declares that the goal of its political order is to achieve "a more perfect Union," and the American communitarian platform is doing nothing to abandon that primary ambition. In light of all the problems community advocates attribute to liberal theory—problems of crime, inequality, poverty, and general dissociation—the recommendations emerging from the communitarian ranks ought to be carefully pondered. Maybe the answers to these problems, communitarians suggest, lie not in granting Americans more freedom and additional rights, but rather in curtailing individual liberty, and instead fostering a deeper sense of solidarity, a stronger faith in the collective. Perhaps the modern American communitarians—both the theoretical and the prescriptive wings—are ostensibly correct in their general accusations of liberal politics. Perhaps, in the end, liberalism, as part of an organizational model that celebrates individualism and freedom of choice, is not all it is cracked up to be. One thing is certain, however: to insist on the claim that we ought to reconfigure the relationship between liberalism and communitarianism in America is to subscribe to a fundamentally different type of constitutional order altogether.

This brings us ultimately back to the founding. To be sure, the debate over ratification pitted two formidable political ideologies against one another. On the one side stood the Federalists, who strongly believed that the way to ensure a powerful United States was to invest authority in the central government. Order required that in many situations the federal government should oversee the administration of America's major political problems. Shays' Rebellion had earlier been subdued without the help of the mostly impotent Congress, and the attitude among proponents of the newly formed constitutional design was that a reconcentration of power in the central government could alleviate identical future conflicts. Republican sovereignty would still prevail, but the mechanics for resolving the county's political conflicts would simply be employed on a much larger scale.[21] Representation, democracy, liberty, and autonomy were, additionally, all principles that would remain under the proposed Constitution, but they would be seriously and importantly redefined.

On the other side of the ratification debate stood the Anti-Federalists, who, by contrast, endorsed the less radical view that the states and localities were more suited to control the political reins. For the most part conservative, the Anti-Federalists differed from their opponents in their belief that the principles of freedom and security that were present at the time of independence were best captured in political design, not by the constitutional text, but by the Articles of Confederation. They argued fervently that in a country as vast as the United States, no central government could effectively and with necessary authority control the variety of political relationships and organizations present at the local and state levels.[22] Civic virtue could only be realized in small territories, with local authorities who were intimately familiar with the customs and traditions of a specific community. What is more, the Anti-Federalists thought, only with a deep and voluntary attachment to the institutions of their own local government could the American people form and develop the proper character to ensure that they would become responsible and active citizens. Finally, the Anti-Federalist argument went, Federalists were seriously mistaken in assuming that granting additional authority to the institutions of the national government would somehow provide the means to greater political stability.

Yet despite these fundamental differences, in at least one way the two most important competing factions in U.S. history should be viewed as forever aligned; for it is all too clear that both the Federalists and the Anti-Federalists were engrossed in the same general project. Each, to be sure, had an opinion on the quality of the proposed constitutional doctrine, but on a much higher level, it should be remembered that each championed a particular and compelling vision for the American political regime. The brilliance of Article VII of the text was that it not only permitted debate on the merits of the Constitution, but it also implicitly encouraged the discussion of alternative constitutional designs.[23] In permitting a nationwide dialogue on the mechanics of the newly drafted text, it opened the door for the Anti-Federalists to organize their movement to combat the new regime through direct appeals to both reason and prudence, or, as Publius so aptly argued in *Federalist* 1, "reflection" and "choice." Indeed, it allowed the opponents of the Constitution to respond to a revolutionary new order by suggesting the return to an old, already-established system.

With that in mind, it is not such a stretch to suggest that the country's liberal and communitarian supporters are the Federalists and Anti-Federalists of our time. Much as the reality of Anti-Federalist thought signaled opposition to the vision espoused by eighteenth-century supporters of the U.S. Constitution, the current presence of the communitarian movement and other alternative antiliberal ideologies reveals a general discontent with the primacy of liberalism in American society. If nothing else, what our current constitutional system allows—and even fosters—is constant reflection on its own fundamental principles. Thus, it is not at all an exaggeration to suggest that the contemporary dispute between liberals and communitarians—a dispute centered on the core tenets of American politics—is one that strongly resembles the earlier debate over constitutional acceptance. Indeed, the ratification of a constitutional vision for America can be described, even in the new millennium, as an ongoing project, with communitarianism representing one organizational ideal, and liberalism representing another. And no matter which ideology ultimately wins, as citizens, we should be pleased that the American constitutional order, mechanically and substantively, is capacious enough to peaceably resolve this enduring debate.

Notes

Preface

1. Abraham Lincoln, "Message to Congress in Special Session, July 4, 1861," in *Abraham Lincoln: Speeches and Writings, 1859–1865* (New York: Library of America, 1989), 253.
2. *Ex Parte Merryman,* F. Cas. 9487 (1861).
3. Lincoln, "Message to Congress," 253.
4. See Stephen M. Griffin, *American Constitutionalism: From Theory to Politics* (Princeton, N.J.: Princeton University Press, 1996).

O N E : Introduction

1. See Herbert Storing, *What the Anti-Federalists Were For* (Chicago: University of Chicago Press, 1981). Throughout the work, Storing discusses the argumentative atmosphere that pervaded the drafting and ratification of the U.S. Constitution. He remarks: "The nation was born in consensus but it lives in controversy, and the main lines of that controversy are well-worn paths leading back to the founding debate" (p. 6).
2. See *United States v Schwimmer,* 279 U.S. 644, 654–55 (1929) (Holmes, J., dissenting).
3. See *Abrams v United States,* 250 U.S. 616, 630 (1919) (Holmes, J. dissenting).
4. See *New York Times Co. v Sullivan,* 376 U.S. 254, 270 (1964).
5. Catherine Drinker Bowen, *Miracle at Philadelphia: The Story of the Constitutional Convention, May to September 1787* (Boston: Little, Brown, 1966), 5.
6. See in particular, Charles Beard, *An Economic Interpretation of the Constitution* (New York: Free Press, 1913).
7. See Wayne D. Moore, *Constitutional Rights and Powers of the People* (Princeton, N.J.: Princeton University Press, 1996), esp. chap. 3.
8. Storing, *Anti-Federalists,* 5. Storing further notes that the lack of consensus was not unique to Anti-Federalists. Federalists were also contradictory in their priorities: "There is an impression of greater unity [among Federalists] because [they] were (in general) unified in supporting the Constitution. . . . The impression has been strengthened by the Federalists' victory and the massive impact on later generations of *The Federalist Papers,* which have tended to occupy the Federalist stage and lend their unity to the whole group supporting the Constitution. There were in fact diverse and contradictory opinions among the Federalists just as there were among their opponents."

Adding confusion to the matter, consider also Paul Finkelman, "Antifederalists: The Loyal Opposition and the American Constitution," *Cornell Law Review* 70 (1984): 182–207, who not only emphasizes Anti-Federalist divisions but also points out the limitations of Storing's overall analysis.

9. Moore, *Constitutional Rights*, 70–71.

10. Jonathon Elliot, ed., *The Debates of the State Conventions on the Adoption of the Federal Constitution, as Recommended by the General Convention at Philadelphia in 1787* (Philadelphia, 1866), 3:579.

11. Suzanna Sherry has argued that the debate between Federalists and Anti-Federalists over the issue of virtue and the public good signaled a paradigm shift in which man abandoned the classical view of republicanism that engendered the primacy of the community and replaced that view with a modernist one that now celebrates above all else the principles of individualism and autonomy. See Suzanna Sherry, "Civic Virtue and the Feminine Voice in Constitutional Adjudication," *Virginia Law Review* 543 (1986): 72.

12. Storing, *Anti-Federalists*, 15.

13. Ibid., 20.

14. See George W. Carey and Bruce Frohnen, eds., *Community and Tradition: Conservative Perspectives on the American Experience* (Lanham, Md.: Rowman and Littlefield: 1998).

15. Barry Alan Shain, "American Community," in *Community and Tradition*, ed. Carey and Frohnen, 55–56.

16. Wilfred M. McClay, "Mr. Emerson's Tombstone," in *Community and Tradition*, ed. Carey and Frohnen, 92.

17. There has been a surge of literature over the last three decades suggesting that late-eighteenth-century America should be characterized more accurately as an era that promoted classical republicanism. See Bernard Bailyn, *The Ideological Origins of the American Revolution* (Cambridge, Mass.: Harvard University Press, 1967); Lance Banning, *The Jeffersonian Persuasion: Evolution of a Party Ideology* (Ithaca, N.Y.: Cornell University Press, 1978); Sherry, "Civic Virtue"; and Carey and Frohnen, eds., *Community and Tradition*.

18. Sherry, "Civic Virtue," 5.

19. Alexander Hamilton, James Madison, and John Jay, *The Federalist Papers* (New York: Modern Library), no. 10.

20. See Storing, *Anti-Federalists*, chap. 3.

21. Alexis de Tocqueville, *Democracy in America*, trans. George Lawrence, ed. J. P. Mayer (Garden City, N.Y.: Anchor Books, 1969), 2:508. See also McClay, "Mr. Emerson's Tombstone," 92–97.

22. Gordon S. Wood, *The Creation of the American Republic 1776–1787* (Chapel Hill: University of North Carolina Press, 1969), 58.

23. Shain, "American Community," 46.

24. Brutus I, 2.9.16, in Herbert J. Storing, *The Anti-Federalist: Writings by the Opponents of the Constitution* (Chicago: University of Chicago Press, 1981), 24.

25. Joseph Lathrop, "A Miscellaneous Collection of Original Pieces," in *American Political Writing During the Founding Era, 1760–1805*, ed. Charles S. Hyneman and Donald Lutz (Indianapolis, Ind.: Liberty, 1983), 1:670–71.

26. Brutus, January 3, 1788, quoted in Storing, *Anti-Federalist Writings*, 146.

27. Wood, *American Republic*, 427.

28. Massachusetts Constitution of 1780, Part I, Art. III.

29. It is perhaps uniquely American because unlike any other political constitutions, the U.S. text, with its liberal foundation, allows for the discussion and consideration of alternative designs that may lead to its own rejection.

30. Michael Sandel is the communitarian most explicitly engaged in constitutional inquiry. See his *Democracy's Discontent: America in Search of a Public Philosophy* (Cambridge, Mass.: Harvard University Press, 1996). Yet even here, Sandel is exclusively interested in constitutional practice—namely, in judicial interpretation of the text—and not in the larger issue of constitutionalism.

31. The debate over the constitutional ideal goes back as far as the ancients. See, in particular, Aristotle, *The Politics*, ed. Ernest Barker (London: Oxford University Press, 1958).

32. The urgent tone of Hamilton's thoughts in the first *Federalist Paper* is illuminating. When pleading for the adoption of the U.S. Constitution, Hamilton wrote: "The subject speaks its own importance; comprehending in its consequences nothing less than the existence of the UNION, the safety and welfare of the parts of which it is composed, the fate of an empire in many respects the most interesting in the world." His words attest to the continued importance of debating constitutions.

33. In Philip B. Kurland and Ralph Lerner, *The Founders' Constitution* (Chicago: University of Chicago Press, 1987), chap. 17, doc. 23.

34. Ibid.

35. Ibid.

36. Albert P. Blaustein and Jay A. Sigler, eds., *Constitutions That Made History* (New York: Paragon House, 1988), XI.

37. See the Constitution of the Republic of South Africa, Chapter 1.

38. Just as the substantive neutrality that accompanies modern liberal statehood is also said to be a self-conscious preference.

39. See Alan C. Cairns, "Citizens (Outsiders) and Governments (Insiders) in Constitution Making: The Case of Meech Lake," *Canadian Public Policy* 14 (1988); and "The Living Canadian Constitution," in *Constitution, Government and Society in Canada*, ed. Douglas E. Williams (Toronto: McClelland and Stewart, 1989). Cairns has described the original Canadian constitution in these words: "The Canadian constitution is defined as a body of understandings which in turn define the basic institutions of government, the relationship between them, plus the relationships between governments in the federal system and between the citizens and those governments" ("Living Canadian Constitution," 31).

40. See O. D. Skelton, *The Life and Times of Sir Alexander Tilloch Galt* (Toronto: McClelland and Stewart, 1966).

41. Certainly, it can be argued that the debates surrounding slavery, and then the ultimate national crisis of the Civil War, provide examples of a time in American history when the question of political modeling or constitutional excellence resurfaced.

42. In many ways the attempt to improve the American political system by considering fundamentally different models resurrects the phrase in the Declaration of Independence that "it is the right of the people to alter or abolish" any "form of govern-

ment" that has become "destructive" to the principles of "life, liberty and the pursuit of happiness." Also, it reminds us of Jefferson's famous plea to change the Constitution, through constitutional convention, every generation.

43. See Benjamin Barber, *Strong Democracy: Participatory Politics for a New Age* (Berkeley: University of California Press, 1984). See also Robert Dahl, *Democracy and Its Critics* (New Haven, Conn.: Yale University Press, 1989); and James Fishkin, *Democracy and Deliberation: New Directions for Democratic Reform* (New Haven, Conn.: Yale University Press, 1991).

44. See Stephen Mulhall and Adam Swift, *Liberals and Communitarians* (Oxford: Blackwell Publishers, 1992), esp. the Preface and Introduction. See also Susan Moller Okin, who refers to the liberal-communitarian conflict as "the central debate in Anglo-American political theory during the 1980's" ("Humanist Liberalism," in *Liberalism and the Moral Life*, ed. Nancy Rosenblum [Cambridge, Mass.: Harvard University Press, 1989], 46).

45. Alasdair MacIntyre, *After Virtue: A Study in Moral Theory* (Notre Dame, Ind.: University of Notre Dame Press, 1981), 2.

46. Charles Taylor, *Philosophy and the Human Sciences: Philosophical Papers 2* (Cambridge: Cambridge University Press, 1985), 187.

47. Michael Sandel, *Liberalism and the Limits of Justice* (Cambridge: Cambridge University Press, 1982), 1.

48. For additional theoretical communitarian works, see Alasdair MacIntyre, "The Privatization of the Good," *Review of Politics* 52, no. 3 (Summer 1990): 344–61; and *Whose Justice? Which Rationality?* (Notre Dame, Ind.: University of Notre Dame Press, 1988). See also Michael Walzer, *Spheres of Justice* (Oxford: Basil Blackwell, 1983); "The Communitarian Critique of Liberalism," *Political Theory* 18, no. 1 (February 1990): 6–23; *The Company of Critics* (New York: Basic Books, 1988); and *Interpretation and Social Criticism* (Cambridge, Mass.: Harvard University Press, 1987).

49. Norman Barry, "Charles Taylor on Multiculturalism and the Politics of Recognition," in *Community and Tradition*, ed. Carey and Frohnen, 122–23.

50. Marx's discussion of alienation and Durkheim's concern over the principle of "anomie" also (implicitly) pervade the work of most prescriptive communitarians.

51. See Amitai Etzioni, *The Spirit of Community: Rights, Responsibilities, and the Communitarian Agenda* (New York: Crown Publishers, 1993).

52. See Barber, *Strong Democracy*.

53. See Amy Gutmann, "Communitarian Critics of Liberalism," *Philosophy and Public Affairs* 14, no. 3 (Summer 1985): 308–22.

54. See "The Responsive Community Platform: Rights and Responsibilities," signed November 18, 1991, in Etzioni, *Spirit of Community*, 253–67.

55. Certainly some liberals and communitarians have found a bit of common ground in the last few years. Theorists such as Michael Walzer and Stephen Macedo, for instance, have admitted to the allure of the opposite position, arguing separately that we are obliged to accept the basic premises of the liberal and communitarian position and try to accommodate each in our policy initiatives. See Stephen Macedo, *Liberal Virtues: Citizenship, Virtue, and Community in Liberal Constitutionalism* (Oxford: Oxford University Press, 1990). Overall, however, much of the debate is still characterized by dissonance. Consider Sandel, who writes in the Introduction to his *Liberalism and*

Its Critics (Oxford: Basil Blackwell, 1984) that the difference between neo-Kantian liberals and communitarians is considerable.

56. Macedo, *Liberal Virtues*.

57. Ibid., 12.

58. As will become clear in chapter 3, we must construct a hypothetical rather than illustrative vision of communitarian politics quite simply because no fully communitarian regime is currently in existence.

59. In Israel, non-Jews are not granted full citizenship, but certain procedural and personal liberties are given to minority constituents. See Gary J. Jacobsohn, *Apple of Gold: Israeli and American Constitutionalism* (Princeton, N.J.: Princeton University Press, 1992); and Joav Peled, "Ethnic Democracy and the Legal Construction of Citizenship: Arab Citizens of the Jewish State," *American Political Science Review* 86 (1992): 432–43.

60. Many of George W. Bush's policies, including his "Faith-based and Community Initiative," are influenced by communitarian philosophy. Additionally, the previous president and vice president were also said to be interested in the communitarian movement. In a *Time* magazine interview with former President Clinton, it was noted that "on his desk were a biography of Woodrow Wilson *and the latest book by sociologist [and communitarian] Amitai Etzioni*" (" 'That's what drives me nuts': An Interview with President Bill Clinton," *Time,* 13 December 1993, 42). Etzioni regularly mentions that he and his communitarian following have the sympathetic ear of former vice president Al Gore. That is not to say that Clinton and Gore fully support a constitutional revolution and the implementation of a communitarian agenda, only that the communitarian movement can boast that it is being taken seriously by some of the most influential political actors.

61. Aside from the liberals, the most prominent critique of contemporary communitarianism has come from the feminists. See, among others, Susan Moller Okin, *Justice, Gender and the Family* (New York: Basic Books, 1989), and "Justice and Gender," *Philosophy and Public Affairs* 16, no. 1 (Winter 1987): 42–72; Marilyn Friedman, "Feminism and Modern Friendship: Dislocating the Community," *Ethics* 99, no. 2 (January 1989): 275–90; Iris Marion Young, *Justice and the Politics of Difference* (Princeton, N.J.: Princeton University Press, 1990), and "The Ideal of Community and the Politics of Difference," *Social Theory and Practice* 12, no. 1 (Spring 1986): 1–26. Also see Donna Greschner, "Feminist Concerns with the New Communitarians," in *Law and the Community,* ed. A. Hutchinson and L. Green (Toronto: Carswell, 1989).

T W O : Theoretical and Prescriptive Foundations

1. See Michael Walzer, "The Communitarian Critique of Liberalism," *Political Theory* 18, no. 1 (February 1990): 6–23.

2. Stephen Holmes, *The Anatomy of Antiliberalism* (Cambridge, Mass.: Harvard University Press, 1993), 3.

3. Daniel Bell, *Communitarianism and Its Critics* (Oxford: Oxford University Press, 1993), 4.

4. Shlomo Avineri and Avner de-Shalit, eds., *Communitarianism and Individualism* (Oxford: Oxford University Press, 1992), 2.

5. Michael Sandel, *Democracy's Discontent: America in Search of a Public Philosophy* (Cambridge, Mass.: Belknap Press, 1996), 24.

6. John Rawls, "Kantian Constructivism in Moral Theory: The Dewey Lectures, 1980," *Journal of Philosophy* 77 (1980): 544.

7. See Will Kymlicka, "Liberalism and Communitarianism," *Canadian Journal of Philosophy* 18 (1988): 181–203.

8. Stephen Mulhall and Adam Swift, *Liberals and Communitarians* (Oxford: Blackwell, 1992), xi–xii.

9. See Michael Sandel, "The Procedural Republic and the Unencumbered Self," *Political Theory* 12, no. 1 (February 1984): 81–96.

10. Ibid., 86.

11. John Rawls, *A Theory of Justice* (Cambridge, Mass.: Harvard University Press, 1971), 560.

12. Sandel, "Procedural Republic," 90.

13. Sandel, *Democracy's Discontent*, 13.

14. Ibid., 16.

15. Charles Taylor, "Alternative Futures: Legitimacy, Identity and Alienation in Late Twentieth Century Canada," in *Constitutionalism, Citizenship and Society in Canada* (Toronto: University of Toronto Press, 1985), 209.

16. Alasdair MacIntyre, "Is Patriotism a Virtue?" in *Liberalism,* An Elger Reference Collection, Schools of Thought in Politics, vol. 2, ed. Richard J. Arneson (Brookfield, Vt.: Ashgate Publishers, 1992), 259.

17. Sandel, "Procedural Republic."

18. Will Kymlicka, *Contemporary Political Philosophy: An Introduction* (Oxford: Clarendon Press, 1990), 213.

19. Michael Sandel, *Liberalism and the Limits of Justice* (Cambridge: Cambridge University Press, 1982), 58.

20. Sandel, *Limits of Justice*, 22.

21. Taylor, perhaps more than any other communitarian thinker, combines both methodological and normative arguments in his general challenge to the liberal paradigm.

22. Taylor, "Alternative Futures," 187.

23. Ibid.

24. Charles Taylor, *Sources of the Self* (Cambridge: Cambridge University Press, 1990), 34.

25. Ibid. The overall premise of Taylor's argument here is that the self and a conception of the good are inescapably linked.

26. Taylor, "Alternative Futures," 188.

27. Ibid.

28. Ibid., 183.

29. Charles Taylor, *Hegel and Modern Society* (Cambridge: Cambridge University Press, 1979), 157.

30. Ibid., 159.

31. Amitai Etzioni, himself a leading communitarian, describes MacIntyre as a "strong" communitarian because of his propensity toward Aristotelian virtue and ancient politics. Etzioni writes: "[MacIntyre's] conception of the exemplary moral community derives from the Aristotelian tradition of civic virtue, where persons are

understood to achieve a *telos* by exercising virtues." See Amitai Etzioni, "Liberals and Communitarians," *Partisan Review* 57, no. 2 (1990): 215–27.

32. See MacIntyre, *After Virtue* (1984) and *Whose Justice, Whose Rationality?* (1988). The "emotivist" self is similar to the "atomistic" self described by Taylor. According to MacIntyre, the emotivist self is one that holds no firm attachment to any shared moral or ethical teaching. "Judgments," he says, "are *nothing but* [individual] expressions of preference" (*After Virtue, 11–12*). Accordingly, the emotivist self, with its liberal reinforcements, is an isolated self.

33. MacIntyre, *After Virtue*, 32.

34. Mulhall and Swift, *Liberals and Communitarians*, 76.

35. MacIntyre, *After Virtue*, 2.

36. MacIntyre, *Whose Justice?* 397.

37. Michael Walzer, *Radical Principles: Reflections of an Unreconstructed Democrat* (New York: Basic Books, 1980), 7.

38. Ibid., 6.

39. Ibid.

40. Charles Taylor, "Cross Purposes: The Liberal Communitarian Debate," in *Liberalism and the Moral Life*, ed. Nancy Rosenblum (Cambridge, Mass.: Harvard University Press, 1989), 166.

41. Sandel, *Limits of Justice*, 62.

42. Sandel, "Procedural Republic," 86–87.

43. Sandel, *Democracy's Discontent*, 69.

44. Ibid., 117.

45. MacIntyre, "Is Patriotism a Virtue?" 250.

46. Ibid., 253.

47. See Michael Walzer, *Obligations: Essays on Disobedience, War, and Citizenship* (Cambridge, Mass.: Harvard University Press, 1970).

48. Michael Walzer, "The Idea of Civil Society: A Path to Social Reconstruction" *Dissent* 38 (Spring 1991): 293–304.

49. Taylor, "Cross Purposes," 166.

50. Ibid., 170.

51. Ibid.

52. Some argue that liberal society does have a "common" good that can be found as a "result of a process of combining preferences, all of which are counted equally (if consistent with the principles of justice)." Therefore, the claim that liberal society can only articulate a "convergent" or "cooperative" good, and not a "common" good is, to some, a matter of interpretation. See Kymlicka, *Liberalism, Community and Culture* (Oxford: Clarendon Press, 1990), 206.

53. Taylor, "Cross Purposes," 170.

54. Kymlicka, *Contemporary Political Philosophy*, 206.

55. In his later works, Rawls has qualified his argument to apply only to western-style constitutional democracies. See in particular, John Rawls, *Political Liberalism* (New York: Columbia University Press, 1993).

56. See Baron de Montesquieu, *The Spirit of the Laws*, translated by Thomas Nugent (New York: Collier Macmillan, 1949), I:XIV–XIX.

57. See Michael Walzer, *Spheres of Justice* (Oxford, Basil Blackwell, 1983), 313–13. See also Walzer, *The Company of Critics* (New York: Basic Books, 1988); and *Interpretation*

and Social Criticism (Cambridge, Mass., Harvard University Press, 1987). See also Christopher Lasch, who, like Walzer, explains that the problem with liberalism lies with its "narrow conception of the public interest." Politics, he says, should regulate "the practices of individuals and groups so as to limit the degree to which they are comprised and corrupted by the pursuit of external goods" ("The Communitarian Critique of Liberalism" in *Community in America: The Challenge of Habits of the Heart*, ed. Charles H. Reynolds and Ralph Norman [Berkeley: University of California Press, 1988], 184).

58. See in particular, Michael Walzer, "The Communitarian Critique of Liberalism," *Political Theory* 18, no. 1 (February 1990), 6–23.

59. Ibid., 20.

60. Michael Walzer, "The Idea of Civil Society: A Path to Social Reconstruction," *Dissent* (Spring 1991): 293–304.

61. Ibid., 303.

62. Ibid., 303 (emphasis added).

63. For a discussion of liberal skepticism and the issue of state sponsorship of particularistic goods, see Kymlicka, *Contemporary Political Philosophy*, chapter 6.

64. Sandel, *Democracy's Discontent*, 28.

65. Ibid., 25.

66. See Kenneth L. Grasso, "Contemporary Communitarianism, the Lure of the State, and the Modern Quest for Community" in *Community and Tradition*, ed. Carey and Frohnen (Lanham, Md.: Rowman and Littlefield, 1998), 17–38.

67. Ibid., 37.

68. Bruce Frohnen, *The New Communitarians and the Crisis of Modern Liberalism* (Lawrence: University of Kansas Press, 1996), 22.

69. Ibid., 22.

70. Bruce Frohnen. "Commitment and Obligation" in *Community and Tradition*, ed. Carey and Frohnen (Lanham, Md.: Rowman and Littlefield, 1998), 179.

71. Frohnen, *New Communitarians*, 36.

72. Ibid., 27. Frohnen believes there is one intermediate institution that is more successful than others in instilling a sense of virtue among individuals—religion. "Without religion or some other putatively transcendent set of standards telling us to do unto others as we would have done unto us, society breaks down," he writes. "Individuals come to see their community as a source of benefits to be exploited rather than the locus of a way of life they wish to protect. We lose our commitment to and our knowledge of virtue and commence lives of selfishness, irresponsibility, and even crime." Despite their similar conclusions about intermediate institutions more generally, other conservative communitarians are not as enamored with religion as the primary source of guidance.

73. Carey and Frohnen, *Community and Tradition*, 7.

74. Ibid., 15.

75. See Alexis de Tocqueville, *Democracy in America*, Book II, Part II, Chapter 4.

76. See Frohnen, *New Communitarians*.

77. Tocqueville, *Democracy in America*, 511.

78. Barry Alan Shain, "American Community," in *Community and Tradition*, ed. Carey and Frohnen, 46.

79. Tocqueville, *Democracy in America,* quoted in Shain, "American Community," 49.

80. George W. Carey, "The Constitution and Community," in George W. Carey and Bruce Frohnen, eds., *Community and Tradition: Conservative Perspectives on the American Experience* (Lanham, Md.: Rowan and Littlefield, 1998), 63.

81. Amitai Etzioni, *The Spirit of Community: Rights, Responsibilities and the Communitarian Agenda* (New York: Crown Publishers, 1993), 23. See also Etzioni, *An Immodest Agenda: Rebuilding America before the Twenty-First Century* (New York: McGraw Hill, 1983); and "Liberals and Communitarians," *Partisan Review* 57, no. 2 (1990): 215–27.

82. Etzioni, *Spirit of Community,* 24.

83. Ibid., 4.

84. See Mary Ann Glendon, *Rights Talk: The Impoverishment of Political Discourse* (New York: Free Press, 1991).

85. In addition to the ongoing work centered on the theory of liberalism, see Bruce Ackerman, *Social Justice in the Liberal State* (New Haven, Conn.: Yale University Press, 1980).

86. See, in particular, William A. Galston, *Liberal Purposes: Goods, Virtues and Diversity in the Liberal State* (Cambridge: Cambridge University Press, 1991). See also Galston, "Moral Personality and Liberal Theory: John Rawls's Dewey Lectures," *Political Theory* 10, no. 4 (November 1982): 492–519; and *Justice and the Human Good* (Chicago: University of Chicago Press, 1980).

87. Etzioni, *Spirit of Community,* 3.

88. Ibid., 3.

89. See, in particular, Etzioni, *Spirit of Community,* and Glendon, *Rights Talk.*

90. Etzioni, *Spirit of Community,* 5.

91. Glendon, *Rights Talk,* x–xi.

92. Ibid., 9.

93. Ibid., 14.

94. Ibid., 44–45.

95. Ibid., 15.

96. Etzioni, *Spirit of Community,* 1.

97. See Morris Janowitz, *The Reconstruction of Patriotism: Education for Civic Consciousness* (Chicago: University of Chicago Press, 1983).

98. Etzioni, *Spirit of Community,* 4.

99. See Glendon, *Rights Talk,* chapter 7.

100. Ibid., 179.

101. See Benjamin Barber, *Strong Democracy: Participatory Politics for a New Age* (Berkeley: University of California Press, 1984). See also Barber, *The Conquest of Politics: Liberal Philosophy in Democratic Times* (Princeton, N.J.: Princeton University Press, 1988).

102. Barber, *Strong Democracy,* 118.

103. Many voting studies reveal America's trend toward political apathy. Among the most interesting are: Paul R. Abramson and John H. Aldrich, "The Decline of Electoral Participation in America," *American Political Science Review* (September 1982): 502–21; G. Bingham Powell Jr., "American Voter Turnout in Comparative Perspective," *American Political Science Review* (March 1986): 17–43; Angus Campbell, Philip E. Converse,

Warren E. Miller, and Donald E. Stokes, *The American Voter* (New York: John Wiley and Sons, 1960); and Norman H. Nie, Sidney Verba, and John R. Petrocik, *The Changing American Voter* (Cambridge, Mass.: Harvard University Press, 1976).

104. Barber, *Strong Democracy,* 4.

105. Ibid., 151.

106. Ibid., 4.

107. Ibid., 155 (emphasis his).

108. Ibid., 123.

109. Perhaps Barber was prophetic in light of the fiasco surrounding the 2000 presidential election.

110. Etzioni, *Spirit of Community,* 23.

111. See Galston, *Liberal Purposes,* chapter 11.

112. Ibid., 242–43.

113. Ibid., 255–56.

114. Barber also has a vision of civic education in which the training of a true citizen comes from constantly engaging the individual in the practice of politics. See Barber, *Strong Democracy,* 233–37.

115. For a more detailed discussion of communitarian ideas for education, consult Etzioni, *Spirit of Community,* chapter 3, as well as "The Responsive Communitarian Platform."

116. Etzioni, *Spirit of Community,* 248.

117. Galston offers a fine exploration of religion and its place in the overall development of American citizenship in chapter 12 of *Liberal Purposes.* Dismayed by the modern radicalization of both secular and religious institutions in keeping politics and the moral teaching of religious communities completely and thoroughly separate, he contends that churches, synagogues, and mosques have much to teach liberal citizens about the ways of sharing, tolerance, and freedom. But until we allow those religious institutions to exist (within limits) as part of the public sphere, we will never fully heed their lessons.

T H R E E : Participation, Consensus, and the Common Good

1. H. N. Hirsch has observed that "it is striking that *none* of the [communitarian] scholars presents a straightforward account of the conditions necessary for creating a community." See "The Threnody of Liberalism: Constitutional Liberty and the Renewal of Community," *Political Theory* 14, no. 3 (August 1986): 433.

2. In fact, John Wallach has written that the problem with communitarianism (and liberalism) is that neither are "political theory at all. None saw what he was doing as fundamental *political* theory or *political* critique, and the starting point for both liberals and communitarians lie outside the political domain." See John Wallach, "Liberals, Communitarians and the Tasks of Political Theory" *Political Theory* 15, no. 4 (November 1987): 581–611.

3. Ian Shapiro has written: "[communitarians] should shift the [liberal-communitarian debate] to a lower level of abstraction and seek to supply substantive content to the various communitarian proposals they advocate." To a certain extent, the prescriptive communitarians have, since Shapiro raised this criticism, supplied the needed content, but Shapiro's claim is still valid in terms of a constitutional communitarian

strategy. See Ian Shapiro, *The Evolution of Rights in Liberal Theory* (Cambridge: Cambridge University Press, 1986), 297. In a related statement, Ronald Beiner, himself a communitarian sympathizer, admits there exists a big gap between theory and practice in the communitarian movement. He writes: "I admit freely that the critical probing of contemporary liberalism in this work has been conducted on the assumption that theory as such is a pure indulgence whose end is simply the enhancement of our understanding, not the supply of nostrums for an improved practice." See Ronald Beiner, *What's the Matter with Liberalism?* (Berkeley: University of California Press, 1992).

4. See Daniel Bell, *Communitarianism and Its Critics* (Oxford: Clarendon Press, 1993), 91. Bell goes on to identify the critics who condemn communitarianism as John Dunn, *Interpreting Political Responsibility* (Oxford: Polity Press, 1990); Nancy Rosenblum, "Pluralism and Self-Defense," in *Liberalism and the Moral Life*, ed. Nancy Rosenblum (Cambridge, Mass.: Harvard University Press, 1989) as well as "Moral Membership in a Post-Liberal State" *World Politics* (July 1984); and Stephen Holmes, "The Permanent Structure of Anti-Liberal Thought," in *Liberalism and the Moral Life*, ed. Rosenblum.

5. See Robert N. Bellah, Richard Madsen, William M. Sullivan, Ann Swidler, and Steven M. Tipton, *The Good Society* (New York: Vintage Books, 1991). See also their *Habits of the Heart* (Berkeley: University of California Press, 1985), and their edited volume, *Individualism and Commitment in American Life: Readings on the Themes of Habits of the Heart* (New York: Harper and Row, 1987). See also Bell, *Communitarianism and Its Critics* (1993); William M. Sullivan, *Reconstructing Public Philosophy* (Berkeley: University of California Press, 1982); and Beiner, *What's the Matter with Liberalism?* (1992). See also Ronald Beiner, "What's the Matter with Liberalism?" in *Law and the Community: The End of Liberalism?* ed. Allen C. Hutchinson and Leslie J. M. Green (Toronto: Carswell, 1989), where Beiner disavows any connection to the communitarian movement. Yet, like Alasdair MacIntyre's, Beiner's normative theory—described by him as socialist—is remarkably compatible with the communitarian endeavor.

6. See, in particular, Alasdair MacIntyre, *After Virtue: A Study in Moral Theory* (Notre Dame, Ind.: University of Notre Dame Press, 1981), 221; and "A Partial Response to my Critics," in *After MacIntyre: Critical Perspectives on the Work of Alasdair MacIntyre*, ed. John Horton and Susan Mendes (Cambridge: Polity, 1994), 302. For an excellent discussion of the issue, see Will Kymlicka, *Contemporary Political Philosophy: An Introduction*, 2nd ed. (Oxford: Oxford University Press, 2002), 261–68.

7. Brad Lowell Stone, "On the Extent of Community: Civil Society, Civil Religion, and the State," in *Community and Tradition*, ed. George W. Carey and Bruce Frohnen (Lanham, Md.: Roman and Littlefield, 1998), 138. See also Bruce Frohnen, *The New Communitarians and the Crisis of Modern Liberalism* (Lawrence: University of Kansas Press, 1996), 215–18.

8. Michael Sandel, *Democracy's Discontent: America in Search of Public Philosophy* (Cambridge, Mass.: Belknap Press, 1996), 6.

9. Ibid., 65–66.

10. See Benjamin Barber, *A Place for Us: How to Make Society Civil and Democracy Strong* (New York: Hill and Wang, 1998), chapter 2.

11. Ibid., 44.

12. MacIntyre, *After Virtue*, 222.

13. Frohnen, *New Communitarians,* 66.

14. MacIntyre, *After Virtue,* 219.

15. See Norman Barry, "Charles Taylor on Multiculturalism and the Politics of Recognition," in *Community and Tradition,* ed. Carey and Frohnen (1998), 103–24.

16. Baron de Montesquieu, *The Spirit of the Laws,* translated by Thomas Nugent (New York: Collier Macmillan, 1949), Book IV, number 5.

17. Jean Jacques Rousseau, *The Social Contract,* translated by G. D. H. Cole (New York: E. P. Dutton, 1950), Book II, chapter 7. See also Stephen Kautz, *Liberalism and Community* (Ithaca, N.Y.: Cornell University Press, 1995), 58–59.

18. In describing the communitarian position, Avineri and de-Shalit write: "From the ontological argument communitarians conclude that, in order to justify the special obligations that we hold to members of our communities—families, nations, and so forth—one must attach some intrinsic (i.e. non-instrumental) value to the community itself and to our relations with other members of the community" (*Communitarianism and Individualism* [Oxford: Oxford University Press, 1992], 6). Also, Markate Daly, in reference to the liberal-communitarian debate, notes, "The debate focuses on the theoretical and social consequences of stressing either liberty or community as the primary value in a society." See Markate Daly, ed., *Communitarianism: A New Public Ethics* (Belmont, Calif.: Wadsworth Publishing, 1994), xix.

19. For a discussion of the concept of "flourishing," see J. Donald Moon, "Thin Selves/Rich Lives: On the Concept of the Self in Liberal Theory," paper delivered at the Annual Meeting of the American Political Science Association, Washington, D.C., August 1986.

20. Bellah et al., *The Good Society,* 139.

21. David Miller, "Community and Citizenship," in *Communitarianism and Individualism,* ed. Shlomo Avineri and Avner de-Shalit (Oxford: Oxford University Press, 1992), 86.

22. MacIntyre, *After Virtue,* 200.

23. Bell, *Communitarianism and Its Critics,* 141. Of course, Walzer's point regarding the distribution of social goods and the theory of justice required for a fair administration of that distribution is instructive in that it supplies the foundation for Bell's argument.

24. For each of these political observers, locating the common character of the inhabitants of a proposed state is essential to the political and constitutional construction of that polity. See, in particular, Rousseau's *Constitutional Project for Corsica;* Montesquieu's *The Spirit of the Laws;* and Cass Sunstein, "Constitution-Making in Eastern Europe: An Interim Report" (1991).

25. Bell, *Communitarianism and Its Critics,* 14.

26. See Stephen Newman, "Challenging the Liberal Individualist Tradition in America: 'Community' as a Critical Ideal in Recent Political Theory," in *Law and the Community,* ed. Allen Hutchinson and Leslie Green (Toronto: Carswell, 1989).

27. In response to the communitarian suggestion that liberalism encourages a neutral state, some have argued that the idea of state neutrality provides a separate and distinct interpretation of the conception of the good. Stephen Holmes, for instance, has noted that liberalism has its own conception of the good that combines individual preferences and personal freedom. Holmes' point is that liberal societies are not without a conception of the good; they simply endorse a different interpretation of the

good. See Stephen Holmes, "The Permanent Structure of Anti-liberal Thought" in *Liberalism and the Moral Life,* ed. Nancy Rosenblum (Cambridge, Mass.: Harvard University Press, 1989).

28. Bell, *Communitarianism and Its Critics,* 37.

29. Benjamin Barber, *Strong Democracy* (Berkeley: University of California Press, 1984), 156.

30. Ibid., 161.

31. I am thinking of the Jewish state of Israel as an illustration of this point.

32. I have combined what Robert Booth Fowler finds to be two separate communitarian ideas—participatory democracy and republicanism—because I believe, unlike him, that in communitarian thinking there are only minor differences between the two. In fact, it is quite clear that these two forms of government are deeply related and perhaps used interchangeably throughout the entire literature on community. Both the communitarian forms of participatory democracy and republicanism claim that ultimate sovereignty is vested immediately in the citizenry. Similarly, both "seek to transform politics from a process to a way of life" by active participation, and "require a life of shared virtues and shared history." For Fowler's discussion of the differences, see his *The Dance with Community: The Contemporary Debate in American Political Thought* (Lawrence: University Press of Kansas, 1991), Part II.

33. Some may claim that democratic majoritarianism accomplishes much the same thing. After all, majority rule is a political decision rule that seeks to produce decisions and policies based on some idea of collective will. The major difference between democratic majoritarianism and the consensus-based decision rule that is popular among communitarian thinkers is that consensualism attempts to execute political decisions based on the principles of full and active participation as well as the idea of cooperation and compromise. As such, it could be a far cry from the mere counting of individual interests in majoritarian societies.

34. See Richard A. Epstein, "The Republican Civic Tradition: Modern Republicanism—Or the Flight From Substance," *Yale Law Journal* 97 (1988): 1633, 1634–37.

35. See Alexander Hamilton, James Madison, and John Jay, *The Federalist Papers* (New York: Modern Library), no. 51, p. 243.

36. See Will Kymlicka, *Contemporary Political Philosophy: An Introduction* (Oxford: Clarendon Press, 1990), 206–7.

37. There are a variety of prescriptive communitarian proposals for ensuring active participation in the political process, and many of these include innovative technological interaction resembling the "electronic town meetings" that first made news during the 1992 presidential election. The common denominator and the important theoretical point throughout all of these proposals, however, is that they undertake to improve the citizens' ability to collectively craft and shape their political communities. For specific proposals, see Robert Dahl, *Democracy and Its Critics* (New Haven, Conn.: Yale University Press, 1989); James Fishkin, *Democracy and Deliberation: New Directions for Democratic Reform* (New Haven, Conn.: Yale University Press, 1991); and Barber, *Strong Democracy.*

38. See Barber, *Strong Democracy* (1984); and *The Conquest of Politics: Liberal Philosophy in Democratic Times* (Princeton, N.J.: Princeton University Press, 1988).

39. Communitarians, like so many other political ideologies, use a variety of different terms to depict one fundamental practice. Barber's understanding of commu-

nitarian politics, for example, uses "mutualism" or "consensualism" to describe the ideal form of political decision making. Etzioni and the Responsive Community Movement, on the other hand, prefer to use "deliberation" to describe the same thing. In the end, however, they are advocating the same type of decision-rule, one that seeks to build compromise and consensus through interaction, discussion, and debate.

40. Barber, *Strong Democracy*, 132.

41. William M. Sullivan, "A Renewal of Civic Philosophy," in *Communitarianism: A New Public Ethics*, ed. Markate Daly (Belmont, Calif.: Wadsworth Publishing, 1994), 194.

42. John Dewey, *The Public and Its Problems* (New York: Holt Rinehart, 1927), 148.

43. Barber, *Strong Democracy*, 145.

44. See Sullivan, *Reconstructing Public Philosophy*.

45. Ibid., 71.

46. Ibid.

47. Barber, *Strong Democracy*, 198.

48. Ibid., 199–200.

49. Sullivan, "Renewal," 190.

50. Bellah et al., *Good Society*, 5.

51. Ibid., 4.

52. Ibid., 10.

53. Ibid., 10–11.

54. Ibid., 40.

55. See Bell, *Communitarianism and Its Critics*, 31–45.

56. See Bellah et al., *Good Society*, especially chapter 1 where the authors consider "why our cultural resources for dealing with [institutional dilemmas] are impoverished."

57. Ibid., 136.

58. Frohnen, *New Communitarians*, 235.

59. Ibid., 205. See also Barry Alan Shain, *The Myth of American Individualism: The Protestant Origins of American Political Thought* (Princeton, N.J.: Princeton University Press, 1994).

60. Bell, *Communitarianism and Its Critics*, 158. There is good reason to believe the communitarian point raised here. After all, both America (with the issue of multicultural education and bilingualism) and Canada (with the French language speakers opposing unilingualism) are currently embroiled in a fight over the possibility of implementing as mandatory a single dominant language. The opponents of these measures often raise the argument that their identity and culture will be lost with the adoption of such a policy.

61. This works, communitarians assert, precisely because language is the most commonly used tool to facilitate collective relationships. Presumably, only those who fully understand the language can actively participate in the shaping of the public good.

62. Kymlicka, *Contemporary Political Philosophy*, 206–7.

63. Bell, *Communitarianism and Its Critics*, 183.

64. As Kymlicka indicates, supporters of this sort of disparate treatment may have a number of justifications for their decision to place more value on one over the other. "Studies may reveal that [art] is stimulating whereas wrestling [or boxing] produces frustration or docility; or that wrestling [and boxing fans] often come to regret their

past activities, whereas [patrons of the arts] rarely regret theirs" (*Contemporary Political Philosophy,* 201).

65. Liberals often refer to this communitarian practice as censorship. But to be fair to the communitarian position, it is less a call to censor certain ideas, and more an attempt to celebrate the thoughts and practices the embedded community already shares in common.

66. See Benjamin Barber, "A Mandate for Liberty: Requiring Education-Based Community Service," in *The Essential Communitarian Reader,* ed. Amitai Etzioni (Lanham, Md.: Rowman and Littlefield: 1998), 237–45.

67. The Responsive Communitarian Platform outwardly disavows any connection to particularistic or intolerant behavior.

68. Bell, *Communitarianism and Its Critics,* 140. See also Peter Singer, *Hegel* (Oxford: Oxford University Press, 1983).

69. See Michael Walzer, "The New Tribalism: Notes on a Difficult Problem," *Dissent* (Spring 1992): 164–71.

70. Stephen Newman writes: "What so annoys communitarians is the distinction liberals insist on making between the political community, or the state, and other levels of human association, or society. Communitarian theorists are inclined to view politics and society as inextricably joined together: the state is a reflection of society (it is the community's political face) and society is, or at least it can become, an expression of the community's political will." See Stephen Newman, "Challenging the Liberal Individualist Tradition in America: 'Community' as a Critical Ideal in Recent Political Theory," in *Law and the Community: The End of Liberalism?* ed. Allen Hutchinson and Leslie Green (Toronto: Carswell, 1989), 255.

71. See Joshua Abramowitz, "The Tao of community," *Public Interest* no. 113 (Fall 1993): 119–21.

72. Bellah et al., *Good Society,* 16.

73. Ibid., 143.

74. Bell, *Communitarianism and Its Critics,* 137.

75. One of the necessary functions of the central state that Bell points to is that of taxation. He says that taxation must be the bastion of the national government because it is the only political institution that has the means and the scope to carry out the function. But fully consistent with the first principle of communitarianism, Bell notes that certain functions (like that of taxation) must be carried out at the national level because it is there (and not at the local level) that most of the citizens feel the highest sense of communalism. "It just so happens that the nation-state has emerged, for whatever concatenation of historical reasons, as the unit within which our sense of solidarity is strongest" (ibid., 138).

76. Ibid., 137.

77. See Kymlicka, *Contemporary Political Philosophy,* 206–7.

78. See Amy Gutmann, "Communitarian Critics of Liberalism," *Philosophy and Public Affairs* 14, no. 3 (Summer 1985); and Robert Thigpen and Lyle Downing, "Liberalism and the Communitarian Critique, *American Journal of Political Science* 31, no. 3 (August 1987): 637–55.

79. Aside from the most obvious feminist critiques listed above, see also Marilyn Frye, *The Politics of Reality: Essays in Feminist Theory* (Freedom, Calif.: Crossing Press, 1983); Jean Bethke Elshtain, *Public Man, Private Woman: Women in Social and Political*

Thought (Princeton, N.J.: Princeton University Press, 1981); Jean Grimshaw, *Philosophy and Feminist Thinking* (Minneapolis: University of Minnesota Press, 1986); Carole Pateman, "'The Disorder of Women': Women, Love and the Sense of Justice," *Ethics* 81 (1980): 20–34; as well as Will Kymlicka, "Some Questions about Justice and Community," in Bell, *Communitarianism and Its Critics.*

80. At the outset it seems clear that the subtle distinction between constitutional theory and constitutionalism must be addressed. When I speak of *constitutional theory,* I am referring specifically to the theory and practice of political order, or self-conscious political design. When I refer to *constitutionalism,* on the other hand, I am mainly considering the (deeply related) principle that power must in some way be created and limited. The distinction is made more clearly by considering the collected works of Harris and perhaps Kuhn on the one side, and chiefly McIlwain and Corwin on the other. For this project, however, both concepts are essential because, as I will argue below, the current construction of communitarianism has difficulty sustaining the principles of modern constitutionalism, whereas the very mission of the communitarian project (and the entirety of the liberal-communitarian debate) is one, as I have argued above, centered most profoundly on the idea of constitutional order.

81. The former Soviet bloc countries, as they seek to stabilize their countries after independence, are currently engrossed in just such a battle. See, among many others, Cass R. Sunstein, "Constitution-Making in Eastern Europe: An Interim Report"; Stephen L. Elkin, "Citizenship and Constitutionalism in Post-Communist Regimes," *PS: Political Science and Politics* 23, no. 2 (June 1990): 163–66; and Jon Elster, "Constitutionalism in Eastern Europe: An Introduction," *University of Chicago Law Review* 58 (1991): 447–82.

82. Herbert J. Storing and Murray Dry, the leading students of the Anti-Federalist movement, have both remarked that those who opposed the ratification of the U.S. Constitution must be thought of as important members of the American founding. See Herbert J. Storing, ed., *The Anti-Federalist: An Abridgement of the Complete Anti-Federalist* (Chicago: University of Chicago Press, 1985). William F. Harris has argued a very similar point in *The Interpretable Constitution* (Baltimore: Johns Hopkins University Press, 1994).

83. Hamilton, Madison, and Jay, *The Federalist Papers,* no. 1, p. 3.

FOUR: The Constitutionalist Challenge to American Communitarianism

1. Robert Cover was perhaps the only clear advocate of a community theory that outwardly addresses the larger issue of constitutionalism. See Robert M. Cover, "Nomos and Narrative," *Harvard Law Review* 97 (1983): 4–68.

2. See H. N. Hirsch, "The Threnody of Liberalism: Constitutional Liberty and the Renewal of Community, *Political Theory* 14, no. 3 (August 1986): 423–49.

3. See Alexander Hamilton, James Madison, and John Jay, *The Federalist Papers* (New York: Modern Library), no. 51.

4. Walter Murphy, "Constitutions, Constitutionalism, and Democracy," in *Constitutionalism and Democracy: Transitions in the Contemporary World,* ed. Douglas Greenburg, Stanley N. Katz, Melanie Beth Oliviero, and Steven Wheatley (Oxford: Oxford University Press, 1993), 7.

5. Here I take exception to Gordon J. Schochet, who insists that "today, a 'constitu-

tion' merely identifies a set of formal political institutions rather than an ideology." If by ideology he includes certain values and principles that inform the polity, then he is wrong to say that a constitution does not include an ideological component. See Gordon J. Schochet, "Introduction: Constitutionalism, Liberalism and the Study of Politics," in *Nomos XX: Constitutionalism*, ed. J. Roland Pennock and John W. Chapman (New York: New York University Press, 1979), 5.

6. Stephen Holmes, "Precommitment and the Paradox of Democracy," in *Constitutionalism and Democracy*, ed. Jon Elster and Rune Slagstad (Cambridge: Cambridge University Press, 1988), 196 (emphasis his).

7. There is an important difference between the sovereign and practical reflections of the sovereign (majorities, representatives, etc.). I do not mean to discount this difference, but merely to point out that the constitutionalist is concerned about both.

8. The word "tangible" here is probably a misnomer. A design for political society—a constitution, in other words—does not have to be written to be understood. Thus, to use "tangible" in this context is not to insist on a physically present constitutional text but rather to recognize that constitutionalist (or even nonconstitutionalist) regimes will have a tangible, interpretable ordering of public institutions. For a detailed discussion of the differences between constitutional texts and constitutional designs, see William F. Harris, *The Interpretable Constitution* (Baltimore: Johns Hopkins University Press, 1993); and "Bonding Word and Polity: The Logic of American Constitutionalism," *American Political Science Review* 76, no. 1 (1982): 34–45.

9. See Graham Walker, "The Constitutional Good: Constitutionalism's Equivocal Moral Imperative," *Polity* 26, no. 1 (Fall 1993): 91–111.

10. In many cases the ruler was limited solely by religious teachings, by what he interpreted as the "word of God."

11. Bolingbroke, "A Dissertation Upon Parties (1733–1734)," quoted in Charles McIlwain, *Constitutionalism: Ancient and Modern* (Ithaca, N.Y.: Cornell University Press, 1940). Schochet adds to Bolingbroke's definition of constitutionalism when he notes, "Constitutional limitations included the accumulated traditions, folkways, and practices of a people as well as the overarching dictates of nature and/or divinity" ("Constitutionalism," 2).

12. See Schochet, "Constitutionalism."

13. Of course not all constitutional limits on sovereign authority were powerless. As an example of a forceful limit, consider the Magna Carta, which contractually bound the king and his barons during the thirteenth and fourteenth centuries. See Arthur Sutherland, *Constitutionalism in America: Origin and Evolution of Its Fundamental Ideas* (New York: Ginn and Co., 1965), chapter 2.

14. Consider the description of the "coronation oath" in McIlwain, *Constitutionalism*, chapter 5.

15. See Hamilton, Madison, and Jay, *The Federalist Papers*, no. 9.

16. See McIlwain, *Constitutionalism*. See also Charles McIlwain, *Constitutionalism and the Changing World* (New York: Macmillan, 1939).

17. For an additional account of the development of the theory of constitutionalism, see Stephen Elkin, "Constitutionalism: Old and New," in *A New Constitutionalism: Designing Political Institutions for a Good Society*, ed. Stephen L. Elkin and Karol Edward Soltan (Chicago: University of Chicago Press, 1993).

18. Among others, see Schochet, "Constitutionalism"; Donald Lutz, *The Origins of*

American Constitutionalism (Baton Rouge: Louisiana State University Press, 1988). Interestingly, others note that the shift to a more potent modern conception of constitutionalism paralleled the movement away from sovereignty of the few and toward democracy, or popular sovereignty.

19. McIlwain, *Constitutionalism*, 23–24.

20. In the early editions of *Constitutional Government and Democracy*, Carl J. Friedrich described the nature of constitutionalism as "restraints upon the arbitrary exercise of governmental power." See Friedrich, *Constitutional Government and Democracy: Theory and Practice in Europe and America* (New York: Ginn and Co., 1946).

21. See Judith Shklar, *Legalism* (Cambridge, Mass.: Harvard University Press, 1964).

22. For a wonderful description of the relationship between fundamental law and ordinary law, see Stephen Griffin, *American Constitutionalism: From Theory to Politics* (Princeton, N.J.: Princeton University Press, 1996), chapter 1. See also H. L. A. Hart, *The Concept of Law* (Oxford: Oxford University Press, 1961); and Larry Alexander, ed., *Constitutionalism: Philosophical Foundations* (Cambridge: Cambridge University Press, 1998).

23. Harris, "Bonding Word." See also Harris, *Interpretable Constitution*.

24. Consider the recent example of South Africa.

25. Chapter 3 in Sanford Levinson's *Constitutional Faith* (Princeton, N.J.: Princeton University Press, 1988) examines the importance of oaths to the continuation of the American constitutional project.

26. In this, the post-Enlightenment era of rationality, where many view government with distrust and apprehension, most regimes have chosen to publicly and permanently announce constitutional limits in writing. As a result, the world has witnessed a substantial increase in formal written constitutional texts over the past two hundred years. Yet formality is not necessarily a requirement of objectivity.

27. Thomas Paine, *Rights of Man: The Complete Works of Thomas Paine* (London: 1793), 302–3 (emphasis his). Commenting on Paine's point, McIlwain notes, "These statements express very clearly the contrast between the new [modern] conception of the conscious formulation by a people of its fundamental law, the new definition of 'constitution,' and the older traditional view in which the word was applied only to the substantive principles to be deduced from a nation's actual institutions and their development" (*Constitutionalism*, 5).

28. See also Thomas Jefferson, who wrote in his "Notes on the State of Virginia" that one of the major defects of the Virginia Constitution was the fact that there was no clear separation between the legislature and the text. He was concerned about the power of the state assembly both in relation to the other branches of government and with respect to the state constitution. The nature of his concern centered on the realization that the state assembly could alter the constitution with ordinary legislation. In *Thomas Jefferson: Selected Writings*, ed. Harvey Mansfield (Wheeling, Ill.: Harlan Davidson, 1979), 28–36.

29. See Hamilton, Madison, and Jay, *The Federalist Papers*, no. 51.

30. Ibid.

31. As Mason and Beaney have suggested, "To all the agencies of government, the Constitution stands in the relationship of creator to creatures." See Alpheus Thomas Mason and William M. Beaney, *The Supreme Court in a Free Society* (New York: W. W. Norton, 1968), 2.

32. McIlwain, *Constitutionalism*, 14.

33. See Graham Walker, "The New Mixed Constitution: A Response to Liberal Debility and Constitutional Deadlock in Eastern Europe," *Polity* 26, no. 3 (Spring 1994): 503–15.

34. See Sotirios Barber, *On What the Constitution Means* (Baltimore: Johns Hopkins University Press, 1984).

35. It is important to note that not only does a constitution organize and confine all actors, it organizes political actors without regard to time. In other words, its main organizational and limiting purpose does not fluctuate when new administrations come to power.

36. To this fundamental point I should add the words of Sunstein, who, in referring to the political philosophy of James Madison, wrote that "constitutions must be insulated from the ordinary operation of politics." See Cass R. Sunstein, "Constitutions and Democracies: An Epilogue," in *Constitutionalism and Democracy*, ed. Jon Elster and Rune Slagstad (Cambridge: Cambridge University Press, 1988), 327.

37. Theodore J. Lowi and Benjamin Ginsberg, *American Government: Freedom and Power*, 3rd ed. (New York: W. W. Norton, 1994), 96.

38. Schochet, "Constitutionalism," 11.

39. See Griffin, *American Constitutionalism*, 15. See also the critically important debate over the proper interpretation of the American Constitution. Some of the most profound works in this ongoing conversation include John Hart Ely's *Democracy and Distrust* (Cambridge, Mass.: Harvard University Press, 1980); Christopher Wolfe, *How to Read the Constitution: Originalism, Constitutional Interpretation, and Judicial Power* (Lanham, Md.: Rowman and Littlefield, 1996); and Laurence Tribe and Michael Dorf, *On Reading the Constitution* (Cambridge, Mass.: Harvard University Press, 1991).

40. See Harris, *Interpretable Constitution*.

41. See Sanford Levinson, "How Many Times Has the United States Constitution Been Amended? (A) <26; (B) 26; (C) 27; (D) 27: Accounting for Constitutional Change," in Levinson, *Responding to Imperfection: The Theory and Practice of Constitutional Amendment* (Princeton, N.J.: Princeton University Press, 1995), 13–36.

42. Jon Elster, "Introduction," in *Constitutionalism and Democracy*, ed. Elster and Slagstad, 2.

43. See Hamilton, Madison, and Jay, *The Federalist Papers*, no. 10.

44. Obviously many of the provisions articulated within the document are continuously being interpreted and reinterpreted, but the point made here is simply that the text's foundational values—liberty, democracy, popular sovereignty—cannot be dramatically altered without significantly changing the substantive meaning of the text.

45. In reference to the main "principles" or "aspirations" of the U.S. Constitution, Arthur Sutherland mentioned five: freedom, justice, equality, segmented rule, and textualism. See Sutherland, *Constitutionalism in America*, chapter 1.

46. See Hamilton, Madison, and Jay, *The Federalist Papers*, no. 10.

47. See Bellah et al., *The Good Society* (New York: Vintage Books, 1991).

48. See Michael Sandel, "The Procedural Republic and the Unencumbered Self," *Political Theory* 12, no. 1 (February 1984); and "Democrats and Community," *New Republic*, 22 February 1988; Alasdair MacIntyre, *After Virtue: A Study in Moral Theory* (Notre Dame, Ind.: University of Notre Dame Press, 1984); and *Whose Justice: Which Rationality?* (Notre Dame: University of Notre Dame Press, 1988); Michael Walzer,

"The Communitarian Critique of Liberalism," *Political Theory* 18, no. 1 (February 1990); and Amitai Etzioni, "Liberals and Communitarians," *Partisan Review* 57, no. 2 (1990).

49. See Michael Walzer, "Philosophy and Democracy" *Political Theory* 9, no. 3 (August 1981): 379–99. In this article, Walzer laments the appearance of "philosophers" (like Rawls) who seek to find truths that transcend the traditions or culture of a particular community. This interesting argument parallels the fundamental disagreement between democrats and constitutionalists and will be taken up in the next chapter. The important point for our present purposes is that Walzer's argument suggests that only those who inhabit the community and actively shape its collective future are in a position to identify constitutive or binding values.

50. Daniel Bell, *Communitarianism and Its Critics* (Oxford: Clarendon Press, 1993), 59.

51. See Michael Walzer, *Spheres of Justice* (Oxford: Basil Blackwell, 1983).

52. Ibid., 312–13.

53. Ibid., 312.

54. Even his argument in *Interpretation and Social Criticism* does not fully save him. There Walzer contends that the social critic must exist internal to the community. There must be some detachment, to be sure, but the real critic is one who understands the particulars of the place he is criticizing. In fact, Walzer has repeatedly favored the idea of ethnic particularism and not universalism. This further demonstrates the fact that his conception of communitarianism cannot fully sustain the requirement of externality. See Michael Walzer, *Interpretation and Social Criticism* (Cambridge, Mass.: Harvard University Press, 1987); and "Roundtable: Nationalism and Ethnic Particularism," *Tikkun* (November/December 1992).

55. Daniel Bell, *Communitarianism and Its Critics*, 141 (emphasis added).

56. Abraham Lincoln, "Message to Congress in Special Session, July 4, 1861," in *Abraham Lincoln: Speeches and Writings, 1859–1865* (New York: Library of America, 1989), 253.

57. See Gary J. Jacobsohn, *Apple of Gold: Constitutionalism in Israel and the United States* (Princeton, N.J.: Princeton University Press, 1990).

58. See Daniel J. Elazar, *The Constitution of the State of Israel* (Jerusalem: Jerusalem Center for Public Affairs, 1988).

59. Quoted in McIlwain, *Constitutionalism: Ancient and Modern*, 9.

60. Graham Walker, "The Idea of Non-Liberal Constitutionalism," 1994.

61. See Sandel, "Procedural Republic."

62. Sandel notes that the United States was largely a constitutive or formative polity up until the mid-century. See ibid., 91–92.

63. Michael Sandel, "Morality and the Liberal Ideal," *New Republic*, 7 May 1984, 17.

64. See Amitai Etzioni, *The Spirit of Community: Rights, Responsibilities, and the Communitarian Agenda* (New York: Crown Publishers, 1993), chapter 1.

65. Frohnen is, of course, influenced greatly by the work of Donald S. Lutz. See Lutz, "Religious Dimensions in the Development of American Constitutionalism," *Emory Law Journal* 39 (1990): 21–40.

66. See Bruce Frohnen, *The New Communitarians and the Crisis of Modern Liberalism* (Lawrence: University Press of Kansas, 1996), 206.

67. Ibid., 206 (emphasis added).

68. Ibid. See also Lutz, "Religious Dimensions."

69. Particular individuals no doubt still view the specifics of religious covenants as ordering their lives. But as far as communities are concerned, only the most radical maintain any primary allegiance to a covenant.

70. Thomas Jefferson, "Letter to Samuel Kercheval, July 12, 1816," in *Thomas Jefferson Selected Writings*, ed. Mansfield, 88–91.

71. Ibid., 90.

72. More likely they are interpreted in a way that aligns them with the governmental initiative. Either way, however, the constitutionalist is troubled by manipulation.

73. See, in particular, Etzioni, *Spirit of Community*; and William A. Galston, *Liberal Purposes: Goods, Virtues, and Diversity in the Liberal State* (Cambridge: Cambridge University Press, 1991).

74. See Etzioni, *Spirit of Community*, 11.

75. One need only look to the events of September 11, 2001, to recognize the seriousness of Etzioni's plan. Individuals of Arab descent face the prospect of significantly weaker civil liberties as a result of the terrorist activities. As I write, the Bush administration is currently calling for, among other things, the suspension of the Fourth Amendment's prohibition against unreasonable searches and seizures, as well as the introduction of military tribunals.

F I V E : Communitarian Democracy

1. Sunstein articulates this point nicely: "For those who believe that there is a conflict between constitutionalism and democracy, the tension stems from the fact that constitutions remove certain topics from public scrutiny and review. The basic institutional arrangements may be changed only with extraordinary difficulty; the rights protected by a constitution are not subject to political revision. For some, the resulting stability is bought at an enormous price, which is the insulation of fundamental choices from collective struggle or deliberation." Cass Sunstein, "Constitutions and Democracies: An Epilogue," in *Constitutionalism and Democracy*, ed. Jon Elster and Rune Slagstad (Cambridge: Cambridge University Press, 1988), 338.

2. Benjamin Barber, *Strong Democracy: Participatory Politics for a New Age* (Berkeley: University of California Press, 1984), 224 (emphasis his).

3. For an interesting and parallel discussion of the abortion debate in the United States, see Laurence Tribe, *Abortion: The Clash of Absolutes* (New York: W. W. Norton, 1990).

4. On a theoretical level, pure democracy may differ from tyranny only in the source of its authority. A single institution still occupies the reins of power. Complete and unfettered rule is once again in the hands of those who fully understand the common principles and values associated with the particular community. Power, again, is not limited—although at first glance it may appear to be more defensible.

5. Much of the contemporary literature on judicial theory and process has been devoted to this issue of self-restraint. For some of the most provocative works, see Robert Bork, *The Tempting of America: The Political Seduction of the Law* (New York: Simon and Schuster, 1990); William H. Rehnquist, "The Notion of a Living Constitution," *Texas Law Review* 54, no. 4 (May 1976); Herbert Wechsler, "Toward Neutral Principles of Constitutional Law," *Harvard Law Review* 73, no. 9 (1959); Benjamin N.

Cardozo, *The Nature of the Judicial Process* (New Haven, Conn.: Yale University Press, 1921); and the comparative Supreme Court decisions of, among others, Justices Felix Frankfurter, Hugo Black, Earl Warren, and William Brennan.

6. At one point in premodern history (and solely with respect to theology) the general consensus among theologians was that God was so omnipotent and powerful that a self-limitation of His own authority was "an expression of His awesome freedom and power." That is to say, the otherwise difficult notion that God could bind himself was partly resolved in the medieval period by suggesting a self-imposed limitation could just as easily be interpreted not as a restraint on power, but as an act of freedom. For it was thought that "the only force . . . capable of binding omnipotence without thereby denying it is the omnipotent will itself." Even Locke echoed this sentiment in section 195 of the *Second Treatise* when he wrote: "[Eternal laws] are so great and so strong in the case of promises that Omnipotence itself can be tied by them. Grants, promises, and oaths are bonds that hold the Almighty; whatever some flatterers say to princes of the world" (*The Second Treatise of Government*, ed. Thomas P. Peardon [Indianapolis, Ind.: Bobbs-Merrill, 1952], 109). See Stephen Holmes, "Precommitment and the Paradox of Democracy," in *Constitutionalism and Democracy*, ed. Jon Elster and Rune Slagstad (Cambridge: Cambridge University Press, 1988). See also Francis Oakley, *Omnipotence, Covenant, and Order* (Ithaca, N.Y.: Cornell University Press, 1984).

7. See Alexander Hamilton, James Madison, and John Jay, *The Federalist Papers* (New York: Modern Library), no. 51.

8. Ibid., no. 47, p. 313. See also Ben O. Nwabueze, *Constitutionalism in the Emergent State* (Rutherford, N.J.: Fairleigh Dickinson University Press, 1973); Carl J. Friedrich, *Constitutional Government and Democracy* (Boston: Ginn and Company, 1946); Holmes, "Precommitment"; and M. J. C. Vile, *Constitutionalism and the Separation of Powers* (Oxford: Clarendon Press, 1967).

9. For another interesting discussion of how constitutionalism "removes certain topics from public scrutiny and review," see Sunstein, "Constitutions and Democracies."

10. Walter Murphy, James Fleming, and Sotirios Barber, *American Constitutional Interpretation* (New York: Foundation Press, 1995), 28.

11. Madison wrote this in a letter to Jefferson dated October 17, 1788. Quoted in Murphy, Fleming, and Barber, *American Constitutional Interpretation*, 28; italics in the original.

12. See William M. Sullivan, *Reconstructing Public Philosophy* (Berkeley: University of California Press, 1982). Yet another similar description of the first principle of communitarianism comes from Miller, who wrote, "The promise of overall community, then, is that it allows people to regard themselves as active subjects shaping the world according to their will." See David Miller, "Community and Citizenship," in *Communitarianism and Individualism*, ed. Shlomo Avineri and Avner de-Shalit (Oxford: Oxford University Press, 1992), 86.

13. For a specific reference to this common element of communitarian thought, see The Responsive Communitarian Platform provision entitled "Not Majoritarian but Strongly Democratic."

14. Sunstein, "Constitutions and Democracy," 347.

15. See in particular, Barber, *Strong Democracy,* chapter 10.

16. Ibid., 282.

17. Ibid. 308–9.

18. See *Newdow v Elk Grove Unified School District,* 292 F. 3d 597 (2002). In response, the Senate passed a resolution condemning the ruling. The vote was 99–0. The corresponding House vote, also condemning the opinion, was 432–3.

19. Barber, *Strong Democracy,* 278–79.

20. Michael Walzer, *Spheres of Justice* (Oxford: Basil Blackwell, 1983), xiv.

21. Ibid., 86–91.

22. This is not really so far-fetched; many, including Walzer, contend that such a shift in attitude has ostensibly occurred in the United States.

23. In discussing why logic dictates that the constitution should be supreme, it was Publius who remarked: "No legislative act contrary to the Constitution, can be valid. To deny this would be to affirm that the deputy is greater than his principal; that the servant is above his master; that the representatives of the people are superior to the people themselves; that men acting by virtue of powers may do not only what their powers do not authorize but what they forbid" (Hamilton, Madison, and Jay, *The Federalist Papers,* no. 78, pp. 505–6).

24. Barry Alan Shain, "American Community," in *Community and Tradition: Conservative Perspectives on American Experience* (Lanham, Md.: Rowman and Littlefield: 1998), 47.

25. Alexis de Tocqueville, *Democracy in America,* translated by George Lawrence (Garden City, N.Y.: Anchor Books, 1969), 644.

26. In Nathaniel Hawthorne's *A Scarlet Letter,* Hester Prynne and Reverend Dimmesdale both eventually suffer at the hand of public opinion.

27. See Alasdair MacIntyre, "Is Patriotism a Virtue?" in *Liberalism,* Elger Reference Collections Schools of Thought, vol. 2, ed. Richard J. Arneson (Brookfield, Vt.: Ashgate Publishers, 1992), 12–13.

28. See Aristotle, *The Politics,* ed. Ernest Barker (Oxford: Oxford University Press, 1946), Book III, chapter X. Aristotle quotes the democrat as saying, "No, by Zeus, it has been done justly, by a decision of the sovereign power." This is, in fact, one of only two places that Aristotle swears in the entirety of the *Politics,* underscoring his point that the sovereign often acts irrationally.

29. Drew R. McCoy, *The Last of the Fathers: James Madison and the Republican Legacy* (Cambridge: Cambridge University Press, 1989), 41.

30. See David Hume, "Of the Origins of Government," in *Essays Moral, Political and Literary* (Oxford, 1963 [orig. publ. 1741–1742]), 35–36, quoted in McCoy, *Last of the Fathers,* 42.

31. Hamilton, Madison, and Jay, *The Federalist Papers,* no. 78, p. 506.

32. Bruce Ackerman suggests that there is only one democratic event that can truly be viewed as fully consistent with constitutionalist principles, and that is the original democratic moment (otherwise known as the ratification). See Bruce A. Ackerman, "Neo-Federalism," in *Constitutionalism and Democracy,* ed. Jon Elster and Rune Slagstad (Cambridge: Cambridge University Press, 1988).

33. For an additional version of this model, see William F. Harris, *The Interpretable Constitution* (Baltimore: Johns Hopkins University Press, 1994), chapters 1 and 4.

34. Barber's general opposition to *representative* government makes the point even more acutely.

35. Agrippa, "Letter to the People," December 3, 1787, quoted in Herbert J. Storing, ed., *The Anti-Federalist: Writings by the Opponents of the Constitution* (Chicago: University of Chicago Press, 1981), 236.

36. Ibid., 235.

37. James Madison, "Vices of the Political System of the United States," quoted in *James Madison: Writings* (New York: Library of America, 1999), 76–78.

38. See Jon Elster and Rune Slagstad, eds., *Constitutionalism and Democracy* (Cambridge: Cambridge University Press, 1988), chapters 5, 11.

39. See William Galston, "Community, Democracy, Philosophy: The Political Thought of Michael Walzer," *Political Theory* (February 1989): 129.

40. By way of illustration, consider a speech delivered by Benjamin Barber in which he noted, "Constitutions do not create democracies, democracies create constitutions." See David Broder, "Independence Day reminders of democracy's challenge," *Boston Globe*, 3 July 1995.

41. Holmes, "Precommitment," 195.

42. Laurence Tribe, *American Constitutional Law* (Mineola, N.Y.: Foundation Press, 1978), 9.

43. See Murphy, Fleming, and Barber, *American Constitutional Interpretation*, chapter 2. In earlier writings Walter Murphy seems to stand strongly behind the claim that constitutionalism and democracy exist in direct tension with each other, but in an interesting more recent piece, Murphy has subtly backed off this earlier proposition. In "Civil Law, Common Law, and Constitutional Democracy," Murphy argues that constitutionalism and democracy, while appearing as contrasting principles, are really separate theories seeking the same ultimate goal: the protection of "human dignity" and "autonomy." See Walter F. Murphy, "Civil Law, Common Law, and Constitutional Democracy," *Louisiana Law Review* 52, no. 1 (September 1991): 91–136. See also George Kateb, "The Moral Distinctiveness of Representative Democracy," *Ethics* 91 (1981): 357–74.

44. Murphy, Fleming, and Barber, *American Constitutional Interpretation*, 27.

45. See Francis Sejersted, "Democracy and the Rule of Law: Some Historical Experiences of Contradictions in the Striving for Good Government," in Elster and Slagstad, *Constitutionalism and Democracy*, 131–52. In the article, Sejersted specifically writes that the "rule of law [or constitutionalism] was meant to curb state authority, while democracy was meant to mobilize society in the exercising of state authority."

46. Consider as an example, Sejersted remarks, early-twentieth-century Germany and the rise of fascism in Europe prior to the Second World War.

47. Murphy, Fleming and Barber, *American Constitutional Interpretation*, 28–29.

48. McIlwain understands this dynamic more thoroughly. He sees an important place for democracy within the general theory of constitutionalism. Implicitly, then, he cautions us against confounding democracy and liberalism. See Charles McIlwain, *Constitutionalism: Ancient and Modern* (Ithaca, N.Y.: Cornell University Press, 1940).

49. See John Hart Ely, *Democracy and Distrust: A Theory of Judicial Review* (Cambridge, Mass.: Harvard University Press, 1980), 7.

50. See Daniel Bell, *Communitarianism and Its Critics* (Oxford: Oxford University Press, 1993), 172–76.

51. Mary Ann Glendon, *Rights Talk: The Impoverishment of Political Discourse* (New York: Free Press, 1991), 171.

52. Robert Bellah et al., *The Good Society* (New York: Vintage Books, 1991), 136.

53. Throughout Glendon's work she constantly laments the fact that the rise of "rights talk" in this country has made it exceedingly difficult for "persons and groups with conflicting interests and views to build coalitions *and achieve compromise.*" "Rights talk in its current form," she continues, "has been the thin end of a wedge that is turning American political discourse into a parody of itself and challenging the very notion that politics can be conducted through reasoned discussion *and compromise*" (*Rights Talk,* 171; emphasis added).

54. John Locke, *The Second Treatise of Government,* ed. Thomas P. Peardon (Indianapolis, Ind.: Bobbs-Merrill, 1954), section 134, p. 75.

55. Holmes, "Precommitment," 227. See also Harris, *Interpretable Constitution,* Introduction.

56. In *Federalist* 51, Publius describes the constitutional transfer of power in the most succinct terms when he writes: "In a single republic, all the power surrendered by the people is submitted to the administration of a single government; and the usurpations are guarded against by a division of the government into distinct and separate departments. In the compound republic of America, the power surrendered by the people is first divided between two distinct governments, and then the portion allotted to each subdivided among distinct and separate departments." See also Friedrich, *Constitutional Government,* chapters X and XI. In the work, Friedrich argues in favor of a distribution of power to separate institutions and political actors.

57. In an illustrative passage prior to his specific discussion of separate powers, Holmes writes: "Constitutions do not merely limit power; they can create and organize power as well as give power a certain direction" ("Precommitment," 228).

58. See Murphy, Fleming, and Barber, *American Constitutional Interpretation,* chapter 3. See also David P. Currie, "The Distribution of Powers after Bowsher," *Supreme Court Review* (1986), 19–36; Peter L. Strauss, "The Place of Agencies in Government: Separation of Powers and the Fourth Branch," *Columbia Law Review* 84 (1984): 573; and Symposium, "The American Constitutional Tradition of Shared and Separated Powers" *William and Mary Law Review* 30 (1989): 209. See also Alpheus Thomas Mason and William M. Beaney, *The Supreme Court in a Free Society,* (New York: W. W. Norton, 1968).

59. Friedrich is also instructive here, as he remarks: "True constitutional government does not exist unless procedural restraints are effectively established. Such restraints involve some division of power; for evidently some considerable power must be vested in those who are expected to do the restraining" (*Constitutional Government,* 170). Friedrich's suggestion is that constitutionalism requires a separation of command so as to ensure a balanced relationship among competing offices. Similarly, the more general observation among modern constitutionalists is that a constitutional delegation of control is required in order to maintain equilibrium and suppress the possible influence of any single institution, while still permitting legitimate political action.

60. Bruce Ackerman refers loosely to these events as "decisions." See Bruce Ackerman. "Dualist Constitutionalism," in *Modern Constitutional Theory: A Reader,* 3rd ed., ed. John H. Garvey and T. Alexander Aleinikoff (St. Paul, Minn.: West Publishing, 1994).

61. See Harris, *Interpretable Constitution*.

62. Ibid., 193.

63. William A. Galston, *Liberal Purposes: Goods, Virtues, and Diversity in the Liberal State* (Cambridge: Cambridge University Press, 1991), 50.

64. Walzer, *Spheres of Justice*, 308.

65. Ibid., 304 (emphasis his).

s i x : Mixed Constitutionalism and the Communitarian Hope

1. Just recently, South Africa drafted and ratified a constitutional text that subscribes most obviously to liberal ideals.

2. Graham Walker, "The New Mixed Constitution: A Response to Liberal Debility and Constitutional Deadlock in Eastern Europe," *Polity* 26, no. 3 (Spring 1994): 504–5.

3. Certainly one must take seriously the recent wave of scholarship, begun by Gordon Wood, which contends the United States was founded on a fervent commitment to the theories of republicanism and community. I do not want to downplay this argument, but I do want to suggest that by comparison, the history of the United States (and the language of the Bill of Rights) suggests that the community-based influence of the founding has given way to a dramatically more liberal public ethos. See Gordon Wood, *The Creation of the American Republic 1776–1787* (Chapel Hill: University of North Carolina Press, 1969), chapter 2. See also Donald Lutz, *The Origins of American Constitutionalism* (Baton Rouge: Louisiana State University Press, 1988); Frank Michelman, "Law's Republic," *Yale Law Journal* 97 (1988): 1493; and Cass Sunstein, "Beyond the Republican Revival," *Yale Law Journal* 97 (1988): 1539.

4. Robert McCloskey's argument that the Court has been most interested in protecting rights over the last three-quarters of a century is appropriate here. See Robert McCloskey, *The American Supreme Court* (Chicago: University of Chicago Press, 1960).

5. See Gary J. Jacobsohn, *Apple of Gold: Constitutionalism in Israel and the United States* (Princeton, N.J.: Princeton University Press, 1993).

6. Gary J. Jacobsohn, "Alternative Pluralisms: Israeli and American Constitutionalism in Comparative Perspective," *Review of Politics* 51 (1989): 167. See also Charles S. Liebman, "Conception of 'State of Israel' in Israeli Society," *Jerusalem Quarterly* 47 (1988).

7. Jacobsohn, "Alternative Pluralisms," 167.

8. Walker, "Mixed Constitution," 512. See also Jacobsohn, *Apple of Gold*. See also an interview with the late legal philosopher H. L .A. Hart in *Israeli Democracy* (Winter 1987), in which he argued that Jewish law was incompatible with the central principles of the liberal creed.

9. See Joav Peled, "Ethnic Democracy and the Legal Construction of Citizenship: Arab Citizens of the Jewish State," *American Political Science Review* 86 (1992). See also Daniel J. Elazar, "Constitution-making: The Pre-eminently Political Act," in *Redesigning the State: The Politics of Constitutional Change*, ed. Keith G. Banting and Richard Simeon (Toronto: University of Toronto Press, 1985).

10. See Emanuel Rackman, *Israel's Emerging Constitution, 1948–1951* (New York: Columbia University Press, 1955). See also George Gross, "The Constitutional Question in Israel" in *Constitutionalism: The Israeli and American Experiences*, ed. Daniel Elazar (Lanham, Md.: University Press of America, 1990).

11. See Daniel J. Elazar, "The Constitution of the State of Israel," *Jerusalem Center for Public Affairs* (1988).

12. Elazar and others have argued that Israel's constitution is an "emerging" text, a text that, while not fixed in time and formality, still acts every bit as constitutive as the more formal examples around the world.

13. See Adam Garfinkle, *Politics and Society in Modern Israel: Myths and Realities* (Armonk, N.Y.: M. E. Sharpe, 1997).

14. Ibid., 155–56.

15. Some may suggest that the three "original" documents—the Declaration of Independence, the Law of Return, and the Covenant Between the State of Israel and the World Zionist Organization—satisfy the requirement of externality, but an appropriate question may be whether these documents truly order the political structures in a way that forestalls the possibility of tyranny. The U.S. Declaration of Independence is certainly external to this country's power centers, but America's political institutions are not accountable to the Declaration of Independence. Similarly, one can easily question the externality of the Basic Law by considering the fact that it can be altered by an absolute majority of the Knesset.

16. Israel's electoral system is one of proportional representation where individual voters choose parties, not individuals, and the parties themselves determine who will be their particular representatives.

17. David Kretzmer, *The Legal Status of the Arabs in Israel* (Boulder, Colo.: Westview, 1990), 24.

18. See *Yardor v Central Election Commission for the Sixth Knesset* (1965).

19. See Peled, "Ethnic Democracy," and Kretzmer, *Legal Status.*

20. See *Neiman v Chairman of the Central Election Commission for the Eleventh Knesset* (1985).

21. Ibid. See also Peled, "Ethnic Democracy."

22. Jacobsohn, *Apple of Gold,* 110.

23. Ireland provides an additional example.

24. Peled, "Ethnic Democracy," 440.

25. Aristotle, *The Politics,* ed. Ernest Barker (New York: Oxford University Press, 1946), IV:XI, 181–82.

26. Among the many American scholars who have devoted their time and considerable intellectual talents over the last few years to the study of Eastern European constitutional change are Jon Elster, Cass Sunstein, Jeffrey Sachs, and Stephen Elkin. In fact, an entire journal is now dedicated to the study of Eastern European constitutional construction. See *East European Constitutional Review,* 1992–present.

27. Walker, "Mixed Constitution," 506 (emphasis his).

28. See Stephen Holmes, *The Anatomy of Antiliberalism* (Cambridge, Mass.: Harvard University Press, 1993). Walker is equally confounded. He writes, "The alternatives to liberalism are as varied and competing (sometimes blood-thirstily competing) as they can be. I unite them as a category only by their negation of the principal liberal affirmations" ("Mixed Constitution," 506).

29. Holmes examines the work of many antiliberals—from Maistre to Schmitt to Strauss—and finds the common denominator to be a bitter hatred of the detached and isolated attitude that goes along with liberal dominance.

30. See German Basic Law, Article 20.

31. See Donald Kommers, *The Constitutional Jurisprudence of the Federal Republic of Germany* (Durham, N.C.: Duke University Press, 1989), chapter 2.

32. *Bundesgerichtshof* Decision of 18 March 1959, 30 BGHZ 7, 11–12, quoted in Mary Ann Glendon, *Rights Talk: The Impoverishment of Political Discourse* (New York: Free Press, 1991), 63.

33. Federal Constitutional Court Decision of July 7, 1970, quoted in Glendon, *Rights Talk*, 71.

34. Glendon, *Rights Talk*, 9.

35. Quoted in Rudolf Dozer, *Property and Environment: The Social Obligation Inherent in Ownership* (Marges, Switzerland: Int. Union for the Conservation of Nature and Natural Resources, 1976), 17.

36. Glendon, *Rights Talk*, 34.

37. See, among others, Richard Epstein, *Takings: Private Property and the Power of Eminent Domain* (Cambridge, Mass.: Harvard University Press, 1985).

38. Article 6, Section 2, reads: "The care and upbringing of children are a natural right of, and duty primarily incumbent upon, the parents. The national community shall watch over their endeavors in this respect."

39. It seems the Germans have taken the famous proverb "It takes an entire community to raise a child" and granted it constitutional status.

40. Kommers, *Constitutional Jurisprudence*, 37.

41. Ibid., 39. For a more specific illustration, see also the Elfes Case, 6 BVerfGE 32 (1957).

42. See Amitai Etzioni, James Fishkin, William Galston, and Mary Ann Glendon, "Editorial Statement: The Responsive Community, Rights and Responsibilities," *The Responsive Community: Rights and Responsibilities* 1, no. 1 (Winter 1990–91). See also Etzioni, "What Community? Whose Responsiveness?" *The Responsive Community: Rights and Responsibilities* 1, no. 2 (Spring 1991).

43. Etzioni et al., "Editorial Statement: The Responsive Community, Rights and Responsibilities," *Responsive Community: Rights and Responsibilities* 1, no. 1 (Winter 1990–91): 2.

44. In the first volume of *The Responsive Community: Rights and Responsibilities*, the question of balancing rights and responsibilities was raised in no fewer than five major articles.

45. Consider what Dallin H. Oaks argues: "We cannot raise ourselves by adding to our inventory of individual rights. The fulfillment of individual rights depends on the fulfillment of individual and group responsibilities." See Dallin H. Oaks, "Rights and Responsibilities," *Responsive Community: Rights and Responsibilities*, vol. 1, no. 1 (Winter, 1990–91), p. 46.

46. See Amitai Etzioni, *The Spirit of Community: Rights, Responsibilities and the Communitarian Agenda* (New York: Crown Publishers, 1993), 4–11.

47. Mary Ann Glendon, " 'Absolute' Rights: Property and Privacy," *Responsive Community: Rights and Responsibilities* 1, no. 4 (Fall 1991): 13. For a similar discussion of free speech, see Jeffrey Abramson and Elizabeth Bussiere, "Free Press and Free Speech: A Communitarian Perspective," *Responsive Community: Rights and Responsibilities* 4, no. 2 (Spring 1994): 22–32.

48. Etzioni, et al., "Editorial Statement," 4. See also William Galston, "A Liberal-

democratic Case for the Two-Parent Family," *Responsive Community: Rights and Responsibilities* 1, no. 1 (Winter 1990–91).

49. See Mary Ann Glendon, "Rights and Responsibilities Viewed from Afar: The Case of Welfare Rights," *Responsive Community: Rights and Responsibilities* 4, no. 2 (Spring 1994).

50. Ibid., 35–36.

51. She may be a communitarian, but she is also a realist. She recognizes that any real alteration of America's constitutional structure will be both difficult and problematic.

SEVEN: Conclusion

1. See Stephen Mulhall and Adam Swift, *Liberals and Communitarians* (Oxford: Blackwell, 1992), Introduction. See also David Rasmussen, ed., *Universalism vs. Communitarianism: Contemporary Debates in Ethics* (Cambridge, Mass.: MIT Press, 1990).

2. See Amy Gutmann, "Communitarian Critics of Liberalism," *Philosophy and Public Affairs* 14, no. l 3 (Summer 1985): 308–22.

3. See Charles Taylor, "Alternative Futures: Legitimacy, Identity and Alienation in Late Twentieth Century Canada," in *Constitutionalism, Citizenship and Society in Canada,* ed. Alan Cairns and Cynthia Williams (Toronto: University of Toronto Press, 1985); and "Cross Purposes: The Liberal Communitarian Debate, in *Liberalism and the Moral Life,* ed. Nancy Rosenblum (Cambridge, Mass.: Harvard University Press, 1990).

4. See Alasdair MacIntyre, *After Virtue: A Study in Moral Theory* (Notre Dame, Ind.: University of Notre Dame Press, 1981). See also his *Whose Justice? Which Responsibility?* (Notre Dame, Ind.: University of Notre Dame Press, 1988); and "The Privatization of the Good," *Review of Politics* 52, no. 3 (Summer 1990).

5. See Michael Walzer, *Spheres of Justice* (Oxford: Basil Blackwell, 1983); *Interpretation and Social Criticism* (Cambridge, Mass.: Harvard University Press, 1987); *The Company of Critics* (New York: Basic Books, 1988); and "The Communitarian Critique of Liberalism," *Political Theory* 18, no. 1 (February 1990).

6. See Benjamin Barber, *Strong Democracy: Participatory Politics for a New Age* (Berkeley: University of California Press, 1984); William A. Galston, *Liberal Purposes: Goods, Virtues, and Diversity in the Liberal State* (Cambridge: Cambridge University Press, 1982); and "Moral Personality and Liberal Theory: John Rawls's Dewey Lectures," *Political Theory* 10, no. 4 (November 1991); Robert Bellah et al., *The Good Society* (New York: Vintage Books, 1985); *Habits of the Heart* (Berkeley: University of California Press, 1985); and *Individualism and Commitment in American Life: Readings on the Themes of Habits of the Heart* (New York: Harper and Row, 1987).

7. It has been argued elsewhere that the rise of communitarian theory has contributed significantly to the substantial narrowing of Rawls' theory.

8. The concern of most pragmatists is that a communitarian regime cannot solve the problem of scale. See H. N. Hirsch, "The Threnody of Liberalism: Constitutional Liberty and the Renewal of Community," *Political Theory* 14, no. 3 (August 1986).

9. Among others, see Charles Fried, "Liberalism, Community and the Objectivity of Values," *Harvard Law Review* 96 (1983): 960.

10. See Herbert McCloskey and John Zaller, *The American Ethos: Public Attitudes toward Capitalism and Democracy* (Cambridge, Mass.: Harvard University Press, 1984).

11. During their respective presidential campaigns, both Buchanan and Bradley tried to incorporate what has become known as "electronic town meetings," where candidates speak directly to their constituents. Communitarians James Fishkin and Benjamin Barber have noted that this style of political communication is perhaps the most active form of participation currently available.

12. Consider the "moderate" stance taken by many Democratic presidential candidates over the last few elections, most notably the unwillingness on the part of Michael Dukakis to admit to being "liberal." Consider also the argument that regularly appears in Lani Guinier's controversial book entitled *The Tyranny of the Majority: Fundamental Fairness in Representative Democracy* (New York: Free Press, 1994). In the book, Guinier makes a number of passing references to the fact that the more extreme members of the liberal wing (Jesse Jackson, for example) have little chance for presidential success because of the shifting tides of American opinion.

13. Specifically, many conservatives have suggested that on such issues as crime, welfare, and education, state and local governments should rightly determine the best policy for their individual territories.

14. Both Etzioni (who calls his proposal "National Service") and Benjamin Barber (who refers to his suggestion as "universal citizen service") specifically call for the introduction of a "Civil Service Corps." See Amitai Etzioni, *The Spirit of Community: Rights, Responsibilities, and the Communitarian Agenda* (New York: Crown Publishers, 1993), 113–15; and Barber, *Strong Democracy*, 298–303.

15. AmeriCorps is run by a larger body called the Corporation for National Service, which oversees additional communitarian and national service programs.

16. The AmeriCorps program was only the most obvious example of the Clinton administration's commitment to communitarian ideas. Consider also the frequency (too numerous to count) with which both Clinton and Gore spoke of "community" or "collective" values. See David Shribman, "National Perspective: Hearing Values of a President," *Boston Globe*, 20 May 1994, 3.

17. In Norfolk and Memphis at least, the feeling was that the state and national curriculums were ineffective and that a "Coalition" approach to education was more suited to the students of the system. As a result, these two systems are now administered by the "Atlas Project," which employs, in a strictly educational setting, many of the main theoretical ideas espoused by communitarian thinkers.

18. The communitarian platform is not limited to the arenas of politics and education. A recent statement issued by America's Roman Catholic bishops cites "individual liberty" as the single most destructive virtue currently plaguing the United States. "Society's high premium on personal freedom and happiness," the bishops argued, "has made it acceptable to abandon personal obligation and resort to easy solutions." See Diego Ribadeneira, "U.S. bishops see society as selfish, hedonistic," *Boston Globe*, 28 September 1995, 1.

19. See, in particular, Mike Allen, "Bush Plans Values-Based Initiative to Rev Up Agenda" *Washington Post*, 29 July 2001, A1.

20. Abraham Lincoln, "Message to Congress in Special Session, July 4, 1861," in *Abraham Lincoln: Speeches and Writings, 1859–1865* (New York: Library of America, 1989), 253.

21. Consider Publius' argument in *Federalist* 10 for "extending the sphere" of Ameri-

can politics so as to stave off the possibility of (majority) tyranny. See Hamilton, Madison, and Jay, *The Federalist Papers* (New York: Modern Library), no. 10.

22. See Herbert Storing, *What the Anti-Federalists Were For* (Chicago: University of Chicago Press, 1981), chapters 3–4.

23. Article VII describes the rules of ratification, suggesting that ratification by the conventions of nine states is sufficient for the "establishment" of the Constitution.

References

Abramowitz, Joshua. "The Tao of community." *Public Interest,* no. 113 (Fall 1993): 119–21.

Abramson, Jeffrey, and Elizabeth Bussiere. "Free Press and Free Speech: A Communitarian Perspective." *The Responsive Community: Rights and Responsibilities* 4, no. 2 (Spring 1994): 22–32.

Abramson, Paul R., and John H. Aldrich. "The Decline of Electoral Participation in America." *American Political Science Review* 76 (September 1982): 502–21.

Ackerman, Bruce A. "Dualist Constitutionalism." In *Modern Constitutional Theory: A Reader,* 3rd ed., edited by John H. Garvey and T. Alexander Aleinikoff. St. Paul, Minn.: West Publishing, 1994.

———. "Neo-Federalism." In *Constitutionalism and Democracy,* edited by Jon Elster and Rune Slagstad. Cambridge: Cambridge University Press, 1988.

———. *Social Justice in the Liberal State.* New Haven: Yale University Press, 1980.

Alexander, Larry, ed. *Constitutionalism: Philosophical Foundations.* Cambridge: Cambridge University Press, 1998.

Aristotle. *The Politics.* Edited by Ernest Barker. London: Oxford University Press, 1958.

Armour, Leslie. "John Locke and American Constitutionalism." In *Constitutionalism: The Philosophic Dimension,* edited by Alan Rosenbaum. New York: Greenwood Press, 1988.

Avineri, Shlomo, and Avner De-Shalit. *Communitarianism and Individualism.* Oxford: Oxford University Press, 1992.

Bailyn, Bernard. *The Ideological Origins of the American Revolution.* Cambridge: Harvard University Press, 1967.

Banning, Lance. *The Jeffersonian Persuasion: Evolution of a Party Ideology.* Ithaca, N.Y.: Cornell University Press, 1978.

Barber, Benjamin. *The Conquest of Politics: Liberal Philosophy in Democratic Times.* Princeton, N.J.: Princeton University Press, 1988.

———. "A Mandate for Liberty: Requiring Education-Based Community Service." In *The Essential Communitarian Reader,* edited by Amitai Etzioni. Lanham, Md.: Rowman and Littlefield: 1998.

———. *A Place for Us: How to Make Society Civil and Democracy Strong.* New York: Hill and Wang, 1998.

———. *Strong Democracy: Participatory Politics for a New Age.* Berkeley: University of California Press, 1984.

Barber, Sotirios. *On What the Constitution Means.* Baltimore: Johns Hopkins University Press, 1984.

Barry, Norman. "Charles Taylor on Multiculturalism and the Politics of Recognition." In *Community and Tradition: Conservative Perspectives on the American Experience*, edited by George W. Carey and Bruce Frohnen. Lanham, Md.: Rowman and Littlefield: 1998.

Beard, Charles. *An Economic Interpretation of the Constitution*. New York: Free Press, 1913.

Beiner, Ronald. *Political Judgment*. Chicago: University of Chicago Press, 1983.

———. *What's the Matter with Liberalism?* Berkeley: University of California Press, 1992.

———. "What's the Matter with Liberalism?" In *Law and the Community: The End of Liberalism?* edited by Allen C. Hutchinson and Leslie J. M. Green. Toronto: Carswell, 1989.

Bell, Daniel. *Communitarianism and Its Critics*. Oxford: Oxford University Press, 1993.

Bellah, Robert N., Richard Madsen, William M. Sullivan, Ann Swidler, and Steven M. Tipton. *The Good Society*. New York: Vintage Books, 1991.

———. *Habits of the Heart: Individualism and Commitment in American Life*. New York, New York: Harper and Row, 1985.

———, eds. *Individualism and Commitment in American Life: Readings on the Themes of Habits of the Heart*. New York: Harper and Row, 1987.

Bentham, Jeremy. *An Introduction to The Principles of Morals and Legislation*. New York: Hafner, 1948.

Bickel, Alexander. *The Least Dangerous Branch: The Supreme Court at the Bar of Politics*. Indianapolis, Ind.: Bobbs-Merrill, 1962).

Black, Charles L. *The People and the Court: Judicial Review in a Democracy*. New York: Macmillan, 1960.

Blaustein, Albert P., and Jay A. Sigler, eds., *Constitutions That Made History*. New York: Paragon House, 1988.

Bowen, Catherine Drinker. *Miracle at Philadelphia: The Story of the Constitutional Convention, May to September 1787*. Boston: Little, Brown, 1966.

Bork, Robert. *The Tempting of America: The Political Seduction of the Law*. New York: Simon and Schuster, 1990.

Buchanan, Allen. "Assessing the Communitarian Critique of Liberalism." *Ethics* (July 1989).

Cairns, Alan C. "Citizens (Outsiders) and Governments (Insiders) in Constitution Making: The Case of Meech Lake." *Canadian Public Policy* 14 (1988).

———. "The Living Canadian Constitution." In *Constitution, Government and Society in Canada*, edited by Douglas E. Williams. Toronto: McClelland and Stewart, 1989.

Campbell, Angus, Philip E. Converse, Warren E. Miller, and Donald E. Stokes. *The American Voter*. New York: John Wiley and Sons, 1960.

Caney, Simon. "Liberalism and Communitarianism: A Misconceived Debate." *Political Studies* (June 1992).

Cardozo, Benjamin N. *The Nature of the Judicial Process*. New Haven, Conn.: Yale University Press, 1921.

Carey, George W., and Bruce Frohnen, eds. *Community and Tradition: Conservative Perspectives on the American Experience*. Lanham, Md.: Rowman and Littlefield: 1998.

Carty, R. Kenneth, and W. Peter Ward, eds. *National Politics and Community in Canada*. Vancouver: University of British Columbia Press, 1986.

Corwin, Edward S. *The "Higher Law" Background of American Constitutional Law.* Ithaca, N.Y.: Great Seal Books, 1955.

Cover, Robert. "Nomos and Narrative," *Harvard Law Review* 97 (1983): 4–68.

Cox, Archibald. *The Role of the Supreme Court in American Government.* New York: Oxford University Press, 1976.

Currie, David P. "The Distribution of Powers after Bowsher." *Supreme Court Review* (1986): 19–40.

Dahl, Robert. *Democracy and Its Critics.* New Haven, Conn.: Yale University Press, 1989.

Daly, Markate, ed. *Communitarianism: A New Public Ethics.* Belmont, Calif.: Wadsworth, 1994.

Dewey, John. *The Public and Its Problems.* New York: Holt Rinehart, 1927.

Dozer, Rudolph. *Property and Environment: The Social Obligation Inherent in Ownership.* Marges, Switzerland: International Union for the Conservation of Nature and Natural Resources, 1976.

Dunn, John. *Interpreting Political Responsibility.* Oxford: Polity Press, 1990.

Dworkin, Ronald. "Liberalism." In *Public and Private Morality,* edited by Stuart Hampshire. Cambridge: Cambridge University Press, 1978.

———. "Liberal Community." *California Law Review* 77 (1989): 479.

———. "Review of Michael Walzer's *Spheres of Justice.*" *New York Review of Books,* 14 April 1983.

———. *Taking Rights Seriously.* Cambridge, Mass.: Harvard University Press, 1977.

Elazar, Daniel J. "Constitution-making: The Pre-eminently Political Act." In *Redesigning the State: The Politics of Constitutional Change,* edited by Keith G. Banting and Richard Simeon. Toronto: University of Toronto Press, 1985.

———. *Constitutionalism: The Israeli and American Experiences.* Lanham, Md.: University Press of America, 1990.

———. *The Constitution of the State of Israel.* Jerusalem: Jerusalem Center for Public Affairs, 1988.

Elkin, Stephen L. "Citizenship and Constitutionalism in Post-Communist Regimes." *PS: Political Science and Politics* 23, no. 2 (June 1990): 163–66.

———. "Constitutionalism: Old and New." In *A New Constitutionalism: Designing Political Institutions for a Good Society,* edited by Stephen L. Elkin and Karol Edward Soltan. Chicago: University of Chicago Press, 1993.

Elliot, Jonathon. *The Debates of the State Conventions on the Adoption of the Federal Constitution, as Recommended by the General Convention at Philadelphia in 1787.* Philadelphia: 1877.

Elshtain, Jean Bethke. *Public Man, Private Woman: Women in Social and Political Thought.* Princeton, N.J.: Princeton University Press, 1981.

Elster, Jon, and Rune Slagstad, eds. *Constitutionalism and Democracy.* Cambridge: Cambridge University Press, 1988.

———. "Constitutionalism in Eastern Europe: An Introduction." *University of Chicago Law Review* 58 (1991): 447–82.

Ely, John Hart. *Democracy and Distrust: A Theory of Judicial Review.* Cambridge, Mass.: Harvard University Press, 1980.

Epstein, Richard A. "The Republican Civic Tradition: Modern Republicanism—Or the Flight From Substance." *Yale Law Journal* 97 (1988): 1633, 1634–37.

———. *Takings: Private Property and the Power of Eminent Domain.* Cambridge, Mass.: Harvard University Press, 1985.

Etzioni, Amitai. *An Immodest Agenda: Rebuilding America before the Twenty-First Century.* New York: McGraw Hill, 1983.

———. "Liberals and Communitarians." *Partisan Review* 57, no. 2 (1990): 215–27.

———. "Restoring Our Moral Voice." *Public Interest,* no. 116 (Summer 1994): 107–13.

———. *The Spirit of Community: Rights, Responsibilities and the Communitarian Agenda.* New York: Crown, 1993.

———. "What Community? Whose Responsiveness?" *The Responsive Community: Rights and Responsibilities* 1, no. 2 (Spring 1991): 5–8.

Etzioni, Amitai, James Fishkin, William Galston, and Mary Ann Glendon. "Editorial Statement: The Responsive Community, Rights and Responsibilities." *The Responsive Community: Rights and Responsibilities* 1, no. 1 (Winter 1990–91): 2–5.

Farrand, Max. *The Records of the Federal Convention of 1787.* New Haven, Conn.: Yale University Press, 1937.

The Federalist. New York: Modern Library.

Ferrara, Alessandro. "Universalisms: Procedural, Contextualist and Prudential." In *Universalism vs. Communitarianism: Contemporary Debates in Ethics,* edited by David Rasmussen. Cambridge, Mass.: MIT Press, 1990.

Finkelman, Paul. "Antifederalists: The Loyal Opposition and the American Constitution." *Cornell Law Review* 70 (1984): 182–207.

Fishkin, James. *Democracy and Deliberation: New Directions for Democratic Reform.* New Haven, Conn.: Yale University Press, 1991.

Fowler, Robert Booth. *The Dance with Community: The Contemporary Debate in American Political Thought.* Lawrence: University Press of Kansas, 1991.

Fried, Charles. "Liberalism, Community and the Objectivity of Values." *Harvard Law Review* 96 (1983): 960–68.

Friedman, Marilyn. "Feminism and Modern Friendship: Dislocating the Community." *Ethics* 99, no. 2 (January 1989): 275–90.

Friedrich, Carl J. *Constitutional Government and Democracy.* Boston: Ginn and Company, 1946.

Frohnen, Bruce. "Commitment and Obligation." In *Community and Tradition: Conservative Perspectives on the American Experience,* edited by George W. Carey and Bruce Frohnen. Lanham, Md.: Rowman and Littlefield, 1998.

———. *The New Communitarians and the Crisis of Modern Liberalism.* Lawrence: University of Kansas Press, 1996.

Frye, Marilyn. *The Politics of Reality: Essays in Feminist Theory.* Freedom, Calif.: Crossing Press, 1983.

Galston, William A. "Community, Democracy, Philosophy: The Political Thought of Michael Walzer." *Political Theory* 17 (February, 1989): 119–30.

———. *Justice and the Human Good.* Chicago: University of Chicago Press, 1980.

———. "A Liberal-democratic Case for the Two-Parent Family." *The Responsive Community: Rights and Responsibilities* 1, no. 1 (Winter 1990–1991): 14–26.

———. *Liberal Purposes: Goods, Virtues and Diversity in the Liberal State.* Cambridge: Cambridge University Press, 1991.

———. "Moral Personality and Liberal Theory: John Rawls's Dewey Lectures." *Political Theory* 10, no. 4 (November 1982): 492–519.

Garfinkle, Adam. *Politics and Society in Modern Israel: Myths and Realities.* Armonk, N.Y.: M. E. Sharpe, 1997.

Gilbert, Neil. "Social Responsibility and Social Accounting: Time For a New Ledger." *The Responsive Community: Rights and Responsibilities* 3, no. 1 (Winter 1992–93).

Glendon, Mary Ann. "'Absolute' Rights: Property and Privacy." *The Responsive Community: Rights and Responsibilities* 1, no. 4 (Fall 1991): 12–20.

———. "Rights and Responsibilities Viewed from Afar: The Case of Welfare Rights." *The Responsive Community: Rights and Responsibilities* 4, no. 2 (Spring 1994): 33–42.

———. *Rights Talk: The Impoverishment of Political Discourse.* New York: Free Press, 1991.

Goodnow, Frank. *Principles of Constitutional Government.* New York: Harper Brothers, 1916.

Grasso, Kenneth L. "Contemporary Communitarianism, the Lure of the State, and the Modern Quest for Community." In *Community and Tradition: Conservative Perspectives on the American Experience,* edited by George W. Carey and Bruce Frohnen. Lanham, Md.: Rowman and Littlefield: 1998.

Gray, John. "The Failings of Neutrality." *The Responsive Community: Rights and Responsibilities* 3, no. 2 (Spring 1993).

Greschner, Donna. "Feminist Concerns with the New Communitarians." In *Law and the Community,* edited by A. Hutchinson and L. Green. Toronto: Carswell, 1989.

Griffin, Stephen M. *American Constitutionalism: From Theory to Politics.* Princeton, N.J.: Princeton University Press, 1996.

Grimshaw, Jean. *Philosophy and Feminist Thinking.* Minneapolis: University of Minnesota Press, 1986.

Gross, George. "The Constitutional Question in Israel." In *Constitutionalism: The Israeli and American Experiences,* edited by Daniel Elazar. Lanham, Md.: University Press of America, 1990.

Guinier, Lani. *The Tyranny of the Majority: Fundamental Fairness in Representative Democracy.* New York: Free Press, 1994.

Gunther, Gerald. *Constitutional Law,* 11th ed. Mineola, N.Y.: Foundation Press, 1985.

Gutmann, Amy. "Communitarian Critics of Liberalism." *Philosophy and Public Affairs* 14, no. 3 (Summer 1985): 308–22.

Gwyn, William P. "The Separation of Powers and Modern Forms of Government." In *Separation of Powers—Does It Still Work?* edited by Robert Goldwin and Art Kaufman. Washington, D.C.: American Enterprise Institute, 1986.

Hand, Learned. *The Bill of Rights.* Cambridge, Mass.: Harvard University Press, 1958.

Hare, R. M. "Rights, Utility and Universalization: Reply to J. L. Mackie." In R. Frey, *Utility and Rights.* Minneapolis: University of Minnesota Press, 1984.

Harris, William F. "Bonding Word and Polity: The Logic of American Constitutionalism." *American Political Science Review* 76, no. 1 (1982): 34–45.

———. *The Interpretable Constitution.* Baltimore: Johns Hopkins University Press, 1994.

Hart, H. L. A. *The Concept of Law.* Oxford: Oxford University Press, 1961.

Hirsch, H. N. "The Threnody of Liberalism: Constitutional Liberty and the Renewal of Community." *Political Theory* 14, no. 3 (August 1986): 423–49.

Holmes, Stephen. *The Anatomy of Antiliberalism.* Cambridge, Mass.: Harvard University Press, 1993.

———. "The Community Trap." *New Republic,* 28 November 1988, 24–25.

———. "The Permanent Structure of Anti-Liberal Thought." In *Liberalism and the Moral Life,* edited by Nancy Rosenblum. Cambridge, Mass.: Harvard University Press, 1989.

———. "Precommitment and the Paradox of Democracy." In *Constitutionalism and Democracy,* edited by Jon Elster and Rune Slagstad. Cambridge: Cambridge University Press, 1988.

Hume, David. "Of the Origins of Government." In *Essays Moral, Political and Literary.* Oxford, 1963; orig. 1741–42.

Hutchinson, Allen C. and Leslie J. M. Green, eds. *Law and the Community: The End of Liberalism?* Toronto: Carswell, 1989.

Jacobsohn, Gary J. "Alternative Pluralisms: Israel and American Constitutionalism in Comparative Perspective." *Review of Politics* 51 (1989): 159–87.

———. *Apple of Gold: Constitutionalism in Israel and the United States.* Princeton, N.J.: Princeton University Press, 1993.

Janowitz, Morris. *The Reconstruction of Patriotism: Education for Civic Consciousness.* Chicago: University of Chicago Press, 1983.

Jefferson, Thomas. "Letter to Samuel Kercheval, July 12, 1816." In *Thomas Jefferson Selected Writings,* edited by Harvey C. Mansfield, 88–91. Wheeling, Ill.: Harlan Davidson, 1979.

———. "Notes on the State of Virginia." In *Thomas Jefferson: Selected Writings,* edited by Harvey Mansfield. Wheeling, Ill.: Harlan Davidson, 1979.

Kateb, George. "The Moral Distinctiveness of Representative Democracy." *Ethics* 91, no. 3 (April 1981): 357–74.

Kautz, Stephen. *Liberalism and Community.* Ithaca, N.Y.: Cornell University Press, 1995.

Kommers, Donald P. *The Constitutional Jurisprudence of the Federal Republic of Germany.* Durham, N.C.: Duke University Press, 1989.

Kornberg, Allan, and Harold Clarke. *Citizens and Community: Political Support in a Representative Democracy.* Cambridge: Cambridge University Press, 1992.

Kraynak, Robert P. "Tocqueville's Constitutionalism." *American Political Science Review* 81, no. 4 (1981).

Kretzmer, David. *The Legal Status of the Arabs in Israel.* Boulder, Colo.: Westview, 1990.

Kuhn, Thomas. *The Structure of Scientific Revolutions.* Chicago: University of Chicago Press, 1970.

Kurland, Philip B., and Ralph Lerner. *The Founder's Constitution.* Chicago: University of Chicago Press, 1987.

Kymlicka, Will. *Contemporary Political Philosophy: An Introduction.* Oxford: Clarendon Press, 1990.

———. "Liberalism and Communitarianism." *Canadian Journal of Philosophy* 18 (1988): 181–204.

———. *Liberalism, Community and Culture.* Oxford: Clarendon Press, 1989.

———. "Some Questions about Justice and Community." In Daniel Bell, *Communitarianism and Its Critics.* Oxford: Oxford University Press, 1993.

Larmore, Charles. "Review of Michael Sandel's *Liberalism and the Limits of Justice.*" *Journal of Philosophy* 81, no. 6 (June 1984).

Lasch, Christopher. "The Communitarian Critique of Liberalism." In *Community in America: The Challenge of Habits of the Heart,* edited by Charles H. Reynolds and Ralph Norman. Berkeley: University of California Press, 1988.

Lathrop, Joseph. "A Miscellaneous Collection of Original Pieces." In *American Political Writing During the Founding Era, 1760–1805,* edited by Charles S. Hyneman and Donald Lutz. Indianapolis: Liberty, 1983.

Levinson, Sanford. *Constitutional Faith.* Princeton, N.J.: Princeton University Press, 1988.

———. "How Many Times Has the United States Constitution Been Amended? (A) <26; (B) 26; (C) 27; (D) >27: Accounting for Constitutional Change." In Sanford Levinson, *Responding to Imperfection: The Theory and Practice of Constitutional Amendment.* Princeton, N.J.: Princeton University Press, 1995.

Liebman, Charles S. "Conception of 'State of Israel' in Israeli Society." *Jerusalem Quarterly* 47 (1988).

Lincoln, Abraham. "Message to Congress in Special Session, July 4, 1861." In *Abraham Lincoln: Speeches and Writings, 1859–1865.* New York: Library of America, 1989.

Locke, John. *The Second Treatise of Government.* Edited by Thomas P. Peardon. Indianapolis: Bobbs-Merrill, 1952.

Lowi, Theodore J., and Benjamin Ginsberg. *American Government: Freedom and Power,* 3rd ed. New York: W. W. Norton, 1994.

Lutz, Donald. *The Origins of American Constitutionalism.* Baton Rouge: Louisiana State University Press, 1988.

———. "Religious Dimensions in the Development of American Constitutionalism." *Emory Law Journal* 39 (1990): 21–40.

Macedo, Stephen. *Liberal Virtues: Citizenship, Virtue and Community in Liberal Constitutionalism.* Oxford: Clarendon Press, 1990.

MacIntyre, Alasdair. *After Virtue: A Study in Moral Theory.* Notre Dame, Ind.: University of Notre Dame Press, 1981.

———. "Is Patriotism a Virtue?" In *Liberalism,* Elger Reference Collection Schools of Thought, vol. 2, edited by Richard J. Arneson. Brookfield, Vt.: Ashgate Publishers, 1992.

———. "A Partial Response to my Critics." In *After MacIntyre: Critical Perspectives on the Work of Alasdair MacIntyre,* edited by John Horton and Susan Mendes. Cambridge: Polity, 1994.

———. "The Privatization of the Good." *Review of Politics* 52, no. 3 (Summer 1990): 345–63.

———. *A Short History of Ethics.* New York: Macmillan, 1966.

———. *Whose Justice? Which Rationality?* London: Duckworth, 1988.

Madison, James. *Notes of Debates in the Federal Convention of 1787.* New York: W. W. Norton, 1987.

———. "Vices of the Political System of the United States." In *James Madison: Writings.* New York: Library of America, 1999.

Mason, Alpheus Thomas, and William M. Beaney. *The Supreme Court in a Free Society.* New York: W. W. Norton, 1968.

McClay, Wilfred M. "Mr. Emerson's Tombstone." In *Community and Tradition: Conservative Perspectives on the American Experience,* edited by George W. Carey and Bruce Frohnen. Lanham, Md.: Rowman and Littlefield, 1998.

McCloskey, Herbert, and John Zaller. *The American Ethos: Public Attitudes toward Capitalism and Democracy.* Cambridge, Mass.: Harvard University Press, 1984.

McCloskey, Robert G. *The American Supreme Court.* Chicago: University of Chicago Press, 1960.

McCoy, Drew R. *The Last of the Fathers: James Madison and the Republican Legacy.* Cambridge: Cambridge University Press, 1989.

McIlwain, Charles. *Constitutionalism: Ancient and Modern.* Ithaca, N.Y.: Cornell University Press, 1940.

———. *Constitutionalism and the Changing World.* New York: Macmillan, 1939.

Michelman, Frank. "Law's Republic." *Yale Law Journal* 97 (1988): 1493–537.

Mill, John Stuart. "Utilitarianism." In John Stuart Mill and Jeremy Bentham, *Utilitarianism and Other Essays,* edited by Alan Ryan. New York: Penguin Books, 1987.

Miller, David. "Community and Citizenship." In *Communitarianism and Individualism,* edited by Shlomo Avineri and Avner de-Shalit. Oxford: Oxford University Press, 1992.

Baron de Montesquieu. *The Spirit of the Laws.* Translated by Thomas Nugent. New York: Collier Macmillan, 1949.

Moon, J. Donald. "Thin Selves/Rich Lives: On the Concept of the Self in Liberal Theory." Paper delivered at the Annual Meeting of the American Political Science Association, Washington, D.C., August 1986.

Moore, Wayne D. *Constitutional Rights and Powers of the People.* Princeton, N.J.: Princeton University Press, 1996.

Mulhall, Stephen, and Adam Swift. *Liberals and Communitarians.* Oxford: Blackwell Publishers, 1992.

Murphy, Walter F. "Civil Law, Common Law, and Constitutional Democracy." *Louisiana Law Review* 52 (September 1991): 92–136.

———. "Constitutions, Constitutionalism and Democracy." In *Constitutionalism and Democracy: Transitions in the Contemporary World,* edited by Douglas Greenburg, Stanley N. Katz, Melanie Beth Oliviero, and Steven Wheatley. Oxford: Oxford University Press, 1993.

Murphy, Walter F., James E. Fleming, and Sotirios Barber. *American Constitutional Interpretation.* New York: Foundation Press, 1995.

"Nationalism and Ethnic Particularism." *Tikkun* 7 (November/December 1992).

Newman, Stephen. "Challenging the Liberal Individualist Tradition in America: 'Community' as a Critical Ideal in Recent Political Theory." In *Law and the Community: The End of Liberalism?* edited by Allen Hutchinson and Leslie Green. Toronto: Carswell, 1989.

Nie, Norman H., Sidney Verba, and John R. Petrocik. *The Changing American Voter.* Cambridge, Mass.: Harvard University Press, 1976.

Nozick, Robert. *Anarchy, State, and Utopia.* New York: Basic Books, 1974.

Nwabueze, Ben O. *Constitutionalism in the Emergent State.* Rutherford, N.J.: Fairleigh Dickinson University Press, 1973.

Oakley, Francis. *Omnipotence, Covenant, and Order.* Ithaca, N.Y.: Cornell University Press, 1984.

Oaks, Dallin H. "Rights and Responsibilities." *The Responsive Community: Rights and Responsibilities* 1, no. 1 (Winter 1990–1991): 37–46.

Okin, Susan Moller. "Humanist Liberalism." In *Liberalism and the Moral Life,* edited by Nancy Rosenblum. Cambridge, Mass.: Harvard University Press, 1989.

———. "Justice and Gender." *Philosophy and Public Affairs* 16, no. 1 (Winter 1987): 42–72.

———. *Justice, Gender and the Family.* New York: Basic Books, 1989.

Oldfield, Adrian. *Citizenship and Community: Civic Republicanism and the Modern World.* London: Routledge, 1990.

Paine, Thomas. *Rights of Man: The Complete Works of Thomas Paine.* London: 1793.

Pateman, Carole. " 'The Disorder of Women': Women, Love and the Sense of Justice." *Ethics* 91, no. 1 (October 1980): 20–34.

Peled, Joav. "Ethnic Democracy and the Legal Construction of Citizenship: Arab Citizens of the Jewish State." *American Political Science Review* 86 (1992): 432–43.

Powell, G. Bingham. "American Voter Turnout in Comparative Perspective." *American Political Science Review* 80 (March 1986): 17–43.

Rackman, Emanuel. *Israel's Emerging Constitution, 1948–1951.* New York: Columbia University Press, 1955.

Rasmussen, David, ed. *Universalism vs. Communitarianism: Contemporary Debates in Ethics.* Cambridge, Mass.: MIT Press, 1990.

Rawls, John. "Constitutional Liberty and the Concept of Justice." In *Rights,* ed. David Lyons. Belmont, Calif.: Wadsworth, 1979.

———. "Justice as Fairness: Political not Metaphysical." *Philosophy and Public Affairs* 14 (Summer 1985): 223–51.

———. "Kantian Constructivism in Moral Theory: The Dewey Lectures, 1980." *Journal of Philosophy* 77 (1980): 515–72.

———. *Political Liberalism.* New York: Columbia University Press, 1993.

———. *A Theory of Justice.* Cambridge, Mass.: Harvard University Press, 1971.

Rehnquist, William H. "The Notion of a Living Constitution." *Texas Law Review* 54, no. 4 (May 1976): 693–706.

Rivlin, Alice M. "Making Responsibilities Clearer: A New Federal/Local Division of Labor and Resources." *The Responsive Community: Rights and Responsibilities* 2, no. 4 (Fall 1992).

Rosenbaum, Alan, ed. *Constitutionalism: The Philosophic Dimension.* New York: Greenwood Press, 1988.

Rosenblum, Nancy. "Moral Membership in a Post-Liberal State." *World Politics* 36 (July 1984): 581–96.

———. "Pluralism and Self Defense." In *Liberalism and the Moral Life,* ed. Nancy Rosenblum. Cambridge, Mass.: Harvard University Press, 1989.

———, ed. *Liberalism and the Moral Life.* Cambridge, Mass.: Harvard University Press, 1989.

Rousseau, Jean Jacques. *Constitutional Project for Corsica.* Translated and edited by Frederick Watkins. Edinburgh, N.Y.: Nelson, 1953.

———. *The Social Contract.* Translated by G. D. H. Cole. New York: E. P. Dutton, 1950.

Ryan, Alan. "Communitarianism: The Good, the Bad, and the Muddly." *Dissent* 39 (Summer 1989).

Sandel, Michael. *Democracy's Discontent: America in Search of a Public Philosophy.* Cambridge, Mass.: Harvard University Press, 1996.

———. "Democrats and Community." *New Republic,* 22 February 1988, 20–23.

———. *Liberalism and its Critics.* Oxford: Basil Blackwell, 1984.

———. *Liberalism and the Limits of Justice.* Cambridge: Cambridge University Press, 1982.

———. "Morality and the Liberal Ideal." *New Republic,* 7 May 1984, 15–17.

——. "The Procedural Republic and the Unencumbered Self." *Political Theory* 12, no. 1 (February 1984): 81–96.

Schlesinger, Arthur M. *The Disuniting of America*. New York: W. W. Norton, 1992.

Schochet, Gordon J. "Introduction: Constitutionalism, Liberalism and the Study of Politics." In *Nomos XX: Constitutionalism*. edited by J. Roland Pennock and John W. Chapman. New York: New York University Press, 1979.

Sejersted, Francis. "Democracy and the Rule of Law: Some Historical Experiences of Contradictions in the Striving for Good Government." In *Constitutionalism and Democracy*, edited by Jon Elster and Rune Slagstad. Cambridge: Cambridge University Press, 1988.

Shain, Barry Alan. "American Community." In *Community and Tradition: Conservative Perspectives on the American Experience*, edited by George W. Carey and Bruce Frohnen. Lanham, Md.: Rowman and Littlefield, 1998.

——. *The Myth of American Individualism: The Protestant Origins of American Political Thought*. Princeton, N.J.: Princeton University Press, 1994.

Shapiro, Ian. *The Evolution of Rights in Liberal Theory*. Cambridge: Cambridge University Press, 1986.

Sherry, Suzanna. "Civic Virtue and the Feminine Voice in Constitutional Adjudication." *Virginia Law Review* 72 (1986): 543–616.

Shklar, Judith. *Legalism*. Cambridge, Mass.: Harvard University Press, 1964.

Singer, Peter. *Hegel*. Oxford: Oxford University Press, 1983.

Skelton, O. D. *The Life and Times of Sir Alexander Tilloch Galt*. Toronto: McClelland and Stewart, 1966.

Smith, Rogers M. *Liberalism and American Constitutional Law*. Cambridge, Mass.: Harvard University Press, 1985.

Soltan, Karol Edward. "Generic Constitutionalism." In *A New Constitutionalism: Designing Political Institutions for a Good Society*, edited by Stephen Elkin and Karol Edward Soltan. Chicago: University of Chicago Press, 1993.

Spragens, Thomas A. "The Limitations of Libertarianism, Part I." *The Responsive Community: Rights and Responsibilities* 2, no. 1 (Winter 1991).

——. "The Limitations of Libertarianism, Part II." *The Responsive Community: Rights and Responsibilities* 2, no. 2 (Spring 1992).

Stone, Brad Lowell. "On the Extent of Community: Civil Society, Civil Religion, and the State." In *Community and Tradition: Conservative Perspectives on the American Experience*, edited by George W. Carey and Bruce Frohnen. Lanham, Md.: Rowman and Littlefield, 1998.

Storing, Herbert J. *What the Anti-Federalists Were For*. Chicago: University of Chicago Press, 1981.

——, ed. *The Anti-Federalist: An Abridgement, by Murray Dry, of the Complete Anti-Federalist*. Chicago: University of Chicago Press, 1985.

——, ed. *The Complete Anti-Federalist: Writings by the Opponents of the Constitution*. Chicago: University of Chicago Press.

Strauss, Peter L. "The Place of Agencies in Government: Separation of Powers and the Fourth Branch." *Columbia Law Review* 84 (1984): 573–669.

Sullivan, William M. *Reconstructing Public Philosophy*. Berkeley: University of California Press, 1982.

——. "A Renewal of Civic Philosophy." In *Communitarianism: A New Public Ethics*, edited by Markate Daly. Belmont, Calif.: Wadsworth, 1994.

Sunstein, Cass R. "Beyond the Republican Revival." *Yale Law Journal* 97 (1988): 1539–90.

———. "Constitutions and Democracies: An Epilogue." In *Constitutionalism and Democracy,* edited by Jon Elster and Rune Slagstad. Cambridge: Cambridge University Press, 1988.

———. "Constitution-Making in Eastern Europe: An Interim Report."

Sutherland, Arthur. *Constitutionalism in America: Origin and Evolution of Its Fundamental Ideas.* New York: Ginn, 1965.

Symposium. "The American Constitutional Tradition of Shared and Separated Powers." *William and Mary Law Review* 30 (1989).

Taylor, Charles. "Alternative Futures: Legitimacy, Identity and Alienation in Late Twentieth Century Canada." In *Constitutionalism, Citizenship and Society in Canada,* edited by Alan Cairns and Cynthia Williams. Toronto: University of Toronto Press, 1985.

———. "Cross Purposes: The Liberal-Communitarian Debate." In *Liberalism and the Moral Life.,* edited by Nancy Rosenblum. Cambridge, Mass.: Harvard University Press, 1989.

———. *Hegel and Modern Society.* Cambridge: Cambridge University Press, 1979.

———. *The Malaise of Modernity.* Concord, Ont.: Anansi, 1991.

———. *Philosophy and the Human Sciences: Philosophical Papers 2.* Cambridge: Cambridge University Press, 1981.

———. *Sources of the Self: The Making of the Modern Identity.* Cambridge: Cambridge University Press, 1989.

Thigpen, Robert, and Lyle Downing. "Liberalism and the Communitarian Critique." *American Journal of Political Science* 31, no. 3 (August 1987): 637–55.

Tocqueville, Alexis de. *Democracy in America.* Translated by George Lawrence; edited by J. P. Mayer. Garden City, N.Y.: Anchor Books, 1969.

———. "Of Individualism in Democracies." In *Democracy in America,* vol. 2, ed. J. P. Mayer. New York: Anchor Books, 1969.

Tribe, Laurence H. *Abortion: The Clash of Absolutes.* New York: W. W. Norton, 1990.

———. *American Constitutional Law.* Mineola, N.Y.: Foundation Press, 1978.

———. *Constitutional Choices.* Cambridge, Mass.: Harvard University Press, 1985.

Tribe, Laurence, and Michael Dorf. *On Reading the Constitution.* Cambridge, Mass.: Harvard University Press, 1991.

Vile, M. J. C. *Constitutionalism and the Separation of Powers.* Oxford: Oxford University Press, 1967.

Vipond, Robert C. *Liberty and Community: Canadian Federalism and the Failure of the Constitution.* Albany: State University of New York Press, 1991.

Walker, Graham. "The Constitutional Good: Constitutionalism's Equivocal Moral Imperative." *Polity* 26, no. 1 (Fall 1993): 91–111.

———. "The Idea of Non-Liberal Constitutionalism." Unpublished article, 1994.

———. "The New Mixed Constitution: A Response to Liberal Debility and Constitutional Deadlock in Eastern Europe." *Polity* 26, no. 3 (Spring 1994): 503–15.

Wallach, John. "Liberals, Communitarians and the Tasks of Political Theory." *Political Theory* 15, no. 4 (November 1987): 581–611.

Walzer, Michael. "The Communitarian Critique of Liberalism." *Political Theory* 18, no. 1 (February 1990): 6–23.

———. *The Company of Critics.* New York: Basic Books, 1988.

———. "The Idea of Civil Society: A Path to Social Reconstruction." *Dissent* 38 (Spring 1991): 293–304.

———. *Interpretation and Social Criticism.* Cambridge, Mass.: Harvard University Press, 1987.

———. "The New Tribalism: Notes on a Difficult Problem." *Dissent* 39 (Spring 1992): 164–71.

———. *Obligations: Essays on Disobedience, War, and Citizenship.* Cambridge, Mass.: Harvard University Press, 1970.

———. "Philosophy and Democracy." *Political Theory* 9, no. 3 (August 1981): 379–99.

———. *Radical Principles: Reflections of an Unreconstructed Democrat.* New York: Basic Books, 1980.

———. Roundtable: Nationalism and Ethnic Particularism. *Tikkun* (November/December 1992): 49–56.

———. *Spheres of Justice.* Oxford: Basil Blackwell, 1983.

Ward, Norman. *Dawson's The Government of Canada,* 6th ed. Toronto: University of Toronto Press, 1987.

Wechsler, Herbert. "Toward Neutral Principles of Constitutional Law." *Harvard Law Review* 73, no. 9 (1959).

Wheare, Kenneth C. *Modern Constitutions,* 2nd ed. London: Oxford University Press, 1966.

Williams, B. "A Critique of Utilitarianism." In *Utilitarianism: For and Against,* edited by J. J. C. Smart and B. Williams. Cambridge: Cambridge University Press, 1973.

Wolfe, Christopher. *How to Read the Constitution: Originalism, Constitutional Interpretation, and Judicial Power.* Lanham, Md.: Rowman and Littlefield, 1996.

———. *The Rise of Modern Judicial Review: From Constitutional Interpretation to Judge-Made Law.* New York: Basic Books, 1986.

Wood, Gordon S. *The Creation of the American Republic 1776–1787.* Chapel Hill: University of North Carolina Press, 1969.

Young, Iris Marion. "The Ideal of Community and the Politics of Difference." *Social Theory and Practice* 12, no. 1 (Spring 1986): 1–26.

———. *Justice and the Politics of Difference.* Princeton, N.J.: Princeton University Press, 1990.

Yudof, Mark G. "Review of Amy Gutmann's *Democratic Education.*" *Ethics* 99, no. 2 (January 1989): 441–42.

Index

abortion, 152

Ackerman, Bruce, xiv, 66, 241n. 32

Agranat, Shimon, 191

Agrippa, 165–66

American constitutional founding, xii, 94–95, 98–99, 122, 128, 139, 150, 216–18; and classical republicanism, 174–75; Constitutional Convention and, 1–3; Enlightenment influences on, 120–21, 174; and Federalist/Anti-Federalist debate, 14–15; ratification debates and, 3–4, 5–11. *See also* Anti-Federalists; Federalists

American Revolution, 5, 94, 206

AmeriCorps, 213–14

ancient republics, 121

Anti-Federalists, 4, 14–15, 28, 61, 65, 108–9, 113, 217–18, 219n. 8; and bill of rights, 6, 8, 164–66; and civic virtue, 6–10, 217, 220n. 11; and communitarian principles, 5–11; and conservatism, 5, 87; and conservative communitarianism, 63–64, 136; and constitutional values, 17–18; and heterogeneity, 5; and individualism, 7; and religion, 10; and republicanism, 6–10, 87, 165, 217; and state constitutions, 167–68

aristocracy, 132, 144

Aristotle, xiv, 95, 199, 221n. 31; and classical republicanism, 9; and mixed constitutions, 184, 195; and rationality, 162

Articles of Confederation, 2, 3, 166, 217

authoritarianism, 146

Avineri, Shlomo, 230n. 18

Barber, Benjamin, 21, 80, 82–85, 107, 137, 210–11, 242n. 40; and citizenship, 73–74; and civic education, 102–3, 228n. 114; and the good, 89–90; and the judiciary, 157; and majoritarianism, 95–96; and political apathy, 71–74; and postal reform, 158–59; and the public/private distinction, 73–74; and referenda, 156–57; and representation, 73–74, 94–96, 135; and strong democracy, 72–74, 89–90, 91, 92–96, 152, 155–56, 179, 231n. 39; and strong democratic civil society, 82–83

Barber, Sotirios, 154, 169–70

Barry, Norman, 20, 84

Basic Law (Germany), 26–27, 183–84, 185–86, 195–203; balancing rights and responsibilities, 204–5; and endorsement of values, 201–2; rights and liberties in, 197–203; and traditions, 201. *See also* semi-liberal constitutions

Basic Law (Israel), 140, 188, 192–93

Beccaria, Cesare, 120

Beiner, Ronald, 79, 229n. 5

Bell, Daniel, 79, 86–87, 101, 103–4; and the conception of the good, 88–89; and constitutional order, 139; and democracy, 171; and institutions, 97; and language, 99; and Switzerland, 105–6; on taxation, 233n. 75

Bellah, Robert, 79, 86, 172; and institutions, 88, 96–100, 105, 210–11

Blackstone, William, 69, 199

Bolingbroke, Lord, 118

Bradley, Bill, 248n. 11

Brandenburg v Ohio, 185

British North America Act of 1867 (Canada's Constitution), 17

Brutus, 9–10

Buchanan, Pat, 212–13, 248n. 11

Bundesgerichtshof (Federal High Court of Justice, Germany), 198

Printed in the United States
56725LVS00007BA/31

9 780801 885389